The Two Worlds of Jim Yoshida

THE
TWO WORLDS
OF
JIM YOSHIDA

By

JIM YOSHIDA

with BILL HOSOKAWA

WILLIAM MORROW & COMPANY, INC.

New York 1972

3   4   5   75   74   73

For Suye Uyesugi Yoshida

Foreword

I AM delighted to have been offered an opportunity to share some of my thoughts on *The Two Worlds of Jim Yoshida*.

This is a most interesting book for two reasons. First, it tells a fascinating personal story about an American who, because of legal technicalities, was impressed into the Japanese Army during World War II. As a reluctant combatant, he offers an insight into the life of the Japanese Army and soldier in this period. These memoirs would be interesting reading for this reason alone.

However, second, and ultimately more important, is his account of his personal struggle to retain his American heritage in a land that also legally and culturally claimed his loyalty. In an age when too many Americans are disdainfully discarding their citizenship and birthright, it is instructive to read how important these were to a man whose American roots reached back only a single generation.

Jim Yoshida had an unusual, if not unique, opportunity to sample life in two vastly different cultures. In spite of the warmth and affection in which he held Japan, in the end he chose to return to the United States, with all its blemishes and defects. Too many Americans have lost sight of the attractions of our nation—the openness of our society, respect for individuality and the individual, and the flexibility and responsiveness of the United States government.

Thankfully this book is not a mindless patriotic paean. Rather it is a stirring personal story of what America meant to one man and how it sustained him in his most dismal hour. In an age marked by deep cynicism, it is refreshing to read of a man who had an opportunity to straddle two different worlds but in the end chose to return to the land of his birth. There are lessons here that we can all learn.

DANIEL K. INOUYE
United States Senator

One

THERE is nothing in the world quite like the waves of sound that greet the home team when it steps out into the football stadium. They surge like the tide, a tactile thing that can be felt as well as heard, communicating the fans' electric excitement to the athletes. In the concentration of game action a player himself may hear nothing. At most he may be only dimly aware of sound beating down on him. But before the kickoff, before the launching of combat, it is impossible not to feel the crowd's vitality and inspiration, to sense its unity, to be charged emotionally and physically by the hammering vibrations.

And now, moments before the opening kickoff, I lifted my face to absorb the strength and support flowing from the throats of the crowd. What marvelous loyalty, I thought. For three wretched seasons our team had failed to win a game. We had not been able to score even a single touchdown. And yet the students were cheering us as if we were champions.

Our opponent this day was Garfield High School whose team, unlike ours, was riding high. Our rivalry reached back over many school generations. Our frustrating season could be salvaged by a victory over Garfield. Downfield, Garfield's purple and white uniforms were spread out in receiving formation. I crouched and tightened my chinstrap, waiting for the referee's whistle to start the game. Then I heard the satisfying thump of foot on football and raced toward the foe, eager to make contact, hungry for the fierce satisfaction of hitting someone—anyone—and knocking him to the ground.

Garfield was over-anxious. We held them for three downs. They punted, and now it was our turn to take the offensive. We lined up, single-wing to the right. I was in the fullback position, two steps ahead of the tailback and just to his right, ready to block for him or take the ball.

The quarterback's voice was high with tension: "Seventy-two, fourteen, twenty-nine . . ." The ball shot back to me. I hugged it tight against my belly, cradling it in the safety of both arms. I faked one step left, just the way Coach had taught us, felt the cleats dig in as I shifted my weight back and plunged into the line. A hole opened for the barest moment over right guard, just where it should be. I broke through, hurtled past the linebacker, driving and twisting until I went down under a ton of weight. I leaped back on my feet, eager to carry the ball again, aware for the first time of the din from the stands. Thirteen yards on that carry. First and ten for Broadway. The linesmen scrambled to move up the chain markers.

Two plays later we had another first down. The plays that had been piled up disastrously by our other foes were clicking now. I made ten more yards, then five, then seven. I threw a key block as the tailback broke around end for twelve. The quarterback sent me into the middle for eight more. Now we were only three yards from a touchdown, the closest we'd been to scoring in three long years. I wanted in the worst way for the quarterback to call my number, and he did.

"I can make it, I can make it," I told myself. "Just give

me a little hole, just a little hole." The line surged forward and I plunged over the goal line with feet to spare. Touchdown! Bedlam in the stands. Bandsmen's horns blaring hysterically. I could hardly hear what the quarterback was saying as we huddled for the point-after try. Our place-kicker wasn't reliable; he was calling my play again. We were going to try to run it over.

Nobody could stop me now. I plunged into a mass of struggling bodies and bulled over by sheer power for the seventh point. Buried under a pile of sweaty, jersey-clad humanity, I relaxed and enjoyed the rare delight of scoring. Now they were unpiling and my teammates were pounding my back, yanking at my headgear in exhilaration.

"Yoshida, Yoshida, get up," someone was shouting.

I grinned insanely and opened my eyes.

And the grin vanished. The stadium was gone.

The crowd was gone.

All around me were men, but they were not clad in the gay colors of football uniforms.

They wore shabby, ill-fitting uniforms of mustard-brown twill, high-collared tunics and leggings wrapped around their calves. They wore helmets of brown-painted steel draped with camouflage netting. And I wore the same uniform—the uniform of the Imperial Japanese Army.

"Yoshida," the voice ordered. "Get up. Quickly. We move out in ten minutes."

"Yes, sir!" My reply was automatic and lifeless. Suddenly I was aware of the dank cold of the pre-dawn mist, the sour smell of the countryside, the misery in my bones, the harsh voice of the sergeant I hated with an intensity I had never known was in me.

I struggled to button the tunic, which was just like the ones the other men wore. I knew it was mine because my name was on it, Yoshida, in Japanese characters, over the left breast pocket, but it had never been designed for anyone my size. The sleeves hit me halfway up the elbow and it was many inches too tight across the shoulders. Instinctively I reached for the boots which I had removed when I lay down to sleep. They were as much too large for me as my tunic was small. Mismatched, at least two sizes too big on the right foot, three on the other, the toes had to be stuffed with rags to keep my feet from swimming around. But badly as they fit, I was grateful to have them. Without them I would have had to walk barefoot across the endless plains and mountains and rice paddies of Central China where the land stretches on and on and on into infinity.

Bone-weary from days of marching, unrefreshed by fitful sleep on the ground, the men made their preparations in sullen silence. The only sounds were of gear being packed, the creak of leather as the horses were loaded, the clink of metal and the crunch of gravel under hobnailed boots. I shouldered my pack and joined my squad, waiting for the order that would send us out once more. The armies of every nation have their own peculiar ways of doing things, but in one respect they are all alike. Enlisted men must always hurry up and wait. It was during waits such as these that I had time to wonder, wonder about many things:

To wonder what weird turn of fate decreed that I, an apple-pie-loving, red-white-and-blue, football-playing American should wind up in the Japanese Army in World War II.

To wonder whether I would ever make it back home to Seattle, on the blue waters of Puget Sound in the beautifully wooded state of Washington, a world away from the weary brown terrain of China. It never occurred to me to wonder who would win the war. There never was any doubt in my mind that the United States would be victorious; the doubt was over whether I would survive to see my country triumph.

To wonder why I dreamed the same football dream night after night, again and again. Always it was the Broadway-

Garfield game, replayed over and over like a movie in a theater. I found myself looking forward to being transported back to a happier time in dream fantasy, but how I dreaded the inevitable moment of awakening.

Still, the dream restored me however briefly to the identity I longed for: Jim K. Yoshida, American of Japanese descent, high school football hero, proud winner of a football scholarship that would enable me to get a college education.

But in bitter reality I was the unwilling, unhappy, confused inhabitant of another world: Yoshida Katsumi, private, Imperial Japanese Army. No. 3 man in an eight-man crew serving a 102-millimeter howitzer in a heavy weapons company of the 2344th Arrow Battalion, based at Yoyang, a village four days' hard march west of Hankow, 600 miles up the Yangtze River in central China. The time: 1943.

There are, I've heard, many kinds of war. Grand and glorious wars that were fought in earlier, less complicated times. Necessary wars for national survival. Sorry-about-that, made-a-mistake wars. I-hate-your-guts wars. My war was a special kind of war, different from all of these, because I was on the wrong side in a war between the land of my birth and loyalty, and the land of my ancestry. And because my heart was American and my face Japanese, because my uniform was Japanese and my dreams American, I went through a personal hell whose fires could be extinguished only by a special kind of atonement.

But then that is getting ahead of my story. It begins on Skidrow, the waterfront Bowery of Seattle.

Two

My father, Ryunosuke Yoshida, was the youngest of five children of a *sake* (rice wine) brewer in Hirao, a village in Yamaguchi Province, at the southwestern tip of Honshu, the main Japanese Island. He and his next older brother, Saisuke, came to the United States together in 1911. I think the expression is "to seek their fortune," but what they found was little enough. Their first jobs were in a lumber camp in Oregon. Several years later they were ready to go into business for themselves. They started a hog farm on the outskirts of Portland, undeterred by the fact that they had no experience with livestock. The United States was gearing up for entry into World War I. Vancouver Barracks across the Columbia River from Portland was filling up with troops. My father and his brother picked up garbage which the Army was happy to give free to anyone willing to haul it away. This they fed to their pigs. It must have been a lucrative business, but it wasn't the kind of future my father was seeking. He sold his share of the business to his brother and moved to Seattle, where he took up barbering. This wasn't much higher on the social scale

14

than running a hog ranch, but it was less odoriferous and he liked it better.

He seemed to like Seattle, too, for about this time he went back to Japan to find a wife who would share his future in America. He found her in Suye Uyesugi who came from a family of teachers and scholars in Kaminoseki-mura, a village of no more than a hundred households on a tiny island in the Inland Sea nòt far from Hirao. In the old tradition, a go-between introduced the two young people who, after a single meeting, agreed to marriage. The go-between must have known his business for the union turned out beautifully. In an arranged marriage the honeymoon is a period of courtship and love must develop after the wedding. In their later years my father and my mother loved each other in a quiet, undemonstrative manner based on mutual respect, understanding and appreciation. But on their wedding day they were virtually strangers. He promised her no luxuries, only the opportunity to share his hard life in a land where even immigrants could get ahead by working diligently. And she was happy to accept.

Ryunosuke Yoshida returned to Seattle with his bride and he leased a small hotel for her to operate in the heart of the Japanese community while he resumed work as a barber. My older sister, Aiko, was born in 1919. I came along on July 28, 1921. Apparently this was an occasion of great rejoicing, for my parents had been yearning for a son.

Soon afterward my father leased a larger hotel and opened a new barbershop three doors away. The hotel was at 212 First Avenue South, a rough area frequented by longshoremen, seamen, unemployed lumberjacks waiting for the camps to open, alcoholics, derelicts and sundry itinerants. Someone with delusions of grandeur had named the hotel the Grand Central, and that was good enough for Dad. It had about seventy units with a bath on each floor. Our family occupied several of the rooms that opened up into a modest apartment. The barbershop also had baths in the rear, and for a quarter a man could get a cake of soap and towel and all the hot water he needed. Two years after I was born I got another sister, Hideko, who was called Betty when she started school.

I was put to work in my spare time as soon as I was old enough—scrubbing out the baths, sweeping out the barbershop, hanging laundry in the steamroom, mopping the uncarpeted lobby of the hotel. I polished the brass banisters, cleaned the cuspidors and was paid twenty-five cents a week for each floor of the hotel I took care of. We grew up in a rough environment. We saw men who tried to drown their loneliness in liquor. I became accustomed to cleaning their vomit off the lobby entrance. We saw them quarrel and fight and bloody themselves, or fall into a drunken stupor in a littered alley and get hauled off to the city jail, which was near the foot of Yesler Way not far distant. We saw prostitutes trying to victimize these lonely men, and we tried to keep our regular guests from getting rolled. But my mother and sisters were never molested and I don't think I was contaminated by what went on around us.

The Yoshidas were a close-knit family. My parents worked hard—the life of Oriental immigrants on the West Coast was never easy—and they impressed on us the need for industry, honesty, and respect for others, particularly one's elders. We never had much money, but there was always plenty of food on the table. In the evening, when all of us were together, the usual meal was rice, together with vegetables cooked up with fish or a little meat. Sometimes we would have hamburger patties with our rice, a happy blend of Oriental and Western cultures.

My father was a sturdily built man, fairly tall for a Japanese, and he became heavier as he grew older. He sported a bristly Charlie Chaplin mustache and one of his indulgences was cigars. He never learned much English, so he always spoke to us in Japanese. I could understand him, but I couldn't express myself in Japanese so I replied in English. This is the way most Japanese American families communicated, and we got along quite well.

I could never seem to penetrate my father's gruff exterior and I feared him as much as I loved him. I can't ever remember hearing him praise me. Whenever I did anything well, he simply said he expected me to do better next time, and eventually I came to understand that this was his way. When I was sixteen years old I picked a hundred-pound sack of rice off the floor and held it up over my head, the way a weight lifter lifts barbells. This was a feat of strength recognized among Japanese families as a sign that a lad had reached manhood. If Dad was proud, he didn't show any sign. But later Mother told me how really happy he was. About the same time I defeated my father for the first time at arm wrestling. We sat at the kitchen table facing each other. With elbows down on the table, we locked right hands and each tried to force the other's arm down. I was surprised at how easily I defeated him, for Dad had a reputation for physical strength. He was proud that I was growing strong and I felt sad that he was getting old, but neither of us said anything. Our relationship was such that we seldom voiced our thoughts to each other, and I suppose that's the way he was brought up.

With my mother, the relationship was altogether different. She was a tiny woman, no more than five feet two inches tall, but she was blessed with enormous vitality. She had a beautiful heart-shaped face. She was gentle; not once did she ever strike me, although I deserved punishment frequently, and I don't recall that she ever raised her voice to me. But she had a way of talking to me when I did wrong; these talks usually left me weeping in remorse.

Mother had an understanding of young people that was extremely unusual in the Japanese immigrant generation. Dad was strict and stern. He wanted to rear his children the way he had been brought up. Mother was wise enough to know that American children could not be reared like Japanese children, that we were products of the new world and we required freedom. Eventually I came to realize she was a mellowing, liberalizing influence on my father. This does not mean she was entirely permissive. In her own way she kept a tight rein on her children. When I became old enough to go out at night she insisted that I let her know when I came home. I would walk by her bedroom door and knock—*tum-ta-ta-tum-tum*. And she would knock back —*tum-tum*. If she slept while I was out, it was only lightly.

Most of our friends were other Japanese American families, with all of us in similarly humble circumstances. My closest friend was Pete Fujino, one of five kids whose family ran a small apartment house in the lower Yesler Way area. Pete was a natural athlete and wore a judo black belt. He was a little taller than I, and could run a lot faster, so that he played end on the Broadway High School varsity. Because we were both of Japanese extraction, and both team mainstays, the newspapers would refer to us as the Bengal Twins, Broadway being the Tigers. Pete's older sister worked as a waitress at the Paramount Cafe on Jackson Street, the heart of Seattle's international settlement, and he and I would go there often after judo practice to have a piece of pie and a glass of milk, and if we had a few nickels, play the pinball machines.

Usually on Friday nights Joe Nakatsu would join us to make plans for the weekend. Joe was about as big as Pete, and we met through judo. Joe's dad owned a fairly good-sized truck farm in Sunnydale, on the southern outskirts of Seattle. Joe didn't say much, but we got along famously. He and I were usually the top boys in judo tournaments, which meant that often we faced each other. In one match we were both fooling around, each not wanting to throw the other, and the referee was about to call it a draw when Joe's dad jumped up and shouted: "Yoshida, if you're good enough to throw my son, I want you to throw him and win." Well, we both went at it, and I threw Joe. As soon as he hit the mat Joe jumped up and embraced me, and I cried because I had defeated my friend. We were that kind of buddies.

Another one of my closest friends was Kay Nakamura who had more brothers and sisters than I can remember. Mr. Nakamura had a little dry-cleaning shop, also on Yesler Way, and I don't see how he supported his family. But they were all close; it was a warm family and the Nakamuras were good to be with. All the Nakamura kids were good at singing or tap-dancing or playing musical instruments, and on Fridays they'd put on a very informal "Amateur Night" at their home just to entertain friends. Sometimes Joe and Pete and another friend, Mud Tsuchikawa, and I and some others would go to the Nakamura home to listen to the singing and watch the dancing, and then we'd play penny ante poker. The winner left his money to buy pies and cakes and soft drinks for the next time we got together. It was a warm, happy time.

Kay and I were graduated from grade school together and started Broadway High School, but he found he liked playing pool better than studying. So he dropped out. Kay was good at anything he tried—football, basketball, track, baseball. He had deadly aim when he threw the newspapers on his route. And he was good at pool. He could start with only a dime in his pocket and play all day, winning consistently. He could cup his hand and imitate Louis Armstrong playing the "Sugar Blues," and he could do a great imitation of Fred Astaire tap-dancing on the sidewalk. At the end of my junior year Kay said he was going to Los Angeles to join his brother in a produce market. He'd write once in a while—with pencil on toilet paper. I really missed him.

Mud Tsuchikawa's name needs explaining. His given name was Masakatsu, which is as bad as Katsumi. Well, he had to have a nickname, but what can you make from Masakatsu? His family name, Tsuchikawa, means "Earth" *(tsuchi)* "River" *(kawa)*. It was easy to get the nickname "Mud" out of "earth river," so that's what we called him. Mud was the best bowler in our group, and also the smoothest dancer. Dancing made me sweat, and I disliked it. Even when I was going with Pete's sister, Aki, I wouldn't dance, so she and Mud would be out on the floor together while I watched from the table. Mud turned out for the football team, too, but he couldn't quite make it.

After Kay left for Los Angeles, Mud, Pete, Joe and I spent a lot of time together, fooling around, talking about girls, eating, getting into mischief but never really creating trouble or winding up in a jam. Sometimes he'd go up to Madrona Park to play tennis or dance with the car radio going full blast. Some evenings we'd drive out to Magnolia Bluffs for a weiner roast and to dig for butter clams. Some of my other friends were George Tatsumi, who we called Dimples because he had them, Eugene Amabe, known as Beefo because he was heavy-set. Tak Shibuya, who was the best baseball pitcher in our group as well as the best student, and Junelow (Junks) Kurose, who stood six feet tall and weighed 235 pounds. Junks was a senior when I was a sophomore and we played on the same team at Broadway. We did all the things white kids our age did for fun, but we never forgot we were Japanese Americans.

We lived an oddly mixed but pleasant life. We celebrated the Fourth of July, Thanksgiving and Christmas as well as the Japanese festivals like Boys' Day and Girls' Day and the Festival of the Dead in late summer. As children we went to public schools and learned about George Washington at Valley Forge and the grand heritage of a people who were willing to revolt for liberty and freedom. And after school was dismissed at 3 P.M., we trudged on to the Japanese Language School to learn a little about that very difficult language of our parents. Although some resented the double dose of schooling, we did not think it strange, because many of our Jewish friends in Seattle attended Hebrew school.

Somehow this life must have agreed with me, for by the time I was fifteen years old and a freshman at Broadway High School—in September of 1936—I stood five feet seven inches tall and weighed 168 pounds. Many of the other fellows signed up to try out for the freshman football team. I couldn't, because I had to go to Japanese school.

Still, it wouldn't hurt to watch for a little while. I sat on the sidelines, glancing at my Ingersoll watch frequently to make sure I would leave in time to get to Japanese school before the bell rang. About the third day the freshmen engaged in a scrimmage, and I couldn't tear myself away. I had played some sandlot football, and I figured I could do just as well as the boys in uniform. Before I knew it, it was too late to get to Japanese school on time. It didn't take me long to rationalize—being absent was only a little worse than being tardy. I was going to get a scolding if I showed up late without a good excuse, so I might just as well play hookey for the day. Before long, nothing seemed to be more important than playing football with the Broadway High School freshman team. I found myself walking over to the coach—his name was Bob Heaman—and telling him I wanted to turn out.

Heaman looked up and down my stocky frame. "What's your name?" he asked.

"Katsumi Yoshida," I replied.

"That's no name for a kid who wants to play football," he said. "I'm going to call you Jim." He reached into a pocket and pulled out a mimeographed form. "You have to get your parents' permission," he said. "Take this home and get your father to sign it. Come down to the locker room after school tomorrow and check out a uniform."

My heart sank. Here I was being invited to try out for the team and parental permission—an impossible obstacle —blocked the way.

Full of apprehension, I went home at the normal time. Apparently my mother was unaware of my absence from Japanese school, and if my sister Betty had noticed, she hadn't said anything. I knew that my mother could sense when I had something on my mind. Besides, I wanted to talk to her before Dad came home, so I came straight to the point.

"Mom," I said, "I want to turn out for the football team at school."

She scarcely looked up from her cooking. "Isn't it a very rough game?"

"Not really," I said.

After a moment she replied: "You are our only son, Katsumi, and I don't know what we would do if you were injured permanently playing football. Besides, what would you do about Japanese school? I think we had better forget about football."

I knew it was useless to try to change her mind, and even more useless to talk to Dad.

Next day, during a study period, I gave myself permission to play football. I carefully forged my father's signature on the slip. My hands were clammy when I gave the slip to Coach Heaman. I was sure he could hear the pounding of my heart and see the look of guilt that I knew was written on my face. But he failed to notice and routinely filed the permission form and issued me an ancient, hand-me-down uniform and a pair of ill-fitting shoes.

I made the team as a running guard. This meant I pulled out of the line and ran interference for the ball-carrier. If I did what I was supposed to do and threw a good block, the ball-carrier had a chance of making a good gain. The position required speed, agility, size, and the willingness to play the part of a human battering ram. I loved the body contact. At the end of the freshman season I was one of several boys invited to suit up with the varsity. In the season finale the varsity coach, Jerry Robinson, let me play half the game.

Meanwhile, for some reason I have never understood, my absence from Japanese school went unnoticed. Perhaps I had dropped out before anyone became aware that I should have been attending classes. At any rate three months had slipped by without my ever setting foot in Japanese school, and I all but forgot that I was really supposed to be studying the intricacies of the ancestral language rather than learning to block and tackle.

I was finally tripped up when Betty brought home her report card from Japanese school right after the football season ended. As usual she had done very well in her studies, and Dad nodded his approval as he examined her record. I knew what was coming next. He turned to me and asked to see my report card.

"Sir," I said, "I don't have one."

His eyebrows shot up. "Why not? Did you lose it?"

"No sir, I haven't been attending Japanese school."

He fixed me with a stare that bored right through me. We were at the dinner table and Mother had served all of us with hot boiled rice to eat with the cooked meat and vegetables. Steam rose from the bowl in front of my father and I could see his temper rising, too. Ordinarily, I was famished by mealtime and made quick work of my dinner, but now I had lost all interest in food.

"Explain yourself," Dad ordered.

So I told him the whole story, including the way I had forged his signature, and his frown grew darker and darker.

"*Bakatare!*" he finally shouted in fury. There is no precise English equivalent for that word. It means fool, or imbecile, but there is much more scorn, vitriol and invective in the word than is indicated by direct translation.

Good old Mom. She averted a very explosive situation

23

by suggesting that the dinner table was not the place for a scolding. She suggested we finish our dinner and then talk about the problem. I picked at my food while all the others seemed to eat with the usual relish. I wasn't too worried about what had happened—that was over the dam. My real concern was whether Dad would let me play football next season.

Sometime during the meal Dad must have seen the humor of my transgression. Perhaps he remembered pranks he had pulled as a boy. I was relieved to see his anger had given way to simply a serious mood when finally the dishes were cleared away.

First, he lectured me about how wrong it was to deceive one's parents, and I had to agree with him. Eventually he got around to football. "I can understand why you would want to play the game," he said. "It is a rough game and it is natural for boys to want to engage in rough sports. But you must remember you are the son of Japanese parents, and therefore you should take an interest in Japanese sports like *kendo* and judo."

Kendo is a form of fencing. The participants wear masks, helmets and armor, and whale away at each other with split bamboo staves which simulate the long, curved steel swords used by the samurai warriors of old. Judo is like wrestling, hand-to-hand combat, in which a smaller and weaker man learns to use his opponent's strength to defeat him. I wanted nothing to do with *kendo;* the prospect of fighting with sticks was too much. And I didn't have much enthusiasm for judo either, for I had heard that clever little fellows could whip big ones, and I was one of the "big" guys.

"Either sport is good," Dad was saying. "Either one will give you the discipline you need because they are Japanese sports. American life is too soft. You must learn to grow tougher, physically, mentally and morally."

Football isn't tough? He had never played football. He

didn't know what it was to get your brains jarred loose in a hard tackle and then come back for more.

Just then I saw an out. I apologized for what I had done. I was truly sorry. I agreed to go back to Japanese school and try my best to make up for what I had missed. And I said I would go to judo class—and here was the hooker —if I could play football again next year.

The smile that had started to take shape on Dad's face vanished. He raised his arm as though to strike me and just as suddenly he dropped it.

"All right," he said with resignation. "Play football if you must, if it's that important to you. But remember there are things that are important to me, too. So go to Japanese school and try to learn a little about the language. And go to judo classes and learn a little about discipline." We shook hands and I think I gained a deeper understanding of Dad that night than ever before.

Several nights later when I came home from Japanese school Dad introduced me to a handsome, curly-haired fellow who was about eight or ten years older than I. His name was Kenny Kuniyuki; he was an instructor at the Tentokukwan Judo School and the son of one of Dad's best friends. Dad told me Kenny would be my judo teacher. Kenny was a little taller than I, powerfully built with broad, square shoulders that tapered down to slim hips and the muscular legs of an athlete. I liked him immediately. We had dinner together and then he drove me to the judo school.

There were perhaps two dozen boys, many of whom I knew, fooling around on the judo mats. All were wearing padded jackets and short trousers. When Kenny entered, their yelling and laughing stopped abruptly and they snapped to attention. Apparently he was a very important person at the school. Kenny led me to the framed portrait of a little, half-bald old man which hung on one wall and told me to bow before it each time I entered the hall.

Later I learned he was Jigoro Kano, father of modern judo and regarded as a near-deity by devotees of the art.

For the next three weeks, every Monday, Wednesday and Friday, I went to the school and learned to sit Japanese-style with my legs folded under me, and to fall. Falling without hurting yourself is an art in itself. Gradually I learned to roll to absorb the impact as I hit the mat, to break the momentum with my arms and legs and shoulders before I crashed to the floor. Then Kenny—I was supposed to call him Kuniyuki Sensei (Instructor Kuniyuki) —began on the holds and throws. He seemed to think the best way to teach was to demonstrate. From seven to nine thirty I would practice with the other boys, throwing and being thrown almost without a break. Then the others were told to shower and change, but my evening was just starting.

"Come on, Yoshida," Kenny would say. He would let me throw him a few times, then *wham*, I would find myself thrown flat on the mat. "Get up," he would say. "We don't have time to sit around." *Wham*, I would go down again. Or he would say something like, "How would you like to see Tokyo?" I would drop my guard for the barest instant to reply, and *wham*, I would crash into the wall. He would pick me up, sweep my legs from under me and slam me to the mat, scolding me all the time for not taking the offensive. Once he put the choke hold on me and I was too exhausted to struggle. The bright lights overhead faded and I blacked out. Next thing I remember, I was sitting up with someone's knee in my back and arms across my chest. He jerked back on my shoulders while jabbing his knee into my spine and miraculously everything was in focus again.

Some of my friends felt that Kenny was picking on me unfairly. "Jim," one of them asked, "how come you take all that punishment? I'd quit if I were in your place." I must admit that I thought about quitting, especially on mornings after a particularly strenuous workout when I was so sore I could hardly crawl out of bed. But I knew that if I dropped judo I could forget about playing football. I also suspected that Dad had given Kenny orders to make it as rough as he could for me, and that only firmed up my determination to stick it out. Then one day it occurred to me that Kenny wouldn't be spending all that time with me if he didn't think a lot of me. And after that I vowed to take all the punishment he dealt out and come back for more. When Mom asked how I was getting along, I assured her that Kuniyuki Sensei was being extra nice to me.

About six months after I began judo lessons, everything began to fall in place. I was tough physically. I had learned, finally, to take the hardest falls without hurting myself, and now I was able to coordinate my skill together with my strength and dish it out as well as take it. I found a new exhilaration in the combat of judo, and excitement in the smell of the judo mats. Judo was as much fun as football.

Once a month we would have an intra-club tournament. The boys at the Tentokukwan School would be divided into two teams; then we would engage in elimination matches starting with the youngest and newest students. If you threw an opponent, or won a decision over him, you took on the next man and remained in the ring until you were defeated. Although I was bigger than most of the fellows, I still wore the white belt of the novice and was about in the middle of our lineup. In my first tournament I threw seven boys in a row, including two wearing the black belt of experts. I was having the time of my life. A black-belter must throw a white-belter or lose face. I had nothing to lose and could go all out. Kuniyuki Sensei gave me an approving look. Not long afterward I was jumped over all the intermediate steps—yellow, green, brown and purple—and given a black belt. It usually takes a student three or four years of hard work to win black-belt rating.

I had done it in a fraction of that time. Dad beamed approval.

He raised no objection when I turned out for football in the fall of 1937, my sophomore year. I had kept my end of the bargain and he kept his. I made the team as running guard and was lucky enough to be an all-city selection even though we didn't win a single game. This was a busy time for I continued with judo after the daily football workouts. Still, I managed to keep my grades up. After football season I returned to Japanese school and made a valiant but futile effort to catch up with the other students trying to master an almost incomprehensible language.

In the summer of 1938 Kenny took me with him to Taku Harbor, Alaska, where he was foreman in a salmon cannery. It was common practice for Nisei teen-agers in Seattle to work as cannery laborers during the two to three months of the summer season. We were paid about seventy-five dollars a month, plus transportation and room and board in a bunkhouse. Some of the boys gave their earnings to their parents to help support the family. Others saved the money for a college education. We ate rice and salmon at every meal and put in heavy physical labor ten hours a day, six days a week. Anything over sixty hours paid overtime—at thirty cents an hour if I remember correctly. I thrived on the hard work. I returned to Broadway High for my junior year with 190 muscular pounds on my five-foot nine-and-a-half-inch frame. We had a new coach and although I was a letterman, I had to start from scratch to earn my position. But I was bigger and stronger than most of the boys, and more experienced, and had no trouble keeping my job. Again we went through the season without a victory, and once more I was named all-city.

These were happy times. As a football star, I was a "big man" in school. My teammates were of many ethnic origins —Italians, Germans, Jews, Irish—but it never occurred to us that we were different. We were all Americans held together by a common love for football and loyalty to our school. I can remember only one fight, and that was with some college fellows. After judo practice one Friday night, Pete, Joe, Mud and I drove to a drive-in for some root beer. There was some difficulty getting out of the parking lot and four big fellows in another car made some loud remarks. One of them made the mistake of calling us "Japs," a fighting word like "Dago" or "Kike." We piled out in a hurry. Pete grabbed one of the fellows and threw him to the pavement. Joe had his man helpless in an armlock. The biggest fellow swung at me. I ducked, came up under him and flipped him to the ground. It was all over in about thirty seconds.

That evening I learned strength is power. When we demonstrated to those college guys that with judo we were their physical masters, they quickly lost their belligerence. They wanted to be friends. They invited us to have a drink with them. We turned them down, feeling like cocks of the walk. But we paid for it at Tentokukwan where, somehow, the officials had heard of the fight. It had been drilled into us time and again that judo skills were not to be demeaned by street brawls. Each night for the next two weeks we had to sit Japanese-style on our knees and meditate about our "sin." Our American knees weren't made for kneeling. We quickly got the point.

By the time my senior year rolled around, both my parents had become ardent football fans. Since someone had to stay at the barbershop, they alternated in coming out to watch me play. We had still another new coach, Al Lindquist. He figured that since I was fast enough to run in front of the ball-carrier, why couldn't I play in the backfield where my size would be useful? He shifted me to fullback and I guess the experiment was a success because, even though we still didn't win a game, we scored a touchdown—the first in three years. I took it over against Garfield High, and this is what I kept dreaming about when everything else in my life had turned to ashes. We eventually lost the game 27 to 7. The crowd had overflowed from the stands onto the field and as I picked myself up after scoring I saw Dad standing just outside the end zone in his big brown overcoat, a cigar in his mouth and a big grin on his face. I think the sight of that grin made me happier than scoring the touchdown. The judo training gave me a better sense of balance that helped me as a football player. I was named to the all-city team for the third successive year, this time as fullback.

A few weeks after the season ended, I came home from judo practice one night and found Mom looking worried. "Please be quiet," she said. "Your father is not feeling well." He had never been ill and I couldn't imagine his trouble was anything serious. I went to bed without thinking any more about it.

About 2:30 A.M. Mom shook me awake. "Your father is very sick," she said. "I want you to get dressed and take the car and pick up some of his friends."

Betty and I went out together into a steady drizzle. I kept the motor running as I waited for friends to get ready. Suddenly the steady click-click of the windshield wiper stopped. I couldn't understand what the trouble was because our Chevrolet was almost new. The clock on the dash showed 3:10 A.M. When we returned home, we learned Dad had died at precisely that time of a cerebral hemorrhage. The date was December 21, four days before Christmas, 1939.

Three

DAD's death seemed to end my hopes of going to college immediately after finishing high school. In winding up his affairs there was too much to be done that Mom could not handle. I had to be at home to help run the hotel until we could sell it. There were lawyers to talk to, papers to read and sign. Perhaps, after skipping a year, I told myself, I would be able to continue my education—and football. And so I was graduated from Broadway High School in June of 1940 and took over responsibilities as head of the household. I was, in effect, simply marking time until we could get our affairs in shape, spending my free hours at the judo school.

One night about a year after Dad died, Mom brought up a subject that had been in the back of her mind for a long time. She wanted to take Dad's ashes back to his home in Japan for burial.

"Do you remember how he used to say he would live in America forever?" she asked. "He didn't expect to die. But he also said 'When I go back to Japan I will go in an urn and not have to pay boat fare.' And so it has come to that."

Mom wanted to be in Japan no more than three months —just a vacation. "While we are there," she said, "Jim can enroll at the Kodokwan Judo College in Tokyo and become a real expert. We can come home in plenty of time for you to start college in the fall."

I had no desire to go to Japan, but the opportunity to study at Kodokwan was too good to pass up. I had earned third grade black-belt rank, and in all probability I could qualify for fourth grade in a relatively short stay at Kodokwan. In a manner of speaking, Kodokwan is to judo what the Vatican is to the Catholic priesthood. It is possible to learn judo and advance up the scale of proficiency without ever setting foot in Kodokwan. But one who has studied under the masters there enjoys a certain prestige, just like a priest who has had the good fortune to spend some time in Rome. To the three months that Mom wanted to spend in Japan, we had to add a month for the round trip voyage. We set April, 1941, when the weather would be nice in Japan, as the date for departure, and I renewed my efforts to find a buyer who would take over our hotel lease. After we came home, Mom said, she would like to find a modest apartment house she could manage and take in just enough income to make a living.

Meanwhile, what I had been hoping for became reality. Willamette University in Salem, Oregon, a small school noted for its academic as well as athletic program, offered me a scholarship if I would play football. I had doubts about my ability to make the team of a big Pacific Coast Conference school like the University of Washington. But I was confident I could perform adequately in a smaller league. When I explained my personal problem, I was assured the scholarship would be held open until I returned from the trip.

We sailed from Seattle on April 7, 1941, aboard the *Hikawa Maru,* a Japanese mail liner. Japan had been at war with China for four years and U.S.-Japanese relations had been strained as a consequence, but it never entered our minds that war between the two countries was imminent. In fact, such a war was unthinkable. Still, Mom knew that Japan's economy was strained. Our baggage included fourteen large steamer trunks in the hold, many of them packed with cans of meat, vegetables, fruits, coffee, tins of butter and other food items we had been used to. Mom feared that my sisters and I would be unable to adjust to rationed Japanese foods and she was taking no chances on our falling ill.

Joe, Mud, Pete and other friends came to see me off. I'm afraid I didn't say very much because my feelings were deeply mixed. I hated to leave Seattle, which was the only home I had known. I hated to leave my buddies and the gang at the judo school. But the idea of visiting a strange country and attending Kodokwan Judo School was exciting, too. The horn cut loose with a deafening blast, and the ship trembled as the engines began to turn. I was trembling, too. As the *Hikawa Maru* slowly eased backward out of the slip, I blinked back the tears. "So long, guys," I shouted to my friends across the widening gap of gray-green water. "I'll be seeing you in about four months. Don't wear out those Glenn Miller records I left with you."

Early one gray morning two weeks later we docked in Yokohama. My first impression of Japan was far from reassuring. Wiry little men, dressed in dark *happi* coats, black split-toed, rubber-soled *tabi* on their feet, small towels wrapped around their heads as sweatbands, scrambled over the tugs guiding the ship to its berth. They shouted to each other in a language that sounded nothing like what I had studied so laboriously in Seattle.

Mom had warned us about how unpleasant the customs inspectors would be. She was anxious to take American cigarettes to her relatives as gifts because Japanese tobacco, produced by a government monopoly, was so poor. Each person entering Japan was entitled to take in so many packages of cigarettes, but we had been told that sometimes the customs inspectors demanded proof that everyone claiming a tobacco quota was indeed a smoker. So she and my sisters had practiced smoking during the voyage. What a sight they were, coughing and choking and holding their cigarettes awkwardly as if they were afraid of being burned. Fortunately the inspectors were not nearly so strict as we feared. They even failed to detect the four packs I had hidden in my coat pocket. Mom was furious when I pulled them out in triumph after we were safely ashore. "Never fool around with Japanese officials," she warned. "It's dangerous." Before much longer I was to find out just how right she was.

The only difficulty was with a small portable radio. An inspector opened the back and tore out the built-in antenna. I guessed he thought the set might pick up shortwave broadcasts from overseas, for listening to foreign newscasts was forbidden. Mom did all the talking, following the customs men around with our declaration, and I couldn't understand more than a few words of what was being said.

Two uncles were waiting for us outside the customs area. There was Dad's older brother, Saisuke Yoshida, who had run the pig farm in Oregon before returning to Japan a few years earlier. I hadn't seen him since grade school days when we visited his place. Uncle Saisuke wore formal black *hakama* with a black cape over his shoulders. I remembered him as a farmer clad in overalls, with a floppy felt hat and heavy, mud-encrusted shoes. But now he looked distinguished and dignified, a gentleman, a man of means. He greeted us with misty eyes, and all of us burst into tears when we remembered Dad. Mom's older brother was there, too. His name was Denmatsu Uyesugi. He was tall for a Japanese, about my height, with fair skin and a long, deeply lined face, a scholar, famed for his skill as a calligrapher. The two men had traveled nearly a day and a half by train to meet our ship. I was moved by the obvious affection with which Mom was received. She had come home to *her* native land. She had status here, while back in Seattle, *my* native land, she was just the immigrant woman who cut people's hair and ran a hotel that was only a notch or two above a flophouse. Here in Japan, she belonged. But she lived in America by preference, and in months to come I was to have many occasions to ponder over this fact.

Before starting the long trip to our uncles' homes, at the southwestern tip of the main Japanese island called Honshu, they took us to an inn to rest for the night. Everything was new to me. There was no furniture in our room, only immaculate mats of rice straw on the floor. A maid hustled some soft, flat cushions to sit on. Later, I learned, bedding would be brought out from a closet and spread on the floor for us. Our dinners were served in the room by the same maid—bits of fish and prepared vegetables, beautifully arranged on tiny dishes. The portions were only slightly larger than appetizers for me, but I was so fascinated by it all that I didn't mind. The innkeeper himself entered our room to apologize for the dark rice he had to serve—half rice and half wheat. It was far from palatable.

"The rice is strictly rationed these days because of wartime shortages," he explained. "Please bear with us and accept the hardship. When the war is won, we shall have all the fine white rice we want."

He turned to Mom. "Make certain that your children do not waste rice, not a single grain. Rice is the life of our nation. We must conserve it for our troops fighting so courageously in China. As you travel, special military police will be on your train. If you buy a box lunch, be sure that every last grain is consumed before you discard the box." Every last grain indeed! I discovered before long that the box lunches were no more than a snack for me. Mom and my sisters felt sorry for me and gave me some of theirs.

That first evening a young Nisei shipboard acquaintance

and I went out to see the sights. We had heard that prostitution was legal in Japan and so it was inevitable that we should decide to find out what it was all about. "If it's a legitimate business, then we have every right to patronize the business," he argued and at the moment my curiosity overcame my prudence. We walked and walked but found nothing that looked like the red light district on lower Washington Street in Seattle. Finally we decided to ask someone, but realized to our chagrin that we couldn't make ourselves understood. As we were returning to the inn in disgust, I spotted a red light in the distance. We hurried toward it and found a very businesslike two-story building with a red light over the door. But now that we were there, we lost our nerve. The two of us must have paced up and down the street in front of the building for a half hour before I got up the courage to peek into the front office. A woman was working at a desk. She was neither young nor pretty, and she wore a white uniform, like a nurse's. "Boy," I thought, "they sure can do it up proper when it's a licensed business."

I ducked back out to the street and my friend and I flipped a coin to see who would enter first. I lost. I knocked on the door, walked in and stuttering and stammering, asked her what the charge was. She looked puzzled so I tried to explain as best I could what I wanted. She asked me to sit down, then picked up a telephone. I could make out that she was calling a doctor. "They even give you a physical here before they let you in," I thought. Then the light dawned. I was in a doctor's office! The red light indicated the office was open. I jumped up and hurried out and my friend and I ran all the way back to the inn, feeling indescribably guilty and foolish.

In the morning our party took the train for the ancient city of Kyoto, nearly a full day's ride to the southwest. Kyoto lay at the foot of wooded hills, with tiled temple roofs visible in almost every direction. It had a serenity and dignity about it that I could appreciate in an awed, inarticulate way. It had a sense of history that I had never encountered before. We checked in at an inn, then walked the next morning to the magnificent Nishi Hongwanji Temple, headquarters for the Buddhist denomination to which Dad had belonged. The main temple was a great wooden structure, as large as a cathedral. Giant columns made of logs as huge as the Douglas fir that grew in the forests near Seattle held up the vast tiled roof. We knelt in a cool, dark sanctuary off the main building for a special service in which a shaven-headed priest offered chants and prayers for Dad's spirit. Finally he opened the bronze urn which Mom had carried from Seattle, scooped out a few of the ashes, and placed them in a smaller urn for safekeeping at the temple. There were more chants, the sound of muffled bells, and then we lit incense to console Dad's spirit. It was a deeply moving ceremony. I had attended the Buddhist church in Seattle, but I had never understood the religion. I still did not understand it, but now I had gained a deeper sensitivity to its solemnity and beauty, and could appreciate Mom's feelings. Mom, too, seemed relieved that at least part of her mission was completed; some of Dad's ashes would be enshrined forever in the spiritual heart of his native land.

Once more we boarded a train to continue the trip to Dad's home town. Our destination was Yanai, a rail center in Yamaguchi Prefecture. Five miles outside of Yanai was the village of Hirao where Dad was born and grew up. Uncle Saisuke lived in the ancestral home next door to his *sake* brewery. A retail shop was on the first floor and the living quarters upstairs. We arrived to find cousins, uncles, aunts all over the place, anxious to make us welcome, but at the moment I wanted nothing more than to go home to Seattle.

The main trouble was that I was sick with a horrible case of diarrhea and the rural toilet on the first floor, which required that I squat—rather than sit—over a porcelain receptacle, was killing me. After each visit I felt almost too weak to stagger up a steep flight of stairs to my bed, which was nothing more than a quilt spread out on the straw mat floor. My back hurt from the unaccustomed firmness of the bed. I felt feverish and a rash was spreading over my body. I was as miserable as I had ever been.

After a few days, when I felt well enough to appreciate the warm hospitality of all my relatives, it was time to continue on to Mom's home. We hired a taxi and drove to the end of a nearby peninsula. There we boarded a ferry, no larger than a tugboat, for the ride to Kaminoseki, one of a half dozen tiny villages on an island in the Inland Sea about a mile offshore. It was the most beautiful spot I had ever seen. Clear blue water lapped at the pine-studded shores. A rocky point jutted out into the water, and Kaminoseki was built around a picturesque cove that it formed. There was no wharf. A small boat, sculled by two men, slid out through the placid water, pulled up alongside the ferry, and we and our baggage were transferred to it for the short trip to shore. There were only a hundred or so homes in the village, and it seemed nearly everyone came out to greet us. Some member from nearly half the families of Kaminoseki had moved to Hawaii or the United States mainland or had been there briefly to work, so the residents seemed to feel a kinship to anyone from abroad. Since there were no automobiles on the island, some of the men put our luggage on carts and trundled them to Uncle Denmatsu's home, the place where Mom had grown up. It was a tile-roofed two-story building surrounded by a whitewashed wall with an impressively ornate gate through it. Uncle Denmatsu's wife, a gray-haired, sweet-faced little woman, was waiting for us. She had lived in Hawaii for a time and could speak a little English. Because we could communicate she became my favorite instantly. She had prepared a sumptuous meal for us, featuring the seafood that abounded in nearby waters, and I was well enough to enjoy it immensely.

Later we walked to a tiny Buddhist temple that lay half hidden in a grove of twisted pine trees back of Kaminoseki. We found seats and Mom placed Dad's urn in front of her and bowed in meditation for a long time. Presently she began to weep. She wept softly, seemingly without bitterness or grief, weeping only as though it were a natural emotional outlet. No one moved to console her, and I sensed that the tears were good for her. Then she dried her eyes of her own accord and spoke to Dad's spirit. "Father," she said, "at last we have brought you back to your birthplace. I hope you can now rest in peace. We all miss you very much. The children are all well. We have sailed the Pacific safely, and before long we will go back home to Seattle. Please continue to watch over us, as you have always done." She bowed in silent prayer, lit some sticks of incense, placed the urn in the priest's hands, and then we left.

As we strolled back to Kaminoseki, I felt closer to Buddhism than ever before. It was more than chanting and listening to sermons and trying to do good. It was a religion that provided a link between me and the distant past, gave me roots that helped me to feel a kinship to ancestors beyond anyone's recall. And yet one point puzzled me. Why had Dad's ashes been placed in a temple near Mom's home rather than his own? I asked her about that and she explained that Dad's older brother, Uncle Saisuke, being the oldest surviving son of the Yoshida family, had the responsibility of carrying on the family name. He had also inherited his father's estate and had come back from America to assume his obligations. Dad, being a younger son, had no real claim to the Yoshida family line although he had been very close to his brother. And so Mom felt it would be better not to cling to the Yoshida ties, now that Dad was gone. She had chosen her family temple for his final resting place and ordered an appropriate headstone.

I learned about the meaning of head-of-family in another fashion that night. Rural Japanese homes have deep metal bathtubs, shaped almost like barrels. They are designed to be filled with cold water and a fire is built under the tub to heat it. One takes a bath by soaping, washing and thoroughly rinsing outside the tub, entering the steaming hot water at the end only to soak and relax. The head of the household takes his bath first when the water is both hot and clean. The others follow in descending order of importance, with the wife being last. That night, my aunt insisted that I bathe first, and I realized she was deferring to my position as head of my branch of the Yoshida family. I couldn't very well decline the honor. I scrubbed and rinsed in the prescribed manner, then tried to climb into the tub. Slatted boards are provided so one doesn't make direct contact and burn himself on the hot bottom of the tub. When not in use, the boards float, and I found it took a certain technique to keep the boards from bouncing away whenever I tried to put my weight on them. Eventually I squatted down in the tub with the water, almost too hot to bear, covering me up to my chin. Outside, I could hear my aunt scurrying around and tending the fire.

"Is the water hot enough?" she would ask through the window.

"Auntie, it is just right. Please do not exert yourself."

She thought I was being deferential. "We have plenty of fuel," she said, "so enjoy a good hot bath." She stoked up the fire and threw more wood onto the coals. For fear of hurting her feelings, I dared not get out of the tub until a reasonable time had passed. When I finally climbed out of the water I was as red as a boiled lobster. After that I managed somehow to avoid my bath prerogative as the head Yoshida.

All too soon the Kaminoseki interlude ended. It was time for me to enroll at Kodokwan Judo College. Mom took the train with me back to Tokyo, and en route we talked more about going home to the United States than we did about all the wonderful people we had met in Japan. Home was on both our minds.

In Tokyo Mom had arranged to have me stay with a cousin of hers who sold sewing materials and fabrics in a little shop. Their living quarters were above the shop. The place was small but neat and clean.

Despite my protests, Mom went with me to Kodokwan to register. I presented my certificates and letters of recommendation from the judo school in Seattle, and everything was in order. Only then did I realize that for the next eight or nine weeks I would be on my own in a strange country. As Mom's train pulled out to take her back to Kaminoseki, I felt utterly alone in a city of many millions, too homesick for Seattle to be excited by the prospect of working out with some of the best judo artists in the world.

Kodokwan Judo College was about an hour's ride by electric tram from where I lived. It was necessary to transfer twice but having made the trip once with Mom, I had no trouble finding it the next morning. The school was housed in a four-story building with shower facilities in the basement. The main practice area looked as big as two basketball courts, a vast expanse of heavy straw mats riding on countless steel coils to provide "give" for falling bodies. As I entered, the only sound was an occasional *ki-ai,* the hair-raising battle cry that sounds like *yeeee-oh!* as someone executed a throw, followed by a heavy thud as his partner hit the mat. There was no horseplay here, only intense, dedicated concentration on judo.

The instructor I was assigned to was Professor Kenzo Fujizawa, a former naval officer and seventh grade black belt. I judged he was in his early fifties. He was about five feet six inches tall, ruggedly handsome with broad shoulders, powerful arms, a small mustache and slightly wavy hair. It was the way he walked that impressed me. He moved with the lithe grace and coiled power of a panther. He spent a good part of the first day testing my knowledge of fundamentals, checking my technique for each of the basic throws. I passed with flying colors; Kenny had trained me well. I wondered if my fears about the Kodokwan had been exaggerated.

Next day the work started in earnest and I quickly changed my mind. In addition to the formal workouts I was subjected to an endless series of practice bouts. Anybody could come up to you, bow formally, and invite you to practice, and the rule was that you couldn't refuse. Perhaps I was a novelty because of my American background. Perhaps some of the experts wanted to test me because I was so much taller and heavier than most of them. At any rate a steady series of challengers would come up to me, bow, and invite me to grapple. All of them were good. Kenny Kuniyuki's training was kid stuff compared to what I went through for eight solid hours. It was not until the second day that I learned I was entitled to a fifteen-minute break for lunch at a tea shop in the basement. In Seattle it was not unusual for me to practice football for two hours in the afternoon, then go to work out with Kenny in the evening. But that was nothing compared to the demands Kodokwan put on its students. My judo jacket reeked with sweat. I bought two more so I could wash and dry the soiled ones and have a fresh jacket each morning. Even so, the collars became stiff as boards from perspiration that would not wash out, and rubbed my neck raw. When the sweat ran down into the sores they would sting almost unbearably.

Eventually, as I worked out day after day, the truth of what Kenny Kuniyuki had tried to teach dawned on me: Judo is not a test of strength alone; judo is a sport of skill and its essence is timing. Judo involves anticipating an opponent's moves and countering them. If two men of equal physical skill meet in a judo match, the one who out-thinks his opponent will win.

This is what Kenny had tried to hammer home to me even as I developed my physical skills. But when you are young and strong, it is difficult to understand this. You try to overpower your opponent, and because I was big and muscular I had been able to move up with a minimum of the real skill of judo. Now, at Kodokwan, I suddenly realized I could not survive the exhausting regimen on physical stamina alone. I was forced to resort to skill, to rely less on brute power and more and more on the art of judo whereby one utilizes his opponent's strength and weight and aggressiveness to make *him* do your bidding. If I learned nothing else at Kodokwan, I was grateful for this vital lesson.

Weary as I was at the end of each day, I was working myself into top physical condition. Little by little the fat disappeared. The muscles in my arms and shoulders stood out like whipcord and my abdomen was ridged like a washboard. My weight was down to 187, nearly fifteen pounds lighter than when I left Seattle.

Each night at home I would cross out the date on the calendar and count the days until Mom and my sisters and I would be going back to Seattle. There would be plenty to tell the gang at the Tentokukwan Judo School, stories they wouldn't believe about how tough the training was in Tokyo. And at this rate I would report for football in the best physical condition I had ever been in.

The only "day" of rest was Sunday afternoon; we even had to work out Sunday mornings. In the afternoon I would hurry home and write letters. The first one was to Mom, written laboriously in the simple characters that I had learned in the language school. I had so much to tell her about my progress, so much to ask about things in Kaminoseki, and my inability to express myself was maddening. She must have laughed over my letters—from a grown man but written as if by a child.

One day at school a frail-looking elderly man in Japanese

street clothes approached me as I was working out. My partner bowed and stepped back. "You must be Yoshida, the boy from the United States," the old man said. "Are you working hard? Show me what you have learned. Try your skill at throwing me."

I was astonished. An old man like this? And he wasn't even in judo garb. I hesitated, but he motioned me to seize his lapels. I reached out tentatively and, *wham*, I flew through the air and landed ignominiously flat on my face.

"That is no position for a judo expert to be in," the old man chided. "Haven't you learned to fall properly? Here, let us try it again."

I reached out even more cautiously, hoping to get a lock on his arm. Again he threw me, and this time I landed hard on my seat, jarring my spine. Everyone in the hall had stopped to watch us. I was furious, anxious to mix it up with the old man, but he stopped me with an upheld hand. "Go to the corner, Yoshida," he said, "and practice the fundamentals of falling. You have much to learn."

"Sir," I said bowing low, "I have been humbled. Please show me your special throw."

He smiled faintly, straightened his clothing and walked away. Everyone bowed as he passed them.

My erstwhile partner was all eyes. "How do you rate? How come you are so special?" he asked. Then he explained that the little old man was Mifune Sensei, the highest ranking judo artist in the world, the only person qualified to wear a red and white belt. He had spent twenty years in developing the *kuuki nage* (literally, "air throw," referring to the fact that he hardly seemed to put a hand on his opponent in throwing him) with which he had dispatched me. How presumptuous it had been to ask him to show me how it was done. Later, as I thought about it, I told myself, "No matter how good you think you are, Jim, old boy, there's always somebody who can knock your block off."

Not long afterward, three days before my final examinations, an opportunity arose to redeem myself. As I was winding up the day's practice, Professor Fujizawa approached. "I have a favor to ask," he said. "Some Navy seamen were to take their tests for the fourth grade black belt the same day you were, but their ship is to sail earlier than scheduled. They will be here shortly for some special tests, and I have no one to represent the school. I know you are tired after a hard day's workout, but will you help me out?"

Would I? What an honor it was to represent the school. My weariness vanished. There were to be eight seamen, all third grade black belt. Theoretically, each of them was equally proficient as I. How would I fare against them? "Here's one Yankee that's going to show up the Japanese Navy," I muttered.

The seamen were big, hulking specimens, deeply tanned, their heads shaved so close that their scalps looked blue. Mifune Sensei, the old man who had humbled me, officiated.

I took on the sailors one at a time. I threw all eight. The last match was the longest and I threw my man in three minutes. Proud enough to burst, I straightened my jacket deliberately, adjusted my belt, bowed with dignity to Mifune Sensei and walked off the mat with my best poker face. Inside, I wanted to dance and shout. Back home, the cheers for such a feat would have rocked the hall. At Kodokwan there was only silence. There must be no unseemly show of emotion. There must be only icy dignity.

But Professor Fujizawa showed he was human after all. Later, he clapped me on the back and exclaimed, "Well done, Yoshida." Only then did I allow myself a smile. Professor Fujizawa explained I had automatically won promotion to fourth grade black belt with that performance. "You are not required to take the regular test, but you may if you wish," he said. Shucks, I was ready to take on anybody. Three days later I threw four men to nail down my claim to the fourth grade black-belt certificate.

I said good-bye to Professor Fujizawa and other friends

I had made at Kodokwan, packed, said my thank-yous, wired Mom and hurried to Tokyo station to take the train to Yanai. Mom and the two uncles were at the depot to congratulate me.

"You've become so thin," Mom exclaimed. "Well, you'll have a chance to rest a few days before we start home."

We spent the first night at Uncle Saisuke's home in Hirao and left the next morning for Kaminoseki. Tokyo had been sweltering. A sea breeze kept Kaminoseki comfortably cool. I gorged myself on my aunt's cooking, slept late, swam and lazed in the sun, unwinding from the weeks of intense training while waiting to start our homeward journey. Meanwhile, along with her packing, Mom was making farewell calls on all her relatives for she did not know when, if ever, she would return to Japan again.

And then our idyllic little world came to an end in the form of a harmless little telegram delivered by the mailman on his bicycle. I remember the date well, August 12, 1941. The telegram was from the travel agency through which we had booked passage. It said simply: "Regret to report all shipping to U.S. suspended temporarily. Will contact you as soon as definite booking can be made."

Shipping suspended? What did this mean? Had the seamen's union gone on strike? What did the telegram mean by "suspended temporarily"? Would I be able to get home in time for the football season? We talked late into the night.

Four

NEXT morning Mom and Uncle Denmatsu left for Yokohama on the first train to find out what the shipping suspension was all about. My sisters and I were cautioned to be ready to join them on a day's notice if passage could be booked.

Mom returned several days later. One had only to see her face to know the news was bad. She explained that the United States had abrogated its treaty of friendship and commerce with Japan, a very drastic act to underline Washington's displeasure after Japan forced the Vichy French government to grant military bases in Indo-China. This meant that Japanese credits had been frozen in American banks. Shipping between the two countries was at a standstill, and no one could guess when commerce could be resumed.

"Does this mean we can't go home?" I asked in near-desperation.

"I'm afraid so, Jim," she told me gently. "There's nothing we can do but wait and see what will happen. The people in Yokohama told me the government has taken a very serious view of these developments and no one seems to hold out much hope that the ships will be sailing again in the near future. But I have been promised reservations on the first available vessel."

Relations between Japan and the United States obviously had deteriorated badly while I had been in Tokyo. I vaguely remembered hearing something about it. But I could not read the Japanese newspapers and had been too busy to keep up with English language publications like the Japan *Times*. No doubt the unscheduled departure of the Japanese seamen I'd met in the judo tests had been connected in some way with the worsening international situation. And in Hirao, a backwater town at the end of the communication line, the news, if it had come at all, had caused scarcely a ripple in the placid pace of country existence.

I was stunned by this turn of events. Slowly the realization sank into my head that we were stranded in a country that might, just might, get involved in a war with the United States. War between America and Japan? Impossible, I told myself. It just couldn't happen. Why, America was so big and powerful and advanced that Japan wouldn't dare start anything. Yet, I listened with sinking heart when Uncle Denmatsu said it appeared to him that things would get worse before they could become better.

Summer slipped into fall. The persimmons ripened and the tiny Japanese maples turned crimson. It was a beautiful season in southern Japan, but I was in no mood to appreciate it. Back home, I knew, the Willamette University football squad was working out, learning plays, toughening up for the campaign ahead, and I wasn't with them. I had rarely used cigarettes, but now I found myself chain-smoking as I wandered along the seashore and climbed the hills by myself brooding, wondering, hoping.

I became aware of an ever-tightening economy as though Japan were cinching up its collective belt to prepare for the ordeal of an all-out war. Mom said sugar and rice were becoming increasingly more scarce in the stores. Government officials visited our village to take stock of rice reserves and to make sure there was no hoarding. Ladies of the Women's Patriotic Organization, dressed in white smocks with armbands proclaiming their mission, called on each household to urge that we blend more wheat with the rice to stretch the supply. I had another theory. The wheat spoiled the palatability of the rice so we wouldn't eat so much. The canned goods that we had brought from America—luncheon meats, fruits, vegetables—were about gone. Mom urged us to eat more fish since beef and pork, which were scarce anyway, now were almost nonexistent.

Although I understood little of what was being said, I listened frequently to the radio, trying to pick up scraps of news. About all that was being broadcast was martial music and exhortations to conserve, to save, to sacrifice for the good of the nation. More strangers came to our village and enlisted most of the teen-age boys into the *Seinen-dan,* a patriotic youth movement. Their first assignment was to help with the harvest. While all this activity passed me by, I was acutely aware of the rising tempo of nationalism. Even distant relatives, who had come to pay their respects to Mom and my sisters and me when we first arrived, were visited by the Secret Police and questioned. For their own safety, people who had been very friendly toward us stopped dropping in. They appeared uncomfortable when they saw me approaching on the street, and fearing I would add to their troubles, I tried to avoid them.

Sunday, December 7, was just another quietly frustrating day. It would be Saturday back home on the other side of the International Dateline. No news from the travel agent. No letters from Seattle since the shipping freeze. I took a hot bath and went to bed early for want of anything better to do.

Next thing I knew Mom was shaking me awake. "Jim," she said, "Jim, listen carefully. I think it has started at last."

"What's started?"

"The radio says *Shinju-wan*—that's Pearl Harbor, isn't it—has been attacked by naval aircraft. Isn't that in Hawaii? The radio says a state of war exists between Japan and the United States."

I sat bolt upright. Mom was kneeling Japanese fashion on the *tatami* (straw mat) beside my bed, looking suddenly tired and old in the harsh light of the single bulb that hung from the ceiling. Tears coursed down her cheeks. "Oh, Jim," she cried, and threw herself into my arms. "What are you going to do? What have I got you into by bringing you to Japan?" I had never seen her like this. She had always been strong, controlled, and now she was weeping openly. I comforted her as best I could and together we went to the radio.

A recording of the Japanese Navy's favorite "Battleship March," was being played. Presently the announcer cut in with excitement in his voice: "Even at this moment the brave pilots of the Imperial Japanese Navy are pursuing their bombing attack on the Pearl Harbor base of the United States Pacific Fleet. First reports indicate the brilliantly executed assault was far more successful than anticipated. The Pacific Fleet has been annihilated. Sunk or seriously disabled at their moorings are the battleships *Arizona, California, Oklahoma, Nevada, West Virginia, Pennsylvania, Maryland, Tennessee* and many smaller warships. Towering clouds of black smoke are rising above the American base. Our pilots report virtually no resistance as the Americans were caught entirely off guard."

I could make out perhaps half of what he was saying and Mom filled in the rest for me. It seemed incredible that so much damage could be wreaked in a single attack. In my mind the Japanese Navy was still represented by the quaint old relics of the Russo-Japanese War that used to call on Seattle in the course of round-the-world training cruises with newly commissioned ensigns aboard. Those ships were spick-and-span, but they were no match for the great, gray capital ships of the U.S. Navy that anchored in Elliott Bay during the summer Fleet Week along with the massive flattops, *Lexington* and *Saratoga*. I searched desperately for something to console my mother and, I suppose, to reassure myself.

"Look, Mom," I said. "American battleships are named after the states, and you know there are forty-eight states. What if the announcer is telling us the truth? Maybe they sank or damaged six or eight battleships, but we must have forty of them still left, plus a lot of cruisers and destroyers and submarines. The United States will win and this war will be over in no time at all."

But deep in the pit of my stomach I felt a cold, hard lump of fear that would not go away, even after Mom fixed breakfast of hot bean-paste soup, pickles and rice. There was great excitement in the village. I kept out of sight, listening to the radio, not knowing what to expect.

That night the village authorities passed the word—black cloth would have to be draped around all interior light bulbs and all windows must be blacked out. There would be no smoking outdoors after dark. I had to laugh. The radio announcers were still telling the nation what a tremendous victory had been scored at Pearl Harbor, but we in our tiny village—of no military significance whatever —were being ordered to take precautions against an air raid or even a possible invasion.

A week passed and life returned to its normal pace in little Kaminoseki. I half expected a visit from the Secret Police, but none showed up. For the moment, apparently, the officials had no reason to confront me directly. For want of anything better to do, Betty left for the city of Yamaguchi to attend school. I missed her terribly; she was the only one I could speak English with. It was now obvious that I wasn't going home for a long time, not for the duration of the war, and already the inactivity was driving me to distraction. I couldn't just sit in the house waiting for the Secret Police to arrive. I couldn't simply wait for the war to end. I had to do something, but the choices were very limited if for no other reason than that I was an enemy alien who understood little of the language. Whatever I sought to do would have to be acceptable to the Japanese, who were at war with my country, and to me, an American trapped against my will inside an enemy nation.

Uncle Saisuke Yoshida came up with a happy answer. Yanai Commercial School, with some 2,000 male students of high school age, had lost its judo instructor to the Army and was looking for a replacement. He had been assured I would be acceptable. The school was only about three miles from Hirao where Uncle Saisuke lived, about midway on the road to Yanai. He offered to let me and Mom stay with his family. Mom, who had been worried about my mental outlook, agreed this was a fine opportunity, and I decided to give it a try. But first, certain preparations had to be made. Among other things I needed a *kokuminfuku,* a semi-military uniform that all men were now wearing. None of the stores had a ready-made uniform that would come anywhere near fitting me, so I had to have one tailor-made. The uniform consisted of trousers and a close-fitting jacket with high collar. The tunic was made to be worn without a shirt, a washable insert being slipped under the collar. The uniform was of brownish-green twill. There was also a short-billed cap worn without insignia, and roll-on woolen leggings like the kind used by American troops in World War I.

As soon as the uniform was delivered I put on the trousers, folded the cuffs under and tried the leggings. They didn't even reach halfway up my calf.

"You have such heavy legs from all that football and judo," Mom said, "I don't think those leggings are long enough."

I ran down to the tailor and bought a second pair of

leggings and Mom sewed them together, end to end, so they were twice the ordinary length. Somehow I got them wrapped around my calves and the ends knotted, but as soon as I tried to walk they collapsed in a ridiculous heap around my ankles. No matter how I tried wrapping those leggings, they refused to stay up. Finally I took them back to the tailor and explained my predicament.

They say Japanese are too polite to laugh in your face, but the tailor had no such inhibitions. He laughed until his face was red and then explained that my mistake was in winding the leggings around and around in a spiral. They had to be twisted, in a herringbone pattern, each time around so that they overlapped. In that way each loop supported the next one, and a man could walk all day without the leggings slipping down. He did it so easily that I had to laugh with him. It was my first good laugh in weeks. I chuckled all the way home at my stupidity.

I also purchased a bicycle for transportation, and two lunch boxes. The regular tires on the bicycle looked too flimsy to bear my weight, so I had heavy duty models put on. The ordinary Japanese lunch box, with a compartment on one side for rice and a second compartment for pickles or vegetables or whatever, simply didn't accommodate enough food to satisfy my appetite. So Mom arranged for me to carry two of them.

"Thanks to judo, you have a good job now," she told me as I prepared for my first day. "For the kind of work you will be doing, your knowledge of Japanese is adequate. I know you will work hard. If there are things you do not understand, be sure to ask. There is no shame in inquiring. The only shame is in remaining ignorant through false pride."

"Okay, okay," I replied. Mom couldn't seem to get it through her head that I was no longer a child.

I was introduced that morning to other members of the faculty. Most of them were slight, thin, mousy-looking

53

men, probably rejected long ago by the Army. They looked me over curiously. I had no doubt they knew who I was and what strange circumstances had brought me into their midst.

I was to share quarters with the *kendo* teacher who taught fencing as a martial art. He took me in hand and showed me about the school, and I liked him immediately. I had five judo classes during the day and worked with the school judo team after hours. Judo was a major interscholastic sport, I found, its position being comparable to football in American high schools. Yanai Commercial's chief rival was Yanai High School, which was about a mile away.

I hit it off very well from the beginning with the young-sters, who were only a few years my junior. For one thing, I gave no lectures, and they appreciated that. I just wasn't capable of delivering a lecture. And they could tell quickly that I knew something about the sport. I soon discovered the boys had nicknamed me "Judo-man." It was an honor. The principal was known behind his back as "Cat" because of his unblinking eyes. The vice-principal was "Baldy" for obvious reasons and one of the math teachers was "Toad." I wonder what name the boys would have picked if they didn't like me.

Shortly after my arrival a formal parade was scheduled to introduce me to the student body. Each teacher had to sign out a military-issue saber and march at the head of his home room class. The boys in my home room showed me how to fasten the saber in place and coached me on the way to draw it as our group passed the principal's re-viewing stand. There was no time to practice marching, so I decided to watch the group ahead of mine and depend on the experience and good judgment of my boys.

The lower grades passed in review first. My group was made up of third-year boys, so we were about in the mid-dle. The marching looked easy until I found that everyone swung into an unnatural, high-stepping walk as they approached the reviewing stand.

It was too late to back out. I marched on doggedly.

About fifty feet in front of the stand I heard one of the boys in back of me whisper, "Now, sir, now."

I shouted a judo-type *"yeee-oh,"* just the way the teacher in front of me had done, and reached down to draw my saber. Just then the scabbard got caught between my legs, and I stumbled forward and fell flat on my face. I scrambled to my feet and tried again to draw the saber, but now it was bent and refused to budge. "Oh, hell," I muttered under my breath. I executed a snappy "eyes right," threw the principal a Boy Scout salute, and marched on. The principal was grinning. I heard snickers behind me. Mom cried with laughter when I told her about the incident that night. It was great to hear her laugh again.

Thirty boys turned out for the school judo team, which would be made up of five regulars and two subs. They were a fine lot and I enjoyed being with them. We had only two weeks before the first match, and the lads wasted no time. I worked out with each of them to test their skills. On these occasions it was easy to forget I was in Japan. The smell of the judo mats, the soft sighing of bare feet shuffling for position, the occasional grunts and thumps of falling bodies, transported me back to Seattle where I had spent endless hours in the same kind of gym with boys who looked little different from the youngsters I was teaching now. Making believe I was home again, doing the things I enjoyed, gave me an inner peace that nothing else could do.

In a few days I trimmed the squad down to fifteen boys. The two best were a lad named Hamada, who had been team captain the previous year, and Nakamura, a shy, quiet youngster who stood nearly six feet tall. Hamada was so confident of his position that I found him loafing several times. Nakamura, on the other hand, never let up. But when he sparred with Hamada, he seemed to hold back, never attempting the spectacular throws that he executed so well. I could not understand why he showed this deference toward Hamada. One afternoon, following a workout with Nakamura, I told him I had chosen him captain.

Nakamura flushed. "Oh, no, sir," he exclaimed. "It cannot be. Hamada must be the team captain."

"Nonsense," I replied. "You are the better man and you deserve to be captain."

Next morning I submitted the team roster to the principal. That afternoon I was summoned to a special faculty meeting.

The principal hemmed and hawed for quite a while before he came to the point, which was that he did not want Nakamura as captain, and in this he was supported by all the teachers.

"But why, sir?" I cried. "I am the judo coach here. I have worked hard with the boys and it is my decision that Nakamura is best qualified and deserves the captaincy. Why is this a matter for the entire faculty's concern?"

There was a long silence, and then Hashimoto, the history teacher, spoke up. "Yoshida Sensei," he said, "we respect your opinion. But you are new here. Hamada was captain last year. Hamada's father is a very prominent businessman in town—"

I interrupted impatiently: "Why should that matter?"

"Please let me finish. Perhaps you did not know, but Nakamura, despite his name, is not Japanese. He is Korean, and I am sure you know what that means."

Anger gave me an eloquence I did not know I possessed. Back home, even though our schools taught us that all men were created equal, that America was a land of liberty and justice for all, we knew that prejudices existed. We knew that when it came to finding jobs and living in the kind of homes we could afford, there was discrimination against

Japanese Americans because we were of a different skin color. I hadn't expected to find racial prejudice in Japan, and suddenly I was outraged.

"Don't you see the injustice of what you are trying to do?" I demanded in my best Japanese. If my words were not entirely clear, the tone of my voice carried the message. "You talk of fighting the war to win Asia for the Asiatics, but that's a lot of bunk when you discriminate against a student simply because he happened to be born a Korean."

My friend, the *kendo* teacher, was first to reply. "Yoshida," he said, "the judo team is your responsibility. You have made your decision. Stick to it."

The retired Army colonel who headed the military training program was next: "What Yoshida says is right. I support him."

And so Nakamura, the Korean, remained team captain and if he ever learned of the debate in the faculty meeting, it was not from me. He proved to be an inspirational leader, and more than that, he was able to get Hamada's support and cooperation as his assistant. Yanai Commercial defeated Yanai High 4-1, Shimonoseki High 3-2, Fukuoka 4-1, and in the Southern Japan finals, we beat Beppu 3-1 with one tie.

We were preparing to meet Sendai High, the northern division champions, for the all-Japan finals when the tournament was canceled. Someone in Tokyo had decided that students had more important things to learn and do. And besides, the Japanese transportation system was overloaded as it was.

The development of Nakamura's personality during the season was something to behold. His confidence grew and he overcame his shyness. But he never threw his weight around; if anything he was more humble. I mentioned this to Mom one day. "A good man is like a stalk of rice," she said. "The heavier the load of grain it bears, the lower the stalk bends as though in humility. It is only the useless weed that stands arrogantly erect." The Japanese have a way of saying things that gets right to the heart of the matter.

The spring of 1942 slipped into summer. I still did not read enough Japanese to make out what the newspapers were saying, and so my war news was limited to what I could understand on the radio. I heard unfamiliar names made even more strange by the phonetic renditions of Japanese announcers—Guadalcanal, Kiska, the Solomons, Coral Sea, Midway. It was impossible to tell how the war was going. I knew only that food rationing was growing more strict, and now even older men were being drafted. I wondered if I would be called up, and what I would do when the call came.

One day late in the fall of 1942 our village representative in the town council told Mom that I was to report for an Army physical.

I knew I had no choice but to report, but I questioned the legality of the order anyway. "Mom," I asked, "what do you think would happen if I stood on my rights as an American citizen and refused to show up for the examination?"

"It would be unwise," she said. "I'm afraid American laws have very little meaning in Japan in times like this. Besides, I think the Japanese Army has a legal right to demand your services"—she paused for a moment, then continued—"because you are a Japanese citizen."

It was the first time I had heard this. I had thought that I was an American by right of birth. I needed an American passport when I traveled to Japan. How could I be a Japanese citizen?

Mom explained it to me. At the time I was born in Seattle, the Japanese government laid claim to my allegiance simply because I was the child of Japanese citizens. The law stated that a child is a Japanese if his or her father is a Japanese at the time of his or her birth. This, I learned later, is called the law of *jus sanguinis* and is practiced by many countries. In 1924, three years after I was born, Japan changed its citizenship laws, largely at the request of Japanese residents of the United States who foresaw complications. The new law stated that a child born of Japanese parents in the United States, Canada and many South American countries no longer would be considered a Japanese subject unless the parents indicated within fourteen days their intention of claiming Japanese citizenship for the child. This meant a child was no longer automatically Japanese. It required a positive act to claim Japanese citizenship. The law also provided that those born prior to 1924, and who consequently possessed dual citizenship, could cancel their Japanese citizenship by filing formal papers. My parents had neglected to do this. Apparently it was just a lot of red tape they didn't understand. And so even though I had known nothing about it, I was legally both Japanese and American.

What a helluva fix to be in. Yet there was nothing I could do about it now. I showed up for my physical as ordered, together with a number of youngsters who had just reached draft age.

An Army nurse weighed me and measured my height. If she was surprised at my size—I was a good head taller than most of the others—she didn't show it. Then she took my pulse and told me to move on to the next room. A sergeant ordered me to strip. I took off my shirt and trousers and was standing there in my American jockey shorts wondering what to do next when suddenly someone kicked me hard from behind. It was the sergeant. "Are you a man?" he shouted. "Are you ashamed of what you've got? Why try to hide it? When I told you to strip, I meant strip." It was my first encounter with the Japanese Army. I could hardly keep from slugging him. I had a lot to learn.

When I told Uncle Saisuke what had happened, he suggested the sergeant was angry because I was wearing American underwear. "These are times," he said, "when everything foreign, even baseball, is being rejected. It would be better if you got rid of your American shorts." He provided me with a long loin cloth that the Japanese wrap around themselves like an athletic supporter. It was quite uncomfortable and I never liked it. Until I got the knack of wearing it, the cloth would come loose, and several times I found an end sticking out from my trouser bottom as I pedaled my bicycle.

A few days after the examination I received a red card in the mail. It stated that I had passed my examination and that I was to report to the 42nd Division in Yamaguchi City on the first Sunday of February, 1943. The notice was not unexpected. In fact, even though I dreaded the thought of serving in the Japanese Army—what would I do if I were sent to the South Pacific to fight the Americans?—it was almost a relief to be called and get the suspense over with.

The attitude of the villagers in Hirao changed abruptly when I received my draft notice. I suppose they had resented the fact that a big, strapping young man like me had not been summoned for military service. But now they came around with delicacies for me. Some of the ladies of the neighborhood sponsored a *sen-nin-bari,* a length of cloth into which a thousand stitches had been sewed. It was worn next to the skin around the waist as a good-luck amulet and to keep the stomach warm. I was assured a warm stomach would protect me from all manner of digestive upsets, and the stitches, each representing the best wishes of some woman, would ward off danger. But I knew that many a local youth who had been sent off to war with the protection of a *sen-nin-bari* came home only as a handful of ashes in a little white-wrapped wooden box. Still, the good wishes of these simple country people were warmly reassuring.

The third anniversary of Dad's death passed, then Christmas. Back home in Seattle, despite being Buddhists, we had observed Christmas as a holiday, exchanging gifts and observing it as a time of family affection and goodwill even though the religious implications had no meaning for us. In Japan we ignored Christmas entirely. New Year's was the important holiday. Mom helped Uncle Saisuke's wife prepare a feast. There was ample food—baked fish, rice cakes, boiled seaweed—although some of the more exotic delicacies so important to the Japanese were missing. The limited supplies had been sent to the troops at the front.

Reminiscing late in the day, I recalled a New Year's celebration in Seattle when I was only fourteen years old. Dad made it a custom of drinking a toast to the Emperor, shouting three loud *banzai's* for his long life and good health. There was nothing political about it. It was just Dad's way of paying his respects to an institution that he had been taught to revere and respect. All of us children were expected to take part in the rite, performed in front of a portrait of Emperor Hirohito, but for some reason I had refused on that morning. Perhaps it was teen-age rebellion. Perhaps I was simply expressing my independence. At any rate, I stubbornly shouted that the Emperor meant nothing to me and refused to join in the toast.

Dad was furious. I suppose he was more angry about my insubordination than any affront to the Emperor. He was also disturbed about dissent in the family on New Year's Day. This was supposed to be a joyous occasion, when all the unpleasantries of the past year were forgotten and we began with a clean slate, and I'm sure he was aggrieved to find me in such a contrary mood. He promptly ordered me to my room. Later, Mom brought me some food, so I wouldn't miss out entirely on the holiday, and asked me to apologize to Dad. I refused. As I recall, I never did apologize, and I guess Dad just decided to forget about the entire incident.

Mom remembered that day very well. "You were so stubborn," she said. "You are still stubborn. I worry about you very much. You must remember that this is Japan, not America, and you are powerless. You must do what you are told to do. In a few weeks you will be in the Army, in the service of the Emperor whether you like it or not. The important thing is that you come back sound of mind and body. It is all very well to stand on principle, as you did back in Seattle on that New Year's Day so long ago, but principle will not mean a thing if you are imprisoned, or perhaps executed, for insubordination. Remember, the military knows no law. To die in battle is one thing, but it is another matter to bring shame to the Yoshida name. I know you will have a very difficult time in the Army, but you can endure anything if you make up your mind to do so. You have an excellent constitution, toughened and disciplined by football and judo. Your body will serve you well if you will only toughen your mind and spirit in the same manner. And don't worry about your mother and sisters. They will be all right. You will be in our thoughts always. Son, take good care of yourself."

This is the gist of what she said and I think I quote her accurately. There was still a communications barrier between us through the fact that her English was halting and my Japanese only rudimentary. We could talk easily about the ordinary, everyday, housekeeping type matters. But when it came to discussing philosophical and moral concepts like honor and responsibility, I could only guess at the meaning of her words. Mom was not accustomed to revealing her feelings, so I knew she spoke from the heart, and I sensed rather than understood the precise import of what she said that day.

I had many occasions to think about her admonitions. What did she mean by the importance of not bringing shame to the Yoshida name? How did she expect me to behave? As an American? As a Japanese? Honor meant as much in the United States as it did in Japan, I knew.

These thoughts always ended up with the question as

to what I would do if by some great misfortune I should meet, face to face, friends like Pete and Mud and Joe on the field of battle. They were almost like brothers. They would be in American uniforms, serving their country. I would be in Japanese uniform through circumstances beyond my control. Would they shoot me? Would I shoot them? Would I shoot other Americans who were simply nameless boys like those I had played football against— and with? I had no answers except this: If I met Pete and Mud and Joe, I could not hurt them. I would let them kill me before I pointed a weapon in their direction and pulled the trigger. Of this I had no doubt whatever.

Such desperate thoughts were interrupted one evening shortly before I was due to report when my judo students, Nakamura and Hamada, and a third boy called on me. After the preliminaries Nakamura said: "Sir, all three of us have volunteered for the Army so that we can be with you. They are taking even high school students now, you know, and we will probably be in the same unit when you are called up."

"But why?" I asked. "You don't have to go until you are graduated, and it is very important that you complete your education."

"Sir," said Nakamura, "I hope you will not mind my saying so, but you are not much of a soldier." The three boys smiled as Nakamura continued: "That day when you stumbled at the parade proved it. Besides, you read and write Japanese only like a child, and you don't speak or understand it much better. You will have a very difficult time in the Army, and we wish to be with you so that we can help and protect you."

I was speechless. These high school students volunteering just so they could help me! I tried to make light of it but could only press their hands in gratitude. I don't know whether they were accepted for service. After that evening, I never saw them again.

The next night Hamada's father came to the house with

a heavy wrapped package under his arm. I was surprised to see him. He was the "very important businessman" who the teachers had feared to offend when I picked Nakamura as judo team captain. I had believed that my action had angered him. Among other businesses, Hamada owned a confectionery shop. Now he had brought us a fifty-pound sack of brown sugar from his dwindling stocks.

"It is strictly rationed already," he said, explaining what we already knew. "Soon there will be no more. I want you to have it so you will not worry that your mother will be wanting for sugar while you are at the front."

My protests were to no avail. He insisted we keep the sugar, explaining he was deeply in my debt and that he would not feel right unless he could repay it in small part. I did not understand, but Mom explained it later. Mr. Hamada felt I had done him and his son a great favor when I demoted the boy from captain because both of them knew he did not deserve the honor. "The boy's sense of values would have been badly damaged if he had been named captain when obviously he was not the best man," Mom said. "Only you had the courage to demote him, and Mr. Hamada is grateful that you put his son in his place. That was Jim Yoshida, the American, who ignored the father's prestige and influence and saw that justice was done."

After that, when we wanted to talk about the sugar without anyone knowing, we called it Jim. Jim was our code name for our private hoard of precious sugar.

On January 31, 1943, my last night at home, many relatives came to the house for a send-off party. Some had tucked money in envelopes for me. Others gave me good-luck charms to guarantee my safe return. Uncle Saisuke dug out some of his best *sake* and it flowed liberally. I excused myself early and went to bed, but sleep did not come. I was frightened and worried, not knowing what was in store for me, aware of my inability to understand the language, terrified by the thought that I might have to go into combat against American troops. I don't think I slept a wink that night. I heard Mom stirring early. She fixed a big breakfast, but I had no appetite for it. Uncle Saisuke had arranged for two taxis to take us to the Yanai railroad station where less than two years earlier we had arrived from the States. Friends and neighbors lined the streets near Uncle Saisuke's home, shouting *"Banzai, banzai, banzai,"* and waving little Rising Sun flags. But here and there I could see women wiping away tears. I sat quietly in the back seat, holding Mom's hand.

A special military train waited at the station. Names were being read over a loudspeaker system, and other recruits like myself were running about in confusion. Suddenly I heard my name called. I hugged Mom, then tore away. Pushing into the third class railroad car assigned to our group, I rudely shoved two other recruits away from a window seat and peered about in search of Mom. She was worming her way through the crowd toward me, my two uncles right behind her.

I heaved on the window, but it was stuck and refused to budge. I yanked at the top portion and managed to pull it down part way. Mom was trying to tell me something, but I couldn't make out a single word over the hubbub. I climbed on top of the wooden seat and stuck my arms and head out, managing to catch hold of Mom's outstretched hands. Everyone was talking and shouting, and I still couldn't hear what she was saying. The locomotive's whistle shrieked and the train jerked forward. Now I could make out her words: "Katsumi, Katsumi." She was calling my Japanese name. "Katsumi, please take care of yourself. Just take care of yourself. Don't worry about your mother. Take good care of yourself."

The train was moving now. Her grip on my hands eased and she ran along the platform, trying to keep up. The sight was more than I could bear. I jerked my head inside and in sudden uncontrollable despair, I drew back my gloved fist and smashed the window. Through the jagged glass I saw Mom's face for the last time, the features contorted in grief, the tears streaming down her face.

Then something belted me across the right ear. The impact knocked my head against the window frame, and for half an instant I was stunned. I swung around, fists clenched to strike back, and came up face to face with a uniformed warrant officer.

"Baka! Fool!" he shouted. "Sit down!"

The train was moving more rapidly. I could hear the wheels clickety-clicking over the rails. I sat and let the tears roll down my cheeks, not caring how I looked. My last tie with home—home in the States—had just been severed. I didn't give a good goddam about anything any more.

Five

FOR what seemed to be a long time I sat staring at nothing as the train chuffed and rattled over the countryside toward the city of Yamaguchi. None of the other men paid a bit of attention to me; many of them had witnessed my outburst, but from a natural sense of reserve they ignored it. Some were talking loudly among themselves in a country dialect unfamiliar to me. Others seemed to be lost in their own thoughts. By the time we reached Yamaguchi Station shortly before noon I had regained my composure, given myself a pep talk, and had vowed to face up to the future like a man. No more emotional breakdowns, I warned myself.

The warrant officer who had clouted me on the ear lined up our section and marched us in formation to the barracks not far from the station. Sentries at each side of the broad entrance to the post snapped to attention and presented their rifles in front of them, straight up and down, in salute as we straggled in. Our group was told to report to Barracks No. 4, a two-story building with stone walls. Similar buildings stood at intervals around a parade ground as large as two football fields.

Forty-two of us, the equivalent of a platoon, were assigned to a large room on the second story. The flooring was of bare wood, neatly swept. Along one wall was a platform about two feet high. It had a straw-mat floor, just like a Japanese house. We could walk on the wooden floor with our shoes, but they had to be removed, just as in a home, when we stepped into the *tatami* area. Mattresses were lined up in orderly rows on the *tatami*. These were our beds. Several tables, about fifteen feet long, were placed at intervals in the room, and there was a glass ashtray exactly in the center of each table. There was also a rifle rack in the center of the room, but no rifles.

A sergeant called our names and each of us was assigned a bed. At the foot of each mattress were blankets neatly folded, uniform and shoes. The sergeant told us to get into uniform and hurry downstairs to have our heads shaved. I was wearing my hair in a crew cut and getting my skull shaved as clean as a billiard ball was not an inviting prospect.

For a moment I wondered how the Army knew what size clothing each of the recruits wore. Then I realized almost all of them were about the same size—about five feet three or four inches tall and weighing perhaps 125 to 140 pounds. I was about six inches taller and outweighed them by sixty to seventy pounds. Naturally my tunic, quite similar to the one I had worn as a civilian, was too tight across the shoulders and the sleeves were too short. Even so, I could squeeze into it. The trousers were an altogether different matter. The waist was much too big. I wondered how the other recruits were doing and discovered that they simply wrapped the trouser tops around their waists and looped a belt over the folds. So that's what I did, too.

After slipping on a pair of heavy white regulation socks, I found my shoes were impossibly small. I couldn't even get my toes inside them. I unlaced the shoes all the way down and spread the tops, but still my feet would not go in. There was no way that I could wear those shoes. One by one the other men completed dressing and hurried down to the barber. I glanced around nervously and saw there were only three of us left in the room. I was in enough trouble already; I didn't want to be the last man. If I had my American oxfords I could have worn them. But they were back in Uncle Saisuke's home. Remembering my experience with the jockey shorts, I had stored my stylish U.S. shoes and worn wooden *geta* clogs so as not to be conspicuous when I reported to the Army. In desperation I folded the tops of the Army shoes down, shoved my toes in as far as they would go so I could wear them like sandals, and tied them on with the strings looped around my heels. Just as I completed the job the sergeant burst into the room, shouting at me, the last man, tail-end Charlie, to hurry. Then he caught sight of my feet and burst into loud laughter.

Let him laugh. He's really not such a bad guy at all, I told myself as I teetered at attention. He could have walloped me for being late.

The sergeant stopped laughing long enough to declare: "I've never seen such monstrous feet. Come on, let's go find the supply sergeant and see if he can help you."

The supply sergeant went through his entire stock. Not one pair came anywhere near fitting. My shoe size is 10½D, not unusual by American standards, but obviously the Japanese didn't make shoes that large. The two sergeants took me to five other supply areas, and still we found nothing to fit.

Hope stirred faintly in my breast. Suppose they couldn't find shoes that I could wear. Would they send me home? I remembered reading about American kids who were too tall or too heavy and had been rejected for service. How wonderfully ridiculous it would be to be rejected by the Japanese Army because my feet were too big.

My sergeant raised my hopes further when he remarked:

"You can't train to be a soldier without shoes. I guess maybe you'd better go home." Then he laughed uproariously.

But the supply sergeant burst the bubble. "Hey," he said, "I happen to remember we had one of those three-hundred-pound *sumo* wrestlers here a long time ago and they made some special shoes for him. He got kicked out of the Army but maybe his shoes are still around here someplace. Let's try the Machinegun Barracks."

I tottered unwillingly after the sergeants like the ancient Chinese women with bound feet that I used to see once in a while in Seattle's Chinatown.

They found the wrestler's specially fabricated shoes. Dusty. Monstrously ugly. And much too large for me. In addition, they were of two different sizes. I figured one shoe was about a size 13, the other 12.

"They don't fit," I complained. "They are too large."

"You can get your feet into them, can't you?" my sergeant demanded.

"Yes, sir."

"Then you can learn to be a soldier in them." He was no longer the kindly, human sergeant amused by the size of my feet. "On the double. You've wasted a lot of time already. Run back to the barracks and get your head shaved." There was nothing friendly about him any more. Once again I was the lowliest of recruits, and he was my sergeant.

The barber ran his clippers up one side of my head and down the other, back and forth, back and forth. Then he lathered my scalp and shaved it billiard-ball bare. Later I looked into a mirror and had to admit ruefully I'd never realized my head was such a topographical map of hills and valleys and bumps and ridges. On my tunic was a red velvet tab with a single yellow star on it, signifying that I was a *shonen-hei*, a buck private in the Imperial Japanese Army. And when I looked down at my shoes, they reminded me of the clown with the enormous flat feet that I had once seen in a circus back home. A helluva soldier you make, Yoshida, I told myself. The Yanks would laugh themselves sick if they saw you.

The rest of the day was spent in rapid-fire indoctrination. A brigadier general, the base commander, made a welcome speech to all the recruits mustered on the parade grounds. A sergeant explained the bugle calls and reviewed the routine we would be exposed to. After a plain but nourishing supper in the messhall, I was ready for bed. Our room was frigid. There was a potbellied, cast-iron stove, but it was not in use. Due to a shortage of fuel, it would have to get a lot colder before we would be allowed to enjoy the luxury of a fire. I fell asleep wondering how Mom was doing.

Our training began in earnest early the next morning. I suppose basic training is about the same in all armies. First, there was calisthenics. Then running to build up stamina, followed by marching drills. Only then were we allowed to go in for a breakfast of hot rice, bean-paste soup and pickled vegetables. After breakfast there was more marching, learning to salute, formation drills, lunch, calisthenics, more drills, and a long run to top off the day.

All that running and marching raised cruel blisters on my feet. I knew from my football experience that ill-fitting shoes would give me more trouble than I could cope with. That night I took a handful of toilet tissue from the latrine and stuffed it into the toes of my shoes. That helped a little.

Despite painful feet the rest periods during the day were the hardest part for me because that's when the recruits were required to study the Military Handbook, issued to each man at the time of his induction. I didn't know enough Japanese to be able to read it. The handbook contained the Imperial Rescript for Soldiers and Sailors (Gunjin Chokuyu) which was in effect the Emperor's personal message to each member of the armed forces ordering him to be brave, loyal and obedient. It also included the Soldier's Code of Conduct in Combat *(Senjinkun)* which spelled out the code of honor and the unquestioning obedience to orders expected of all troops. There were long passages that had to be committed to memory and we were tested at frequent intervals. The men were called on at random to recite, with the next man continuing where the first man left off. Try as I would to memorize the code by rote, I never got beyond the opening article which stated: "First, a soldier conducts himself properly at all times."

The code was shouted out in a loud, vigorous voice, and I trembled each time we had a *Senjinkun* session, fearing my ignorance would be revealed, ridiculed and punished, but for some reason I was never ordered to recite. Nor did there seem to be any hope that I could learn. I didn't have a single friend I could ask for help.

Monday, Tuesday and Wednesday passed quickly. Late Thursday afternoon, after we had returned to our barracks, a messenger came to the room and said I had a visitor at the main gate. Officially, no visitors were permitted during the week. We had been told that we would be allowed to see relatives on Sunday. Had something gone wrong? Was there an emergency of some kind? I half ran to the main gate and reported to the sergeant of the guard.

"Your sister is waiting for you in the orderly room," he said. He smiled. "You may spend up to an hour with her."

What a delight it was to see Betty, even though she was dressed like any other Japanese schoolgirl in an ill-fitting middy blouse and long blue skirt, her hair parted in back and pigtails hanging to her shoulders.

"Gee, Betty," I said in English, then stopped short. There was a very noticeable bulge along her waistline. Good golly, I thought, my kid sister's in trouble. What Japanese punk had got her pregnant?

Betty broke into a big grin as though she had read my

thoughts, and lifted her blouse. Beneath it, tied around her waist, was a neatly wrapped package.

"I know you too well, Jim," she said. "You're more interested in food than in your sister. So I brought you some goodies." She unwrapped the package. There were rice balls, fried chicken, fishcake, sweetened black bean cake, and even an orange.

"Betty, you dumb kid," I whispered in horror. "You want to get in trouble? They could shoot you, you know."

Betty winked at me. "Don't worry. I hid the food under my blouse in case I had to smuggle it in. But it wasn't necessary. I bribed the guards with some of the sweets. Why do you think they let you come out here?"

As I gobbled down the food, Betty told me how she had been unable to get away from school in Yamaguchi City to see me off. So she made up her mind to come and see me at the barracks, and somehow got the food together and cooked it. Betty had always been a shy, retiring girl, and what she had done was entirely out of character, especially that part about bribing the guard. I marveled at how she had grown up. I know that you don't hold hands with your sister, but I did. She wanted to talk in Japanese for fear of getting both of us in trouble, but it didn't seem right. We talked in low tones in English, just the way we used to do at home late at night sometimes after the folks had retired and we weren't quite ready to go to bed. We talked now about all the things we'd been doing, about Mom, and what we'd do when the war was over and we could go home. We remembered the good times we'd known and the odd experiences we encountered at school and in the Army. The hour passed before we knew it. I embraced my sister. "Good-bye, Jim," she said, and then she turned and walked firmly out the gate. Once she turned to wave, but I could hardly see her through the tears that filmed my eyes. The wind was cold and damp as I made my way back to the barracks, my oversized shoes making crunching noises on the gravel. All I could think of was the mischievous things I had done to Betty while we were growing up, and I wondered why I had been so mean to the sweetest, most considerate little sister in the world. Now I was twenty-two years old, and she was twenty. Whoever married her would be a lucky fellow.

On Saturday morning, our seventh day in the Army, the forty-two men in our room were ordered to assemble instead of going out to drill. Each of us was issued a knapsack, six pairs of new white woolen socks like the sweatsocks we wore for football, mess kits, heavy woolen overcoats and caps. Twenty of us were given rifles—it was the first time I had held a firearm—but no ammunition. The others were issued no arms at all.

"These rifles are the property of the Emperor," the sergeant told us in a loud voice. "The Emperor's chrysanthemum seal is embossed into the steel near the rear sight. The weapon is precious. You will guard it carefully, the way a samurai guards and cares for his long sword. You must let no harm come to the Emperor's property."

I wondered if the fact that I had been issued a rifle meant I was destined for the infantry.

"After dark today we embark on a special training program," the sergeant continued. "Now, go to the warehouse and fill each of your new socks with rice. The six pairs will enable each of you to carry about thirty pounds of rice, a month's supply for each man, in your knapsacks. An Army must be prepared to be self-sufficient regarding its provisions, and this is part of the training. After you have done this, pack up all your belongings and wait for further orders."

It was 11 P.M. before the orders came. We men, bowed under our packs, were marched out the Division gates we had entered only a week earlier and down to the railroad station. A freight train was waiting at the far end. Two noncoms herded all forty-two of us into a boxcar. We were ordered to remove our packs and make ourselves comfortable. There was a little straw on the floor and a five-gallon can at one end to be used as a urinal. I sat with my back against the boxcar's steel wall. Suddenly someone slammed the door shut and we were in complete darkness.

"Where are we going?" someone yelled. "What kind of night maneuvers is this?"

"Quiet!" the sergeant shouted, and the men settled down. Almost immediately the train began to move. Soon it was rumbling and swaying over the tracks. Eventually the rhythm and my weariness put me to sleep. I don't know how long I slept but the train stopped and I awoke. The air of the boxcar was foul and clammy from the condensed breath of the men. I was cramped, stiff and dirty.

The door was opened. I judged by the light that it was shortly after daybreak. The sergeant ordered us out. We were in a railroad station, and I saw a sign with characters that I recognized as reading Shimonoseki. Mom and my sisters and I had once spent a night in an inn at Shimonoseki, a bustling, noisy old port city on the southern tip of Honshu. On the other side of the Straits of Moji, a channel about a mile and a half wide, was the island of Kyushu, famous for the hot springs resort of Beppu which we had visited. Now I could smell the sea. Shimonoseki was the jumping-off place for the Asian mainland, the closest Japanese port to Korea. I wondered if our night training was taking us all the way to China.

Some of the men hurried off to relieve themselves in the station rest room. Obviously they couldn't find the five-gallon can in the pitch-dark freightcar. We washed our faces and hands in the cold water dripping from faucets into concrete troughs at intervals along the station platform. About that time a group of Japanese women appeared. Each of them wore a white smock over her kimono and armbands identified them as members of a patriotic organization. They were carrying some tubs and covered buckets.

75

The tubs held boiled rice and the buckets contained hot bean-paste soup. These were ladled out to us for breakfast, which we washed down with green tea. The hot food was invigorating and some of the weariness vanished from my bones. One of the women had a slight resemblance to Mom. I yearned to talk to her, but I was too shy. I didn't want to display my ignorance of the Japanese language. So I just stood around until the sergeant assembled the group and marched us to a small Shinto shrine on a hill back of the station. We rested there for perhaps two hours.

I had barely dozed off when we were assembled again and marched this time to the waterfront. A small, nondescript freighter, the rust showing through the black paint, was just completing loading at a dock. The crew was securing the booms and tightening the tarpaulins over the hatch covers as we boarded her. We were ordered below decks and a section of the bare hold was assigned us as quarters. Many of the men in the platoon were from the country and had never been aboard an ocean-going vessel. The stale ship smell was overpowering and several of them became ill. Before long the engines started up. Obviously we were about to sail. I asked for permission to go on deck and surprisingly I received it.

The clouds hung low over the pine-covered hills around Shimonoseki. Many small craft plied the choppy waters, each busily intent on its particular mission. I searched the wharf for a familiar face—Mom, Betty, Uncle Denmatsu, Uncle Saisuke—anybody. But there was no one, only a handful of stevedores. Where was the ship taking me? Certainly not home to America! The sudden surge of nostalgia was overwhelmed by a wave of bitterness. Wherever the damned Japanese Army was taking me, I wouldn't get back to the barracks in time for the Sunday visit with friends and relatives.

The freighter turned into the channel, threading its way

between scores of tiny, rocky islands. Presently it headed into the open sea and the engines settled down to a steady rhythm. Only then did it dawn on me that we were not going on any maneuvers. We were headed for the Asian mainland, either Korea or China. It had to be the mainland, not the Southwest Pacific, because of the heavy coats we were wearing. We were headed for the front—with only six days of training, and only half of us armed. And I had never even fired my rifle! What miserable, godawful shape the Japanese Army must be in!

My deduction was right. Early next morning we docked in Pusan, Korea's chief port city on the southern tip of the peninsula. I knew it was Pusan because the sergeant finally told us. It was the first solid bit of information any of us had received. Pusan Harbor was crowded with small ships, sooty, noisy with the throb of exhausts and the hooting of ships' sirens. It didn't look too much different from Shimonoseki. Once more we shouldered our packs and marched off the ship through cobblestone streets to the railroad station. The only way that I could tell the Koreans from Japanese was that the women wore long, flowing white dresses; only most of them looked gray. They wore odd shoes, shaped almost like canoes, with the toes pointed up. The younger men wore trousers and jackets just like the people in Japan, and in every other respect the Koreans looked exactly like the Japanese—short, slight, with straight black hair and prominent cheekbones. Later, I learned that Koreans have a distinct culture and language of their own, but the country was annexed as a Japanese colony in 1910 and only the Japanese language was taught in Korean schools.

At the railroad station we were met by another group of Japanese women with white aprons over their kimono and the now-familiar armbands. Once again they fed us, and I was grateful to get hot food. I didn't know it at the

77

time, but we were to meet similar groups of kindly, bustling, motherly Japanese women many more times in the next few days.

Immediately after our meal we boarded a dusty old railroad car with unpadded wooden seats, just like the standard third class coach on the Japanese railroads. But there was one important difference. The railroad in Korea was standard gauge, as contrasted to the narrow gauge Japanese system. This meant more leg-room. It was a blessing for me.

We rode almost continuously in that car for the next eight days and nights, a grimy, dreary, weary journey broken only by fifteen-minute meal breaks and other infrequent stops while we were hitched to another train, or the locomotive took on fuel, water and a new crew. Our route wound steadily northward up the Korean peninsula, past the cities of Taegu, Taejon and Seoul which the Japanese called Keijo, past mile after mile of frozen rice paddies hemmed in by towering mountains, through tunnels too numerous to count, across steel trestles bridging slow-moving rivers. We saw innumerable villages, one indistinguishable from the next, for each was only a haphazard cluster of straw-thatched houses. Despite the cold, oxcarts moved along the winding dirt roads, and sometimes we saw men on bicycles and coolies trudging along with towering loads of firewood lashed to the A-frames on their backs.

The next stop after Seoul was Pyongyang, which the Japanese called Heijo, and suddenly we were into the increasingly more rugged mountains of northern Korea. Finally, at Antung, we crossed the ice-choked Yalu River on a long steel bridge into the vast, flat, brown valleys of Manchuria. At each meal stop the inevitable little Japanese housewives appeared as if by magic. They were wonderfully well-organized and dedicated. I learned most of them had come as colonists to the mainland many years earlier, and they considered it their patriotic duty to make the journey to the front as comfortable as possible for the thousands of

Japanese troops who traveled the route we were following. A half day after leaving Antung the train struggled up a long slope. Just after topping the last rise we saw the smokestacks of Mukden (now called Shenyang) spread across a huge bowl. Manchuria's largest city had been converted into a vast, sprawling industrial complex in the Japanese drive to colonize this northern province. Mukden was also headquarters of the Kwangtung Army, the crack, semi-autonomous Japanese expeditionary force that had carved an empire out of the mainland. Obviously the Japanese had come prepared to stay a long time.

But we were in Mukden only long enough for the car to be switched to the back end of a China-bound military freight train. Mukden obviously was the marshaling yard for a vast supply network. However, about all I could see of military activity through the grimy windows of our car was scores and scores of sealed boxcars. Presumably they were filled with food and supplies for the Emperor's armies scattered over the endless expanse of China.

Now we turned west and south. The rails led through the parched, rolling hills of Jehol where the frigid north wind sweeping in from the Mongolian steppes whipped the dust off the barren land, past the Great Wall and down to Tientsin at the mouth of the Pai River. The rails led on across the North China plains, as flat and windblown as Kansas, past the ancient cities of Tsinan and Suchow. The terrain was not the only hostile thing. Now, at dusk we were instructed to pull down the shades in our cars, apparently so Chinese guerrillas would not be tempted to put a bullet through the lighted windows. And now the Japanese ladies were missing at the stations. Probably the Japanese women and children had been evacuated from this area. No matter. We were near the end of our endurance, numb with weariness, caked with grime, wanting nothing so much as a hot bath and a place to lie down and sleep.

The ordeal ended at Nanking, or more accurately, Pukow, a town that looked about the way its name sounds, on the north bank of the Yangtze River. Nanking, which had been China's capital until captured by the Japanese, was across the river on the south bank. The ocean was more than 200 miles downstream, but even so I had never seen a river as broad as the Yangtze at Nanking. We boarded a ferryboat for the crossing. The Yangtze was at its winter's low; I wondered how much more impressive it would be in spring flood.

By the river route, it is another 400 miles upstream from Nanking to Hankow, central China's great industrial city. The way we traveled, by train and truck over rutted country roads when finally the rails gave out, it was much farther. It was at Hankow that we finally learned our destination. It was to be the old crossroads town of Yoyang, about ninety miles southwest of Hankow. A battalion, cut down to 180 men and officers because of the demand for manpower elsewhere, was garrisoned there. Our platoon was to reinforce the garrison while we completed basic training. The unit's primary duty was to police the area, occasionally sending out patrols to keep guerrilla forces in check. Division headquarters were at Nanchang, 150 miles to the east on the other side of the Wan Fou Mountains. Even I could see that the outpost wasn't going to get much help from Division if we got in a jam.

We covered the last leg of our journey—the ninety miles from Hankow to Yoyang—on foot even though the Army had plenty of trucks. They showed up regularly with hot meals for us three times a day. But we had to march under full pack, and the only conclusion I could draw was that this was part of our toughening-up process. Because my shoes were so large, I tripped and stumbled frequently. Soon the toilet tissue that I had jammed into the toes disintegrated and I raised a crop of excruciatingly painful blisters. The march took us four days and three nights. Two of the recruits fell, exhausted, and were driven into Yoyang in the supply trucks. I showed my blisters to the sergeant but failed to get any sympathy. We were a sorry crew when we finally reached Yoyang. "Look sharp, soldiers of Japan," the sergeant called out, and we tried in vain to maintain proper military bearing as the hobnails in our boots slipped and clattered over the ancient cobblestones.

The Japanese compound was surrounded by a high barbed wire fence at the northern edge of the city which seemed to be something of a marketplace as well as crossroads. The reddish-orange meatball of the Japanese flag, on a white field, flew from a pole near the front of the compound. A sentry, standing at the at-ease position, looked on curiously as our column approached.

So this was Yoyang, my home-to-be. Dreary, dusty and flea-bitten as it appeared, I was mighty happy to see it. But a bath and rest had to wait until our welcome was completed. We stood at attention while an officer assured us that while Yoyang was off the beaten path it was an important outpost in Japan's plan of empire. Yoyang was a key point in central China's land and waterborne commerce, he said, and it was our responsibility to maintain surveillance over it. In fact, a river flowed directly through the post. During daylight hours a parade of barges and sampans utilized the river, and each vessel was stopped and inspected by Japanese guards for arms, ammunition, unregistered foodstuffs and other contraband. At sunset the river was closed off and all traffic came to a standstill. Inspection stations on the main roads leading in and out of Yoyang were manned twenty-four hours a day, but by far the bulk of the traffic moved over the river.

The Yoyang garrison was known as the 2344th Arrow (*Yari*) Battalion. In effect, it was partly a heavy weapons company and partly an artillery company. Half of the men were assigned to the *daiti-ho,* a light cannon of about 60-mm. bore. There were four of these guns. The other half serviced the two *rentai-ho*, 102-mm. howitzers, assigned to the battalion. There were two flimsy wooden barracks for the enlisted men, one for the *daitai-ho* men and the other for the *rentai-ho*. In addition, there was an administrative building, an officers' billet, combination kitchen-messhall, and a stable for about sixty horses.

The officer assured us that there had been very little hostile activity in the Yoyang sector, and we recruits would be given six months of basic training in all aspects of a soldier's responsibilities. The forty-two men were divided into two even groups, apparently without any rhyme or reason. I was among those sent to the *rentai-ho* barracks where we were assigned quarters and told to get cleaned up. When we were through, the bathwater was as dirty as the river flowing through the camp.

That evening I met the other men in my unit, learned about the buddy system used in the Japanese Army and was introduced to my buddy. He was to work with me, keep me out of trouble and teach me the various duties expected of me. In return, I was something of a private servant to him. I was expected to do his laundry, shine his shoes, run his errands and keep his weapons cleaned and polished. A buddy could be a real friend and help to the recruit, or he could take advantage of a new man and make life miserable for him.

I was fortunate. My buddy was a quiet young fellow named Mizuno. His rank was private first class, called *Joto-hei*. The proper way to address him was Mizuno Joto-hei. He had a way of keeping his eyes glued to the ground when he talked to me, and I noticed he was somewhat stooped, as though his back hurt. He told me to take it easy and everything would be all right. He also told me that one of his main responsibilities was to care for a horse named Enyu. Four-horse teams were used to draw the *rentai-ho* cannon and Enyu was one of them. Mizuno took me out to the stable to meet Enyu. He was a big, strong chestnut-colored beast with a handsome blond mane. Enyu was well-groomed; his coat had a sheen and his hooves had a luster to them. Enyu immediately recognized Mizuno when we came in, and obviously there was a good deal of affection between them. My first impression was that Mizuno was a loner, unhappy with his life in the Army and anxious to return to his farm in southern Japan, and later developments proved that impression to be right.

Just before lights-out Lieutenant Hamasaki, the officer in command of *rentai-ho,* came into the barracks with his noncoms. The lieutenant was fresh out of officers' school, seemed to be ill at ease, and slipped out after a brief word. Sergeant Nakamura was the senior noncom. The Japanese Army gives noncommissioned officers a great deal more authority than the Americans do, as I was to learn very quickly. Nakamura was a small, wiry man with a habitual smirk on his face, and whenever he spoke his heavy glasses slipped off the almost nonexistent bridge of his nose.

Nakamura's chief assistant was Sergeant Shigemi Kido who was unusually lanky for a Japanese, perhaps five feet eight inches tall, and I guessed he weighed about 140 pounds. He had a mole on his left cheek and gold teeth that gleamed in the light. Most of the other men were chunky and square-set, indicating rural backgrounds. Somehow Kido struck me as a city office worker, a pen-pusher who really didn't belong in a line combat outfit. The third man in seniority was Corporal Ohama, a gunnery specialist, of medium height and weight. His face was round and perpetually flushed and thick black eyebrows pointed upward at the end.

One by one the other men introduced themselves. Some of them were tough-looking customers. I was particularly impressed by one named Private Ohiro, a powerfully built man with a mouth full of gold teeth and tattoos on both arms. He had a heavy scar on his left cheek, and he reminded me of a gangland "enforcer." He said he had been in the Army four years. Four years and still a buck private! I put him down as bad news and a fellow to avoid.

Someone said, "We're real happy to see you recruits. We've been buddies doing the dirty work for our superiors for fourteen months. Now you can do the buddy work for us until the next bunch of recruits gets here."

Low men in the pecking order for fourteen months! We laughed, but not very heartily.

Six

As long as I live I will never forget my first morning at Yoyang, even though it started very routinely. After reveille I reported to the stable, just as I had been instructed. Mizuno was already there, busily brushing Enyu, and he asked me to get a bucket of water.

At the far end of the stable was a fifty-gallon steel drum with a firepit under it. The drum was nearly full of boiling hot water. I dipped out about half a bucket and went outside to the trough to mix it with cold water. The trough was frozen over. Just as I set the bucket down to crack the ice, I was kicked from behind. For an instant I thought it was a horse. I whirled and saw Sergeant Nakamura, his face contorted in fury.

"You dumbshit recruit," he screamed, "who do you think you are?"

Before I could answer he kicked at me again. My reflexes acted before I could think. I grabbed his foot in self-defense. Sergeant Nakamura hopped about trying to keep his balance, shouting furiously at me. Sergeant Kido, Corporal Ohama and two lance corporals poured out of the barn. One of them braced me against the stable wall and kicked me in the shins. Another hit me in the face and head, and a third belted me across the middle. As I doubled up in pain, Sergeant Nakamura yelled for me to stand at attention. I stood rigidly, my arms at my sides, while the beating continued. Finally I slumped to the ground, only half-conscious. Only then did the punishment stop. It was the worst physical beating I had ever taken. Sergeant Kido lifted me off the ground and held me erect while Sergeant Nakamura, his livid face only inches from mine, shouted: "Only noncommissioned officers can use the hot water! You break the ice and use the cold water! Understand?"

"Yes, sir. I understand, sir," I replied through bleeding lips.

I poured the hot water back into the drum, got a bucket of cold water and took it back to Mizuno. He was brushing his horse, working diligently as though nothing had happened. Only when the noncoms left did Mizuno turn to me. "I'm sorry, Yoshida," he said. "I should have warned you. But it is just as well. As a recruit you will have many such experiences, and you will be better off for having learned your bitter lesson on your first day." I was too bruised and sore and heartsick to dispute his philosophy.

"Now let me show you about horse care," Mizuno went on in a kindly manner. "First, of course, we brush and curry him. Like this." Then Mizuno showed me how to rake the wet straw out of the stall and spread it thin to dry, salvaging as much as possible for reuse. The manure was carried out to a pile. He showed me a tool that looked like a can opener. "This is to clean the manure from his hoof, around and under the shoe. Don't lose it. It belongs to the Army and we must account for it." He showed me how to seize a foreleg, sidestep in front of the horse, lift the leg and brace it against the thigh while cleaning out the hoof. For the hind leg, he said, face away from the horse and lift it carefully. After you have cleaned the hoof, guide it down slowly as you move away. If a horse jerks or tries to kick, hang on, talk to him calmly and look for an opening and jump aside. Remember, a horse that bites will have a red cloth tied to the mane. The kickers have a red cloth tied to the tail. Mizuno showed me how to put a little oil on the hoof, then wipe it dry to give it the proper sheen. Then he led Enyu to the trough. He placed my hand under the horse's throat and said, "Make sure he drinks about fifty gulps. You can feel him gulping. He needs that amount of water to remain healthy." Then we led Enyu back to the stall and spread dry straw on the floor. After that he showed me how to mix the grain ration of barley, corn, wheat and oats.

"Take good care of him, Yoshida," Mizuno cautioned. "To the Army, Enyu is more valuable than either of us. If we die, they will find another man. But horses are scarce. It is not easy to find or train a suitable replacement. So it is our responsibility to see that nothing happens to this horse."

I couldn't help but admire Mizuno's affection for his animal. And be a little envious. The Army wouldn't beat a horse for making a mistake. They would teach him. I wondered why no one had warned me about the use of hot water instead of beating me half to death after I had broken the rule out of ignorance.

The horse chores taken care of, I had five minutes to rush back to the barracks, wash up, and report to the kitchen to pick up breakfast for the men in my unit. There were three buckets of rice to be placed on the tables, the inevitable bean-paste soup, vegetables cooked with meat, and pickled turnips. Several other recruits and I dished out the food, then waited for the noncoms to sit down.

That's when my second ordeal of the day caught up with me. Sergeant Kido, between mouthfuls of rice, ordered one of the recruits to recite the first chapter of the Military Handbook. He rose and sang out several paragraphs flawlessly.

"Enough," Kido said. "Private Yamamoto, carry on."

Yamamoto finished his assignment, and then it was my turn.

"Private Yoshida, continue."

I couldn't. Not one word. I didn't know a single word. I stood helplessly, in agony, completely dumb.

Sergeant Kido rose menacingly from the table. The only sound in the room was of men eating, studiously staring into the rice bowls in front of them.

"Yoshida!" He was inches from my ear. "Are you deaf? Did you not hear me? I ordered you to continue with the recitation!"

Still I could not speak. He whacked me across the mouth with the back of his hand, reopening a cut inflicted at the stable. I could feel the blood trickling down my chin.

"If you are too stupid to memorize the Military Handbook," Kido continued coldly, "perhaps we can make an impression on you some other way. Get me a rifle."

At the moment I didn't care if he shot me.

Someone brought in a rifle with bayonet attached. Kido handed it to me. He told me to raise it up to firing position, the stock against my right shoulder, my left arm holding up the barrel. Sergeant Nakamura slipped a heavy steel helmet over the bayonet. "Now, let's see how strong you are."

Kido and Nakamura went back to their breakfast. I continued to stand with the rifle still in firing position. The gun was incredibly heavy. I arched my back trying to hold the rifle level so the helmet would not fall off. Kido came back and plunged his fist into my belly. "That is no stance for a Japanese soldier," he remarked. "Stand straight!"

I was perspiring heavily now. The rifle weighed a ton. My back was numb from strain. I wanted to pass out, but couldn't. I wanted to run the bayonet through Kido and Nakamura and every other noncom in the room, but I didn't dare. When Kido finally released me I was bathed in sweat, and now there was no time for breakfast.

I was to go through this ordeal dozens of times for failing to memorize the Military Handbook, and almost always it was Sergeant Kido who started it. I asked my buddy Mizuno to help me, but he confessed he could hardly read. Finally I made a deal with one of the other recruits. I gave him my tobacco ration (five packs of British Player cigarettes, ten to the pack), my beer ration (two pint bottles of Asahi a week), and my share of the *sake* rice wine (one bottle for eight men each week) in return for help. He proved to be no friend of mine. He was more interested in prolonging the supply of tobacco and alcohol than in helping me to learn the manual.

My only consolation was that I excelled in *ju-kenjitsu*, or bayonet practice with a wooden rifle and a rubber-tipped wooden bayonet. My superior weight and height and judo skills enabled me to handle all comers. I could take on a dozen men, one after another, flip them, shove them over, and pin them down. I enjoyed the physical contact; it was something I could understand. I would have liked nothing better than to meet any or all of the noncoms in *ju-kenjitsu*, but they permitted the recruits to take on only each other.

The weeks sped by and I settled into a routine. There was time now to write home. We were issued official military postcards. Letters in sealed envelopes were forbidden as everything was censored. In scrawling handwriting, like a child, I managed to write Mom: "I am well. Everyone is good to me. Miss you very much. Take care of yourself." There was much more I wanted to say, but found it impossible to express it on paper in Japanese. Mom could have understood what I wished to say if I had written in English, but it would have been foolhardy to try to send her a message in an "enemy" language. Her first letter came about two months after I had entered the Army. It said simply: "I hope you are well. We are all healthy and doing our daily chores, so please don't worry. Jim is getting along very well." I smiled at the last sentence. In our code it meant she was enjoying the hoard of brown sugar. And so we kept up our communication in only the barest form, surmounting the language barrier through the knowledge that love and understanding filled the space between the brief sentences.

After the elementary phases of our training at Yoyang reached an end, the recruits were organized into crews to operate the cannon. The *rentai-ho* was a versatile gun that could be drawn by horses, hauled by manpower, or dismantled and its parts carried by either men or horses. Eight men made up a standard team. When the gun was set up on its three-foot wheels, No. 1 man would sight the gun in the general direction of the target. I was No. 2 man, and my assignment was to manhandle the gun in the direc- tion ordered by the No. 1 man. I had no illusions about my job. All it required was no brains and a strong back, and that was all right with me. No. 3 pulled the lanyard to fire the gun. No. 4, so far as I could tell, just squatted beside No. 1 and took over if he was disabled. No. 5 zeroed in on the target, refining the work of No. 1, and gave the order to fire. The other three men were ammunition load- ers, and they were trained to relieve any of us. I don't know why the positions were numbered in this sequence, but that's the way it was. The recruits who didn't have gun assignments were given jobs as ammunition carriers and horse tenders.

We drilled with the cannon every day in all kinds of weather. We practiced at night. We would run at top speed, pulling the cannon behind us with heavy ropes, then stop and dismantle it and load it on horses. We learned to take the cannon apart and reassemble it in the dark. When the cannon was dismantled and moved manually, my job was to carry the barrel, which weighed at least two hundred pounds. The frame on which the barrel slides was much heavier, but two men carried the great load on their shoulders. I had that assignment first, but since I was so much taller than anyone else, it just didn't work. So I got the cannon barrel. It wasn't much fun but still, I could handle the two-hundred-pound barrel without too much sweat.

As a soldier I performed reasonably well. I fitted smoothly into situations requiring teamwork, as in serving the cannon. I was stronger and more agile than most of the others and could perform feats of strength that amazed my comrades. But I still faltered during recitations from the Military Handbook. Sergeant Kido seemed to take a perverse delight in testing me. And when I failed as I invariably did, sometimes he gave me the rifle treatment. Sometimes he slapped me across the mouth or struck me on the cheeks, jeering and ridiculing me. "Yoshida, you are the most stupid private I've ever seen," he would say. "How long have you been studying the Gunjin Chokuyu? Three months? Six months? And still you cannot recite properly. Stupid, stupid, stupid." Then, *whack,* a blow across my face.

The long passages of Gunjin Chokuyu were so much gibberish to me, couched in a very difficult, scholarly form of Japanese that was alien to everything I knew. Even if my tutor had been more diligent about helping me, it wouldn't have done much good. But I could not understand why Kido seemed to have it in for me. He was harsh toward the other recruits but the harshness seemed to turn to cruelty when he was dealing with me. Gradually I developed a hatred of Sergeant Kido. I had hated no man in all my life, but I hated Kido.

One afternoon as we were working with the *rentai-ho,* Lieutenant Hamasaki came out of the headquarters building and summoned the troops around him. "Men," he said, "we have just received intelligence that enemy units have been seen not far from Yoyang. We are going after them. Now we will have a chance to see how well you have learned to handle the cannon. We march in fifteen minutes."

Excitement swept through the ranks. We had never faced the enemy before. We wanted to meet them, yet we were not quite sure how we would perform under combat conditions. Hurriedly we hooked the cannon behind the four-horse team. Other men loaded ammunition, water and food supplies on the pack animals. Lieutenant Hamasaki, a warrant officer, and Sergeants Nakamura and Kido mounted their horses and led the column out of the compound.

We marched for more than three hours without a sign of the enemy. Scouts ranged far ahead and the officers searched the hills with their binoculars but found nothing. The sun had set and dusk was closing in when suddenly along a treeline to the north a purplish flash erupted. "Down, hit the dirt," someone shouted. I heard a whining, whirring sound overhead, the death song of an artillery shell that, once heard, is never forgotten. An instant later the shell landed on the banks of a river behind us, throwing up a fountain of dirt.

Lieutenant Hamasaki knew what he was doing. He shouted sharp orders. Unhook the cannon! Get the horses under cover down by the river! Wheel the gun toward the foe! The gun in the distance fired again. The flash was pinkish in the gathering darkness. I shoved the cannon barrel in the general direction of the enemy—but there was nothing to load into the cannon! In the excitement of the moment the shell bearers had taken the horses with the ammunition down by the river without unloading a supply.

Lieutenant Hamasaki was furious. "Someone get the ammunition," he shouted. I leaped up and ran for the horses. Later, I asked myself why I had been the first to react. Perhaps it was my football training where I had learned to respond swiftly to orders. Anyway, I got up and ran. The toes of my oversized shoes bent back and I stumbled and fell. I got up again and suddenly was aware of the whistling of small arms fire over my head. Someone yelled, "Yoshida, you fool, get down." It was Sergeant Kido. At the same moment he tackled me, and we went rolling down an embankment. "Stay here," he shouted, and scrambled up the bank. I could hear him calling for the ammunition bearers.

Only then did I realize what had happened, how foolishly I had exposed myself. Crouched against the bank, I began to shake. In a moment our cannon opened up. I counted two, three, four, five shots. Then silence. The enemy had vanished. I made my way back to the gun crew. Sergeant Kido had taken over my No. 2 position on the gun. We reformed ranks and marched back to our barracks in silence. Even though we had driven the enemy off, our performance as a unit had been miserable and we knew it. But more than that, Kido's actions had baffled me. He had shown himself to be a cool, resourceful soldier under fire. Perhaps he had saved my life by stopping me when I exposed myself to the enemy. All this did not jibe with the sadistic punishment he dealt me. I couldn't understand the man.

It was past midnight when we returned to Yoyang. We were ready to hit the sack but Sergeant Kido had other ideas. He followed us into the barracks. "The eight men making up the *rentai-ho* crew will line up facing each other, four on a side," he ordered. "Now listen to me. You were failures as soldiers today. Your performance was abominable. You forgot everything we ever taught you. We will now help you to remember."

What happened then was a nightmare. Kido ordered the men on one side to strike those on the other side. In the face. With closed fists. Then on signal the men on the other side were to strike back. We were to punish each other, first one side, then the other, hitting as hard as we could. I was aghast. Outweighing my opponent by sixty pounds,

I could kill him if I punched him full in the face while he stood without attempting to protect himself. I pulled my first punch. Surprised, my opponent pulled his punch when it was his turn. Sergeant Nakamura caught on immediately.

"Yoshida, you aren't going to get off that easy," he growled. Pushing my opponent out of the way, the sergeant took the man's place. If he saw a gleam of triumph in my eyes at the prospect of slugging him legally, it was because I could hardly restrain my enthusiasm. But Sergeant Nakamura outfoxed me again. He traded places with me after each blow so that he was punching every time and I was always on the receiving end.

He bruised my cheek and cut my lip. I could feel a welt rising on my right cheek. My left eye was half closed, and still Kido called out the cadence—one, two, one, two. I could hear the men weeping, not so much in pain but in anger at the stupidity of all this, the inhumanity of punishing a friend for nothing, the utter nightmarish bestiality of this exercise in sadism. If there was any consolation, it was in noticing with my good eye that Sergeant Nakamura had sprained a knuckle. He winced each time he hit me, and his blows became much less forceful. Finally it was Nakamura who told Kido: "That's enough. We don't want to overdo it." The throbbing pain in my head made sleep come hard that night. I heard one of the men sobbing quietly.

Next morning, just before roll call, I encountered Lieutenant Hamasaki in the hallway. With a surprised look he stopped me.

"Yoshida, what happened to your face?"

For a fleeting moment I felt an impulse to tell him the truth. And then I remembered an age-old code. Men don't snitch. If I got a knee in the gut in a football game, I didn't complain to the referee. I took care of the dirty player myself. When Kenny Kuniyuki slammed me against the wall, I told Mom he was giving me a lot of attention. I would take care of Nakamura and Kido in my own way when the opportunity came.

"Sir," I replied, "due to my clumsiness, I walked into a pole in the dark."

"Hmm," the lieutenant replied thoughtfully. "You are a clumsy fool. Be more careful hereafter."

"Yes, sir. Yoshida will be more careful in the future, sir."

The lieutenant saw the other bruised faces and told Sergeant Nakamura to dismiss us for the day.

The respite was only temporary. Knowing the enemy was still in the area, the officers kept us on constant alert. Meanwhile, day after day we trained with the *rentai-ho,* racing about at top speed under the lashing tongues of the noncoms until everyone was near exhaustion. My fatigue was more mental than physical. Not knowing when I would be kicked or slapped, not being able to hit back, afraid that I would say the wrong thing at the wrong time, afraid I would be called on to recite a code that I could not understand, my nerves were on edge.

The pressure began to tell on the others, too. The first to crack up was a recruit named Shimoda who had come to China with our group. He had developed into a skilled technician who knew all about the operation of the weapons. He could recite the manual backward and forward. But he just wasn't able to take the brutal physical punishment. One night he went into the latrine, pressed a grenade to his belly and pulled the pin. He was dead before anyone reached him. Later, I learned that he had a mother and two sisters back in Japan—just like me. Shimoda's death saddened me because it was so unnecessary, but it also gave me a strange and alarming sort of satisfaction; I, a soft, pampered, American-born, American-reared Nisei had not been the first to crack up. After that, I knew I could endure anything any of the other men could take.

Shimoda's remains were cremated at a makeshift crematorium just outside the compound after Lieutenant Hamasaki said a few words to console his spirit—and ours. But Sergeant Nakamura had much more to say. "This coward has died a useless death," he declared. "How did his death benefit the Emperor? In no way at all. If you want to die, I can find more useful ways of death for you."

We knew he was referring to suicide missions, and none of us said a word. I was detailed to gather wood for Shimoda's funeral pyre but excused to go back to sentry duty before the fire was lit. For this I was grateful; I had no desire to watch the unfortunate Shimoda's mortal remains being consumed. After the fire had died down, several handfuls of the ashes would be placed in a small pine box, no more than eight inches square. It was wrapped in a plain white muslin cloth and stored away until someone returning to Japan on rotation could escort it back to the homeland. In all the time I was at Yoyang I never saw a military chaplain, nor were we ever visited by a Buddhist or Shinto priest. The Army itself took religious rites seriously, but they failed to reach out as far as our little outpost.

Seven

AFTER the first brush with the enemy the pace of action stepped up quickly. In the next six months we took part in three major campaigns that took us to many parts of central China. Being on combat missions had its compensation. When we were out in the field, in constant danger of losing our lives, the Mickey Mouse hazing that we experienced in the barracks no longer took place. I could understand why some of the troops said they preferred combat to garrison duty.

But combat was no snap either and I was grateful for the rigorous training that had hardened us. In our first push our company was attached to a division to give it more firepower for a big sweep designed to eliminate a large and active band of guerrillas who were raising hell with the Japanese communications network. Our advance took us into heavily mined enemy territory. After taking a few casualties we were ordered off the roads and into the hills. Most of the marching was done at night. This meant no smoking, canteens wrapped in cloth to prevent noise (a useless precaution since there was so much clatter anyway), and daytime bivouac where, no matter how we tried to conceal our camp, the natives knew every move we made.

Marching in the mountains also meant the *rentai-ho* cannon was dismantled and carried, sometimes by the horses but more often by the men. I shouldered the cannon barrel —two hundred pounds of cold steel—and it was reassuring to feel its hard, smooth surface on my cheek as we felt our way through the darkness. All of us in the heavy weapons company were cruelly laden so we could not keep up with the infantry. We were supposed to get a ten-minute rest every hour, but by the time we caught up with the riflemen they were ready to move again, so in effect we were never able to rest. On the rare occasions I could take a break I preferred to stand with the gun barrel supported in the fork of a tree or on a rock, just so it would take the weight off my shoulder, rather than lowering it to the ground and having to lift it all the way up when it was time to move again.

On and on we marched until, overwhelmed by weariness, our motions were automatic. Forced to maintain silence, the men's thoughts were their own. This is when I "sang" in my mind all the popular American songs I could remember, repeating the lyrics, recalling the tunes, buoyed by the memories of the happy times that these songs meant for me.

Sometimes the march took us through the low country which was turned into a morass by monsoon rains that fell steadily, leaking down between my neck and the poncho until I was soaked through. These areas were a checkerboard of rice paddies. If we could not use the roads, we had to walk single file along the dikes between the paddies, and often we slipped thigh-deep into the slimy mud. If the sun came out the mud would dry into a concrete-like cast before we had time to clean it off. My feet inside the oversize boots were wet constantly, and on the rare occasions I could take the shoes off, I found the skin on my toes white and peeling.

Recalling childhood experiences in Seattle helped me

keep my sanity. I remembered that Dad used to take me salmon fishing in Elliott Bay, on the Seattle waterfront, in his little rowboat. When I was about fourteen years old a regulation had been passed limiting each fisherman to one line. They used to troll for salmon with a line on each side of the boat, and if I was with Dad, he could still use two lines. So I sat in the back with a heavy bamboo rod and conventional reel with a fifty-pound test monofilament line, a thirty-pound leader, and three small hooks rigged to a fresh herring spinner. The other one was a heavy hand line with a piano wire leader, one-pound lead sinker and brass spoon. The line was attached to a stubby bamboo stick, propped up near the oar lock, by an inner tube rubber sling to which was attached a little bell. The rubber sling provided enough "give" when a salmon struck, and the bell jingled the alarm.

We would leave home about 4 A.M. and walk to the boathouse at the foot of King Street. Someone with an outboard motor would tow a dozen or more rowboats similar to ours to the most productive area on the west side of the bay, near the mouth of the Duwamish River. About 8 A.M., when the best of the fishing was over, the tug came back to tow us home to the boathouse.

We were trolling one morning when I got a big strike. My pole was almost jerked from my hands and the reel started to hum. In great excitement I turned the pole over to Dad, who instructed me to pull up the hand line so it wouldn't get in the way. We had hooked a whopper and it was putting up a whale of a fight. We changed positions, Dad in the back so he would have more room to play the fish, and me at the oars to maneuver the boat. Dad was working cautiously, taking in line when he could, letting the salmon run when it insisted, and I became so fascinated by the battle that I didn't notice the boat was drifting closer and closer to the Duwamish Bridge. The waters upstream from the bridge were forbidden; we had to remain outside the river mouth. Just as Dad worked the fish—a magnificent king salmon—to the side of the rowboat I noticed the dark mass of the bridge looming overhead.

"Katsumi," Dad cried, "row us out past the bridge."

"But Dad," I protested, "if I start rowing now we may lose the fish."

"Then gaff him. Be quick about it."

What a beauty it was. When we put him on the scales later, he weighed forty-three pounds. But just as we got him aboard, a patrol boat slid alongside. Dad's protest that we had hooked the fish out in the bay and had been dragged by the tide past the bridge fell on deaf ears. He was given a citation that called for a twenty-five-dollar fine.

Everyone admired the salmon but Dad was furious. "Gotdam sakanabetch," he muttered, which was about as close as he could get to the oath. "No more fishing!" That night we had grilled salmon steak, but Dad refused to eat it.

Slogging through the mud of central China with a cannon barrel on my shoulder, I had to smile at Dad's anger. He didn't go fishing for five months. When we went again, it was blackmouth salmon season. Dad used fresh minnows for bait. We'd caught a couple of good-sized fish. Dad had just rebaited the hook and tossed it out when a seagull sighted it. Before we knew what had happened, he had a screeching, fluttering seagull on the end of his line. Along came the inevitable patrol boat, and Dad was stuck with another twenty-five-dollar fine. He didn't go back to fishing for ten months that time.

China's monsoon rains filled the waterholes and swamps, and before long a plague of mosquitoes descended on us. Have you ever tried to swat mosquitoes without making a sound? It's not possible. So if you don't want to draw the ire of the noncoms by slapping the insects during night patrol, you let them bite you. Within a few hours you find yourself with dozens of angry red welts on arms and neck, and within a few days you're down with the fever. For three days a fever rages, and you don't care very much whether you live or die. Then suddenly the fever breaks, and you feel fine aside from a weakness that is overcome in a few days. When the fever struck we called off our patrols, and those of us who hadn't been stricken went from one barracks to the next to tend the sick. We would wring out towels in cold water and place them on feverish foreheads, change sweat-soaked bedding and try to get the patients to sip water. There wasn't much else we could do, but that really didn't matter. Almost invariably the patients needed only time to make their recovery.

Fortunately I didn't catch the fever but the mosquitoes gave me a bad time in another way. One night, on the way to the latrine, I caught my head in one of the long green nets that had been draped over our beds in an effort to protect the men from the insects.

When I tried to untangle the mess the entire net came tumbling down, dragging the supports with it. The noise attracted Sergeant Nakamura who summoned Sergeant Kido. They were angry about being awakened. "It's careless guys like you that cause the fever to spread," Kido charged, then *whap, whap, whap* across the face. Kido made me bring in two straight-back chairs. I was ordered to support my weight on the chair backs and pump my legs as though riding a bicycle. This wouldn't have been so bad except that one of my knees had been acting up. The same knee had been injured in football and once I had to have it drained. Lately I'd been putting hot packs on it, but it was still very tender. Now, every time I bent the knee, pain shot up the entire leg and I almost blacked out several times before the sergeants let me off the "bicycle." I had no doubt that they knew about my bad knee and had deliberately chosen that particular form of "discipline."

The mosquitoes finally did catch up with me a few nights later. I was standing sentry duty at the front gate when suddenly a chill struck. I felt cold all over, shivering uncontrollably. By the time I was relieved forty-five minutes later, I was so weak I had to sit down and rest before I could make my way back to the barracks. Soon I was burning with fever. A medic drew some blood from my ear for analysis and told me I seemed to have *netai-netsu,* a virulent form of fever. Later, I discovered it was malaria, and I was to have many recurrences before it was finally under control. On this first occurrence I spent a week on my back, taking heavy doses of quinine, before I began to feel halfway decent.

About this time the passage of months, if not our growing proficiency, finally won our group promotion from buck private to private. The advance enabled me to wear two yellow stars on the red felt collar tab, but it made no difference in status around the post. As long as a new crop of replacements did not arrive we still had to serve our buddies. Even the busted privates like Ohiro, the one I thought looked like a gangster, held seniority over us and delighted in ordering me around.

Frequent combat began to take its toll in manpower. One day, while out on patrol, a Chinese mortar shell landed near our column and three men were killed almost instantly. Two of them were recruits who had made the trip to China with me. Another time, when we were being sent to the Nanking area by train a landmine tore two freight cars apart, killing seven and wounding about fifteen men. No one in our outfit was close to the blast but we got the job of gathering up the remains. Shortly after that my buddy Mizuno won rotation to Japan and was assigned to escort some ashes back home. Poor, gentle Mizuno. He never made it. About a week later I heard that the military bus he had taken from Yoyang to Hankow on the first leg of the trip was blown to bits by a landmine.

Mizuno's departure meant that I inherited his horse, Enyu. I spent many hours with him, talking to him in English as though he understood. On the mornings when we were allowed to gallop the horses, I would mount him bareback, lean over his neck and pretend I was a jockey, whispering in his ear, "Come on, baby, we're going to win this one for the U.S.A."

Enyu let me down only once. That was during an inspection by some high-ranking officers from Hankow. We had spent days preparing for them, cleaning our weapons, the barracks and stables, and currying our horses until their coats shone. We grooms finally lined up with our horses as the inspection party approached. The officers were only a few horses away when Enyu, who had been growing restless, raised his tail and did what was only natural for any horse. Hurriedly I stepped back and kicked the pile of fresh manure to spread it around evenly over the parade ground.

The officers were admiring my horse when Sergeant Kido suddenly called me. "Private Yoshida," he said, "you were supposed to have this horse clean. He's dirty. Clean him up."

I gave him a blank stare and that only infuriated him. "Here, look here," he shouted, lifting Enyu's tail. I looked. Kido shoved my head hard, right into the horse's hind end. Unaccustomed to such indignities, the horse heaved, bringing his tail down hard against my head. I was too angry to tell whether the officers were laughing, but of course there was nothing I could do but add another black mark to the mental record I was keeping on Kido.

Immediately after the inspection we were ordered to join the Hajime Regiment to close a trap on Chinese troops guarding the approaches to the Nationalist capital of Chungking. Two full divisions were assigned to what was described as a sweep that would crush the Chinese resistance, but I had heard that phrase before; it never happened. We took buses to Hankow and again marched and marched and marched, resting only ten minutes every hour with twenty minutes for meals of rice balls, pickled turnips and dried fish cooked in soy sauce. Even at night there was little rest.

By day the horses drew the cannon along the dirt roads that led through the countryside. At dusk, the cannon would be disassembled, the horses led to safety, and men would shoulder the parts and head for the high country. All our efforts were in vain. We could never get the Chinese to stand still long enough to fight. Their tactics were to hit us when we were off balance, killing a few men, then fading away before we could retaliate. This was supposed to be a major battle, but they were running and we were chasing, and never quite catching up with them for a showdown.

Finally the drive on Chungking was abandoned and we were ordered to make our way back toward Yoyang, destroying towns along the way. So instead of firing against troops, we blasted houses, bridges and stores of food. Most of the villages were abandoned long before we reached them, the residents having fled into the hills. It was an eerie feeling to march through the seemingly abandoned countryside knowing hostile eyes were watching our every move, and that some of those who were watching us were armed and capable of picking us off, one at a time, if they chose. The Chinese were experts at guerrilla warfare. We saw the enemy only seldom, and I rather suspect they wanted to be seen on those occasions.

Finally we neared our base at Yoyang. For some reason whenever we left Yoyang, or when we were returning to it, we assembled the cannon and let the horses draw them. Was this done for the simple reason that the roads were better around Yoyang and it was easier to put the horses to work? Or was there the subtle matter of face—that we had to look good, look like conquering heroes (and not like beasts of burden) in front of the Chinese residents of the city? I was never able to figure it out. We marched behind our horses into the compound, relieved to know that we had lived through another campaign and that we would be getting hot meals and regular rest for a change, but also worried that the hazing that was part of garrison life would begin again.

We spent the first day and a half cleaning our weapons, washing the horses and grooming them, and finally taking care of our laundry. That was the order of importance—first our weapons, second the horses, and last our personal comfort and cleanliness.

I was on guard duty the second night back at Yoyang when an infantry platoon marched into our compound with a dozen miserable-looking Chinese prisoners. Their hands were tied behind their backs and none of them was in uniform. Most wore pajama-like peasant costumes. The platoon commander explained to the sergeant of the guard that these were guerrillas who had been captured in a raid.

What impressed me most was the hooting, jeering local Chinese civilians. Spitting and throwing stones at the prisoners, the villagers followed them until they were safely inside the compound. I could not understand why the civilians should demonstrate such hatred for their countrymen. Our relations with the citizens of Yoyang were proper but not warm. When we went into town, we paid for anything we took. Peasants from nearby farms delivered their produce to our commissary and were paid on the spot. We could walk the streets without fear, but there was never any fraternization in Yoyang except, of course, in the Army-operated brothels. We never lost sight of the fact that we were invaders in a hostile country. Why should the villagers vent such spite and scorn on the guerrillas? Perhaps they hated the guerrillas because they had pillaged the countryside before the Japanese came. Perhaps they resented the guerrillas because they attracted fighting the way a lightning rod attracts lightning. Or perhaps they were trying to impress the Japanese with their "loyalty" toward the invaders. I couldn't figure it out.

Next morning our platoon was called out for bayonet drill, a somewhat unusual order since the only enemy troops we had seen—and were likely to see—were miles away. At the far end of the parade ground, where we practiced *ju-kenjitsu*, were three straw dummies. We formed three lines and on order three men at a time charged the dummies. I was third in line. When my turn came I ran swiftly at the dummy, stopped abruptly about two feet away, raised the rifle and drove the bayonet through the straw man with a blood-curdling yell. We ran through the drill several times before the noncoms ordered us to take a breather.

What happened next is still unbelievable. The Chinese prisoners I had seen marched into the compound the previous night were brought out onto the field. Sergeant Naka-mura unsheathed his sword and prodded three of the prisoners forward. A man was forced to kneel in front of each straw dummy, each with hands still tied behind his back.

"Now," said Sergeant Nakamura, "we shall see how well you have learned to use the bayonet."

With that he gave the order for the first three men to charge and bayonet the human targets. I could feel my stomach churning, yet I watched in utter fascination as the three charged with rifles held high, screaming as they drove the steel home. The Chinese toppled backward, their faces twisted in agony, but not a sound escaped their tightly clenched teeth. A noncom standing behind each victim lifted him upright again and ordered the second wave to charge. Again three soldiers raced forward. Again they plunged their bayonets into the tortured bodies as blood gushed from the first wounds in a crimson torrent. Mercifully, the Chinese were dead or dying.

Now it was my turn. I watched in horror as the three bodies were dragged away, and new victims prodded into place. My hands were clammy and the rifle felt too heavy to lift. With Sergeant Nakamura's shout ringing in my ears, I felt myself running forward. My man was twenty yards away. For a moment I had the incredible, ridiculous feeling that I was bearing down on a football ball-carrier, poised to make a bone-jarring tackle. The glint of steel quickly shattered that illusion. Ahead I saw only an ashen face, horror-stricken eyes waiting for death.

"*Yeee-ohhh,*" I shouted, and there was more terror than anger in the cry. I lunged with my rifle. At the last moment I averted my face. The bayonet went in too high, into the rib cage instead of the unresisting abdomen. I felt the steel hit hard bone. The gun was nearly wrenched out of my hands as the victim twisted backward.

"*Baka!*" I heard someone yell. "Fool! Withdraw your bayonet." I jerked it back, but it would not come. In desperation I shoved my left foot against the man's chest for leverage and heaved back with all my might. Blood poured from the wound. I ran back and took my place in line again.

On the second round my man had already been bayoneted. He sat limply on the ground, held upright by a noncom, his head lolling like a rag doll. This time I aimed low. The bayonet plunged in easily, deep into the gut. It felt as if I had stabbed a bag of barley, and the blade pulled out without resistance. I found myself panting, sweating, trembling, but the full impact of the enormity of my action did not hit me until later. Numb, perhaps in shock, I had washed up and gone with the others to the messhall. I ate a hearty meal, then went into the kitchen for K.P. duty. That's when I felt it coming. I barely made it to the latrine. There I heaved in wrenching expurgation of the morning's horror. I retched and retched until it felt as though my very guts had been turned inside out. Presently I crawled over to some shade and lay face down. It was a long time before the trembling stopped.

Sleep came very hard that night. I kept seeing the steel plunge into the helpless body, the blade slithering out of the gaping wound, the ashen face of the man I had never known and had no reason to hate and no reason to kill other than that he was a Chinese and I a Japanese. I wondered whether he had a family, whether he had a mother like mine waiting for him to come home. Finally I fell asleep.

Next morning I was among a handful of soldiers singled out for additional bayonet practice—on straw dummies this time. My performance the previous day had not measured up to Sergeant Nakamura's standards. I worked the dummies over furiously. They didn't bleed.

Eight

I'VE been telling you about the beatings I suffered in the
Japanese Army, and you may wonder why I continued to
endure them. I endured them for the simple reason that
there was no choice. Nor was I the only recruit to suffer
punishment for trivial offenses. In the Japanese Army, in
fact in all branches of the Japanese armed forces, iron discipline was enforced by the noncommissioned officers. They
were the law. They were the prosecutors, the judges, and
the ones who dealt out the punishment. Their authority was
traditional and unchallenged, the theory being that we recruits, having suffered such punishment, would gain bound-
less respect for the military hierarchy. A second purpose of
the brutality was to build up our resistance to hardships.
A young soldier who had learned to take savage beatings
without whimpering would, so the theory went, march
endless hours without complaint, sleep on the ground, go
without food if necessary.

I knew that if I struck back against this system, that if
I should attempt to defend myself, I wouldn't even get
the benefit of a kangaroo court trial. All the noncoms would
have ganged up on me and beaten me so badly that death

would be a relief. And I didn't want to die. So I submitted to their discipline, trying to steer clear of trouble but not always succeeding. Almost invariably when I was punished the fault was not mine. I just couldn't do things right—their way—and not because I was stupid or lazy or uncooperative. I couldn't do things the right way because I was an American—by birth, education, training, inclination, loyalty—impressed against my will into the Japanese Army. I could learn their customs. I could adjust to the food and the daily routine. But without a strong working knowledge of the language and the culture and folkways, it was inevitable that I should bungle, and be punished for it. On top of this, however, there was the cruelty that seemed to be a part of the makeup of the noncoms in our outfit, particularly Sergeant Kido who seemed to go out of his way to punish me. Even when he was trying to be nice.

That happened on the day I suffered the worst beating I've ever experienced.

It began pleasantly enough. It was a week or so after the live bayonet practice. Our outfit had pretty well caught up on its garrison responsibilities after the long spell of combat, and almost everyone was given permission to go into Yoyang for the day. I decided not to go, mainly because I was fed up with the *don'ts*—don't eat in a native restaurant, don't harass the civilians, don't get drunk, don't go into the officers' brothel, etc., etc. To heck with it, I thought, I'd rather spend a quiet day in the compound, catching up with my laundry and letter-writing.

The peace was short-lived. By mid-afternoon Sergeant Nakamura, Sergeant Kido and some of the senior privates came back to the compound boisterously drunk. Kido yelled for someone to help him get out of uniform. He stretched out in a chair while I removed his shoes like some valet and neatly rolled up his leggings. Next, Sergeant Nakamura ordered several of the privates to run to the stock room to pick up the weekly beer, *sake,* tobacco, candy, and soap rations.

Because we had been out in the field so long, we got triple the usual amount of beer and *sake,* and that, coming on top of the liquor the men had consumed in town, caused the trouble.

"We're going to have a party," Nakamura shouted in the messhall as soon as the supper dishes had been cleared. "We had a hard time together in the field. You men did pretty well, but you are far from being full-fledged soldiers yet. Today is a very good day to drink together and get to know each other better."

I had enough experience with Sergeant Nakamura to suspect his motives; I suspected he was just trying to latch onto our *sake* ration. Some of the other men were taken in by his apparent sincerity, and before long a great old drinking party was going full blast. The Japanese, unfortunately, seem to have a low tolerance for alcohol. They don't sip their drink to relish it. They make a practice of belting it down as fast as they can, and in no time at all their inhibitions are gone and they become boisterous, sometimes quarrelsome, usually contentious and almost always very demanding, even when they are happy drunk. First, they *banzai*-ed everybody from the Emperor on down, and then they got into a singing mood.

I tried to make myself as inconspicuous as possible, pretending to sip *sake,* which I couldn't tolerate. Someone suggested a singing competition with extra liquor as prizes. A few of the fellows were so anxious to perform they waited in line to get a chance to sing, and several of them weren't bad at all. I was beginning to enjoy the entertainment when Sergeant Kido called out my name. "Yoshida," he shouted above the hubbub, "Yoshida, let's hear you sing."

I just froze. The sound of his voice had that effect on me. I tried to remember a Japanese song, any Japanese song, and drew a blank. The fellows were yelling for me to get up and sing, and Nakamura and Kido were giving me the eye, as if challenging me to get up before the crowd. I stood up slowly and made my way up front, still trying desperately to think of a Japanese song. The only songs that came to mind were the popular American tunes, but of course they wouldn't do. So I just stood there, feeling embarrassed and foolish, until Sergeant Kido staggered up to me and offered me a drink out of his *sake* cup. This is a time-honored ritual. In a friendly drinking bout, you offer your friend a drink out of your little porcelain cup. He drinks, then offers you one out of his cup. To refuse is an insult. Kido thrust his cup under my nose. "Sir," I said quietly, "I appreciate your friendly offer of a drink, but I would like to sing first." I pushed Kido's hand away gently. Snarling, he threw the *sake* in my face and staggered back to his seat.

"Fellows," I began, "I'd like to sing you a little song I learned from my mother a long time ago when I was very young. I have forgotten the title, but this is the way it goes." And I sang:

"*Yu yake ko yake te hi ga kure te,*
"*Yama no otera no kane ga naru . . .*"

It's a simple little song about dusk settling down after a flaming sunset, and the bell sounding from the temple on the hill—a child's song, a soothing sort of lullaby. There was a long moment of silence when I finished. It certainly wasn't my voice that charmed them. Perhaps the men were remembering their own childhoods, and how their mothers had sung the same song to lull them to sleep. Suddenly there was a long burst of applause and cries for me to sing again, but I declined and sat down.

Kido called, "Yoshida, come here. You have some unfinished business."

I went. He thrust another cup of *sake* in front of me and demanded that I drink.

"Thank you, sir," I began, "but I cannot drink . . ."

A belt slashed me across the face. Someone kicked me in the gut. I doubled over in pain and Kido shouted to me to stand at attention. As I tried to straighten up I got another lashing across the face. I heard Private Ohiro's voice demanding that I drink, then someone poured *sake* over my head. The vinegary smell was sickening. Someone kicked me in the stomach again and I went down. Gasping for breath, I could see Nakamura and Kido grinning down at me. Their mouths were moving, but I couldn't hear a word they were saying. Blows were raining on my back. A boot caught me in the back of the neck and I blacked out.

I don't know how long I was unconscious, but when I came to, the party was over. "Yoshida," someone said, "help the men clean up the mess." I managed to get to my feet and straighten the chairs and tables and wield the broom. Several of the men were still out on the floor, their blouses covered with their own vomit. Those able to stand were ordered to line up. Sergeant Nakamura, suddenly sober, addressed us:

"The party is over. You men must remember your place. When you are told to drink, we expect you to drink. But I repeat, the party is over. Never forget your place in this Army. You are still recruits. You will remain recruits, you will not be considered full-fledged soldiers until replacements arrive at this garrison, and only then will you be entitled to move up one step. Dismissed."

I crawled off to bed, shaking my head in disbelief. The day had started so quietly, so pleasantly. And it had ended in no better than a drunken brawl in which I was an innocent victim. The last thing I remember before falling to sleep was vowing to get even with Kido, no matter how long I had to wait. Some day the war would be over and we would be out of the Army, and then I would hunt him down and even the score for the senseless beatings, the humiliation, the unprovoked malice that he vented on me. I wondered if there was such a plea as justifiable homicide in Japan.

The hazing let up the next few weeks, but we were on almost constant alert. This meant garrison routine was suspended while we waited, prepared to move at a moment's notice. This gave me plenty of time to think—about myself, the Japanese, the Army, the war, and to wonder how the war was going elsewhere, particularly in the Southwest Pacific. I knew the situation for the Japanese Army in China wasn't altogether good. The last big drive on Chungking had bogged down. Now our outfit was issued white phosphorus shells and I wasn't sure what that meant. Rifles were distributed among some of the artillery men, and this could only mean that some close-up fighting might be expected. The thought of death had come to me many times. Long ago, in boyhood, I had feared death. Now I was no longer afraid, but I resented the thought of having to die because there was so much I wanted to do. I wanted to go back home to Seattle. I wanted to see Mom and my sisters again. I wanted to live long enough to even accounts with Sergeant Kido. But there were times when I wondered how I would face death if it came. Would I have the courage to die bravely? And what is a brave death?

Back in Seattle during my impressionable years Mom and Dad had told me Japanese soldiers died shouting *banzai* for the Emperor. But here in China, where I had seen many men die, not one had gone to glory with the Emperor's name on his lips. But I had heard many men whisper, "*Okaasan, koraete kure* [Mother, forgive me]," as they lay dying, feeling somehow that they were letting their mothers down by losing their lives.

Winter had set in when we marched forth again, marching by day and marching by night, and never seeing the enemy. I marveled at the way my mind took me back home during those endless treks. My feet, aching in those oversized boots that had never been replaced, reminded me of the pinch

I felt the time I bought my first pair of Florsheim shoes. I remembered the rich gloss of the leather, and how proud I had been of them. Brushing the branch of a winter-dormant tree, I recalled instantly a walk through Madrona Park in Seattle where the maples and elms had shed their leaves. When we stopped for a break, it was just another opportunity for me to relive in my mind the warm memories of life in another world. Sometimes I wondered if these reveries meant I was losing my mind. But I knew that these brief escapes into the world of memory, the world of a happier past, relieved me if only briefly from the harsh realities and gave me the strength to carry on.

Christmas was just another day in the field—cold, wet, mud-caked, weary, dirty, stinking with filth. Finally, on New Year's Day the supply unit caught up with us, and also the mail. Usually several letters arrived together. This time there were twelve, all from Mom. I always opened the last one first, just to make sure everything was all right. She said she was well and keeping busy, and that Jim was still doing fine. I smiled at that one. If the same censor was reading all my mail, he must be thinking that Jim was the name of a pet dog or something. Then, one by one, I went through the rest of the mail. Each letter said about the same thing: Mom was well, thinking of me, praying for my safe return, and don't worry about her. If there were deeper thoughts she wanted to express—and I'm sure there were—they remained unwritten because she knew I could not understand. But it was enough to get these simple little messages that told me all was well back in Japan.

In celebration of the new year all of the troops were given the traditional *mochi*, a glutinous rice cake that I found quite tasteless but considered a delicacy by the Japanese. When toasted, it swells up like a bun and is very sticky. I didn't have anyone I wanted to give my *mochi* to, so I decided to share my cakes with Enyu, my horse. Enyu was about as unenthusiastic about *mochi* as I was, but he made a valiant effort and downed all the cakes even though he had trouble chewing them.

About 3 A.M. someone kicked me in the ribs. A warrant officer shouted that one of the horses was ill and several of us were being summoned to help the men on duty. I ran down to the makeshift corral where the horses were penned and found Enyu on his side, foaming horribly at the mouth. We tried to get him up, but his legs wouldn't support him. He was in obvious distress from gas or indigestion. Finally we got Enyu up and all of us took turns rubbing his sides with balled-up hay. One of the men who was a sort of unit veterinarian found a big syringe in his kit, filled it with soapy lukewarm water, and gave Enyu an enema. Then we rubbed his sides some more while deep-seated rumblings told us the enema was taking effect. Finally the pressure built up to the point where the blockage gave way and Enyu cut loose with a mighty stream. What a welcome sight that was for me. The fellows all shouted *"Banzai, banzai, banzai,"* and went back to their bedrolls, leaving me to clean up the mess. No one ever suspected what had caused Enyu's monumental bellyache, but I knew it was the *mochi.* I apologized in English to Enyu and I wondered what the Army would have done to me had he died. Would they have shot me? Just thinking about it gave me goose-pimples.

Next morning Enyu seemed none the worse for his experience and he resumed his place in the line of march. We were to link up with the division, but lost contact and wandered about seemingly without aim for nearly two weeks. Then a divisional runner caught up with us and ordered us into position for an impending battle. I suppose it's the same in all armies, but it was almost impossible to find out what was going on, or what role we were playing in the broad picture of a single battle, let alone a war. All we knew was what we saw with our own eyes. On this occasion we fired about fifty shells at targets we couldn't see, and that was it for the day.

That night we got promise of much more significant activity. The order was passed to wrap all metal with cloth to eliminate sound. We were also given white bands to wear across our helmets for identification. Finally, we were told that shortly we were to crawl forward ahead of the infantry with our cannon and blast the entrenched enemy at point-blank range. Normally we would use our sights to zero in on the target. This time we were to open the breech and sight through the barrel, firing shells with the fuses set for instantaneous explosion.

With straw and tree branches stuck in our helmets for camouflage, we inched forward as quietly as we could. The moon peeked out from behind the clouds and we could see a broad valley ahead. All through the night we waited and waited. When daylight came we were ordered back without having fired a single shot. Once again the Chinese had drifted away like the night mists and we had been unable to make contact. Now we began the long march back to our base at Yoyang, up and down endless mountains, across vast expanses of fields. Eventually we reached a small town secure enough so that we were promised two days of rest. After the horses were taken care of and the chores done, we were to have our first hot bath in over a month. I was unwrapping my leggings when a fellow exclaimed, "Hey, Yoshida, I think you have beriberi!" He used the word *kakke,* which I had never heard before.

"What's *kakke?*" I asked.

He pointed to my legs. The skin was shiny and the legs looked slightly bloated. The leggings had left deep indentations and the flesh showed no signs of filling in.

"*Kakke* is a nutritional disease caused by a lack of vitamins," he explained. "It can be serious. You better see the doc."

I had felt unusually tired the last several days but thought it was due to the long march. Nonetheless, after my bath I went to the infirmary tent. The major on duty ran his hands over the swollen legs, then sat me down to test my reflexes. I crossed one leg over the other while he tapped the knee with a rubber hammer. Nothing happened. There was no reflex action at all. The doctor asked how I'd been feeling. I replied that I seemed to be unusually tired and my malaria seemed to be kicking up from time to time. He told me to come in for a thorough checkup after we got back to Yoyang.

I couldn't tell for sure whether my trouble was physical or mental when we resumed the march, but my legs seemed to be heavier than they'd ever been. I felt feverish frequently, and I just didn't seem to be hungry any more. I just barely made it back to Yoyang on my own power. By then my fever was so high that I was ordered to the infirmary immediately. I was there four days, sleeping most of the time, before being released to go back to my outfit.

A lot of things had happened in that short time. Division was being reorganized. New recruits were coming in as replacements, but not one was being assigned to our Yari Battalion. We were still low men on the totem pole. But something much more important had happened while I was away. We had a new set of noncoms. Sergeant Nakamura, Sergeant Kido and three others had been rotated back to Japan and were already gone!

I couldn't suppress a cheer when I heard the news. No more beatings for no reason at all! No more hazing and dirty duty and stupid make-work jobs just because my name was Jim Yoshida! The new noncom team was tough—they had waited a long time for their promotion and were out to take every advantage of their new authority—but their discipline was kindergarten stuff compared to the old regime. I could live with strict discipline if it was administered fairly; Nakamura and Kido had frustrated me by seeming to go out of their way to make my life miserable, to give me a beating at the slightest provocation.

One day soon afterward I was told to report to the administrative office for desk duty. This had never happened before. Perhaps, I figured, they were giving me an easy job temporarily because I was still weak from my bout with the fever. I was no more than an office boy, dusting the desks and tidying things while the officer of the day and his noncom did all the paper work. When the lunch hour came I was told to watch the office while they went to get a bite to eat.

For want of anything better to do, I opened the steel files containing personnel records. I could recognize the characters for my name, found my file and went through it. Most of the material was beyond my reading ability—I could just make out my name, address, place and date of birth, etc.

Then I found Sergeant Kido's file. Apparently it hadn't been transferred back to Japan yet. My eyes widened and I broke out in a cold sweat at what I read.

Name: Kido, Shigemi
Place of Birth: Island of Maui, Hawaii
Education: Graduated McKinley High School, Honolulu, Hawaii; some courses in Japanese universities.
Home Address: Yamaguchi Prefecture, Kumage-gun, Hirao Village.

Kido was born in Hawaii! Educated in Hawaii! That made him a Nisei, just like me! And he lived in Japan in the same village where my father was born, the village where I had lived before being conscripted!

"You goddamned no-good bastard, Kido!" I screamed in the empty room. "You Hawaiian son of a bitch! You no-good punk! You, a Nisei, treating me, another Nisei, like I was shit!"

I slammed the file shut and, unable to control my trembling, I sat down in my chair. I couldn't believe Kido was a Nisei.

As calm returned, I muttered to myself, "Kido, if I live through this godforsaken war, I am going to track you down, no matter where you are, no matter how long it takes. I am going to find you and I am going to beat you within an inch of your life. And then you're going to tell me why you treated me like you did, you lousy son of a bitch bastard."

Nine

THE headquarters noncom returned from lunch and found me staring at the wall. "Yoshida," he said, "you look terribly pale. Obviously you haven't recovered from the fever yet. Why don't you go see the doctor?"

"Thank you, sir," I replied, "I appreciate your concern, but I'm all right. All I need is a little lunch."

But in the messhall the smell of food nauseated me, and all I could see was Kido's face leering at me from the tea in the cup. How could a fellow Nisei do what Kido had done to me? I simply could not understand it. I don't know how I got past the rest of the day back in the office. I could think of nothing but Kido. I wanted to look into the personnel files again to make sure I had read Kido's record correctly, yet I didn't dare while the others were present. The last thing I remember before falling asleep that night was shaking my clenched fist at the barracks ceiling and vowing silently: "Kido, you are going to pay for all the lousy misery I suffered. I promise." I had never felt such deep, burning hatred for anyone in my life.

Next morning my legs were so badly swollen I reported directly to the medics. They promptly placed me in the infirmary, which had sleeping space for eight men, and began the long-postponed physical checkup. The doctor's report was not reassuring—malaria, beriberi and malnutrition. I was relieved of roll calls, guard duty, horse duty, all other duties that I had lived with for so long. I had nothing to do but eat and sleep, and I did plenty of both. After a week the swelling had not gone down, and my legs felt incredibly heavy whenever I tried to walk. The doctor shook his head the last time he checked me.

The next thing I knew someone was helping me into my uniform and I was placed in an Army bus for the Yoyang railway station. A day and a night later the train reached Hangchow, a major city about a hundred miles south of Shanghai, not far from the coast. There was a large Japanese Army hospital at Hangchow. Most of the patients had suffered wounds.

At the hospital I was stripped of my uniform and given a green kimono-type robe. Someone took away my oversized boots and replaced them with rubber-soled slippers. In a way I was sorry to see the boots go; they had served me well. But I also hoped I'd never see them again, for they symbolized my role as a misfit in the Japanese Army. The only item they left me was the regulation Army cap. I was assigned to a ward with about thirty patients, and for the first time since leaving Seattle, I had a real bed to sleep in.

The sheets were clean, cool and soothing, and nurses—the first Japanese girls I'd seen since coming to China—flitted about quietly and efficiently. The hospital was so crowded it took the doctors several days to get around to giving me a complete physical. The very next day I was put on a strict diet made up mainly of red *azuki* beans boiled without salt. White rice and anything containing sugar was forbidden. I also got regular doses of quinine to control the malaria. I continued to feel reasonably well so long as I lay quietly in bed. But when I tried to stand or walk, I was alarmed at how weak I had become, and although my legs were still somewhat swollen, my weight was dropping rapidly. One day, after I weighed myself, I made a quick calculation from Japanese *kin* to American pounds and I was shocked to find I had lost forty to fifty pounds. No matter how I figured it, my weight was down to no more than 150 pounds.

Several mornings later I noticed some spots of hardened candle wax on my blanket. I thought nothing of it until a few days later I found more wax spots. I remarked on it to the patient in the next bed and he told me that a nurse would come in with a candle, stand by my bed and watch me while I slept, then cover me gently and return to her rounds. One night soon after that I awoke from a restless sleep and there she was, standing over me with the soft candlelight casting a faint glow over her face. For a split second I thought it was my sister Betty. The nurse took my hand, placed it beneath the covers, gave it a little squeeze, then slipped away. I looked for her during the day but did not see her until one morning she brought me a doll she had made with gauze. It was a pink and white ballerina; the edges of her skirt had been dipped in mercurochrome for coloring. She said it was a going-away gift because I was being transferred to one of the Army's major hospitals in Shanghai.

Suddenly it dawned on me that I was ill, seriously ill, maybe even ready to die. Strangely, though, I felt no pain, only a great weariness that left me with little appetite and only an overwhelming desire to rest. Maybe, I thought, I might even be a mental case. The nurse must have seen the questioning in my eyes. She assured me I would be all right and promised to visit me in Shanghai.

That evening I was placed in a stretcher and loaded into a hospital train with large Red Cross markings on the sides of the coaches. It took a day and a half to reach Shanghai. A military ambulance took me and the other patients to what appeared to be a huge hospital on Shanghai's out-skirts. The jostling of the ambulance was soothing and I fell asleep. Or had I passed out from fatigue? When I awoke I was already between the sheets of a bed in a two-man room. The second bed was vacant. I remember opening my eyes and looking around and saying to myself: "Jim, you must be in terrible shape, or they wouldn't put you in a semiprivate room." It was the most privacy I'd had since being drafted into the Army. I was more tired than I'd ever been in my life—too tired to lift my arms, too tired to keep my eyes open, and terribly tired of being tired. I fell asleep again. I don't know how long I slept, but when I awoke I heard the rustling sound of a starched uniform and felt someone brush against me.

Two nurses were working at the other bed. As I watched, they turned a patient over and hurriedly stuffed cotton into the body orifices. I remembered vaguely that this is what they did when someone died. I realized with a start that a patient had been brought into the room while I slept and that he had died. A cart was rolled into the room and the body taken away. Quickly the nurses changed the sheets and a second patient, lying very quietly, was brought into the room. I fell asleep again as they were placing him into the bed. When I awoke next, the same patient was strug-gling noisily for breath the way a man in a coma does just before death takes over.

I don't know how long I alternately slept and awakened in that little room, drifting in and out of consciousness, nor do I know how many soldiers were brought in to die and then carried away. Later, someone told me twenty-one men had occupied the bed next to mine during that time, but somehow I clung tenaciously to life. All that is a blank now and I shall never know how close I was to death and why I didn't go as the others did. What I do know is that I awoke one morning with my mind clear, as from a long, long sleep, with a firm resolve that I must not die just yet.

I was incredibly weak. I had not the strength even to raise an arm and take a drink of water. I had no desire for food. Yet I realized that I must take nourishment if I was to make it.

"Nurse," I whispered, "do you have any cookies?"

She brought me a single thin wafer, lightly sweetened, perhaps a tea cookie confiscated from British stocks in Shanghai. The nurse broke off a tiny crumb and placed it in my mouth. I was too tired even to chew. I let the saliva soften it and finally I swallowed the morsel. With infinite patience the nurse helped me eat the entire cookie. I knew then I wasn't going to die. I smiled and fell asleep again.

When I awoke intravenous feeding began through a needle inserted into a vein in my thigh. The first time I saw that thigh I turned away in shock; my once massive legs had deteriorated into little more than bone wrapped in flaccid skin.

Slowly, ever so slowly, I regained my strength. Together with the intravenous feeding I received heavy doses of calcium and vitamin B-1 to overcome the effects of the beriberi. The days dragged on into weeks, then months, as the savagely ravaged body fought back with excruciating slowness. There were long hours when I had nothing to do but stare at the ceiling and think about Mom and home and what I had learned about Kido. In the dark moments of loneliness and frustration, I buoyed my spirits with the determination to get back to Japan and see the folks again. In the bitter hours of hopelessness, when I doubted that my body ever would be restored, I would work myself into a seething rage with thoughts of the unfinished business with Kido. One day, long before my legs were strong enough to carry me, I asked my nurse to find me a rubber ball. I squeezed it hour after hour, first in the right hand, then in the left, thousands of times a day to build up my hands and arms. When I became bored with the exercise I would think of Kido again, his neck between my fingers, and return to that endless squeezing. They say hate never built anything. In my case a savage desire for revenge sped the painful road back to health.

In time I was permitted to walk. With a nurse at each side I tested my legs. Two steps were all I could make. Each day I could totter a little farther. The flesh returned to my legs and the muscles became more firm. By early spring of 1945—a year after I'd been stricken—I was finally strong enough to have the run of the hospital.

In all that time I had not written once to Mom. At first I had been too ill. Then, when I became stronger, I had hesitated to write for fear of alarming her. How could I explain in my inadequate language, on one side of a postcard stamped with the name of the hospital, that I had been ill but had made a full recovery? I feared that she would suspect I had been horribly maimed—minus an arm or leg or worse—and was trying to conceal the bad news from her. It would be difficult for her to believe that her 200-pound son, who had never been ill a day in his life, had been felled by something like beriberi. I must have written her twenty times, but each time I tore up the card, fearing to send it. I kept rationalizing that by failing to write to her, I was sparing her the even greater punishment of doubt. The Army, I knew, would not be in touch with her since I was not a battle casualty, and so I hoped she would consider no news as good news. The thought that she might be torn by uncertainty never entered my young mind. And so the days passed.

One morning in May I noticed a call for English-speaking personnel on the bulletin boards. Immediately I saw myself being transferred to the Pacific Theater, perhaps the Philippines, for action against the Americans. I decided to ignore the notice.

A few days later I was summoned by Captain Kunizo Iwata, the hospital supply officer. My apprehension vanished quickly when I met him. His tunic collar was open and his uniform rumpled. He was the farthest thing possible from a spit-and-polish Japanese Army officer. In fact he hardly looked Japanese, having fine features, long eyelashes, large laughing eyes and a perpetual five o'clock shadow. He had my personnel folder in front of him and promptly put me at ease by remarking with a smile that it was obvious I wasn't much of a soldier.

Then he explained that he wanted me to join his staff as his liaison aide, and at the same time tutor him in English. I broke into a wide grin; I was for anything that would keep me out of a combat unit. But the best news was yet to come.

"Of course we'll arrange to get you out of the Army because it wouldn't be right to have a private taking on the responsibilities you will have. You will work as a *Gunzoku* (a civilian attached to the military) with the simulated rank of major. Is that agreeable?"

Was it! In this single interview the misery of military service was made a thing of the distant past. The official orders were signed two days later. I was discharged from the hospital as a patient, discharged from the Army, and officially transferred to the Shanghai Army Hospital. So that we could spend more time conversing with each other in English, Captain Iwata asked me to move into his private quarters with him. For months I had lived in fear that I might talk in English in my sleep and be punished for it. Now I was being paid to speak English! My uniform was khaki shorts for Shanghai's humid heat, open-neck shirt, calf-length white stockings and low-cut civilian shoes that fit—size 10½D oxfords from some well-stocked Shanghai shop. What a relief that was!

My first assignment was to accompany Captain Iwata to Army Liaison Office headquarters in the Broadway Mansions Building just across teeming Soochow Creek from the International Settlement. As we passed out the main gate of the hospital compound the sentry snapped off a salute. Captain Iwata, who had to wear his uniform, saluted back. I could hardly suppress a snicker. It was the sloppiest salute I had ever seen. He was at heart a civilian and, if possible, he was a worse soldier than I had ever been.

"This damned sword," he remarked as we waited for a car outside the gate. "I have to wear it as part of my uniform and I can't even get it out of the scabbard. I think it's rusted in there." When I offered to clean it in my spare time, he replied: "No, don't bother. I never make use of it and I wouldn't know how to use it if I had to." That was the kind of soldier I liked.

I was astonished at the size of Shanghai and the volume of traffic in the streets. Most of the motor vehicles were Army trucks or military vehicles. But thousands of bicycles and rickshas crowded the thoroughfares from curb to curb. Coolies, with tow ropes over their shoulders like beasts of burden, tugged at heavily laden four-wheeled carts. Even two-wheeled hand trucks were being used to transport the city's commerce.

Soochow Creek was lined with junks of all sizes and shapes, with only a narrow channel in the middle for barges taking coal and other raw materials farther up the stream. The iron trusses of Garden Bridge linked the Hongkew, or Japanese sector, with the Bund in the International Settlement. Although the Japanese in effect controlled all of Shanghai, a certain measure of autonomy was still exercised by the International Settlement council, and Japanese sentries checked traffic crossing Garden Bridge.

Broadway Mansions was a huge brick hotel that before the war had been a headquarters for Japanese commercial activity. The Liaison Office, which was responsible for the Army's relations with other national groups, occupied a suite of offices. I waited in the main lobby while Captain Iwata went up to conduct his business. About a half hour later he came down with a black briefcase. We went to a quiet coffee shop where he explained his mission.

"I was told the war is far from over," Captain Iwata said. "The Army is expecting a great many more casualties and we must prepare facilities to take care of them. This briefcase is full of money, Chinese money, in large denominations. If I told you exactly how much I have, you would find it hard to believe. I have the responsibility of using this money to negotiate for more hospital space. Money alone won't buy cooperation, but it will help us make friends, and in this assignment I will have to depend heavily on you because you speak English and I don't. Do you understand?"

During the next few weeks we called on and negotiated for the use of space at St. Luke's Hospital, St. Francis Hospital and Aurora Girls' College, all close to each other in the French Concession. None of the buildings was taken over completely, but we contracted for the use of wards and administrative offices. Soon afterward many of the patients and personnel were moved out of the overcrowded Shanghai Army Hospital into the new hospitals.

One of my favorite contacts was the Mother Superior at the Aurora Girls' College. She and her nuns were very standoffish at first, looking on me with suspicion and with good reason, for the Japanese troops had not always been charitable toward her order. I tried to explain to her that I really wasn't Japanese, but an American whose parents had happened to be Japanese. This didn't make much sense to her. Americans were Americans and Japanese were Japanese, and she could not understand how a person could be both, particularly when the two countries were at war. I finally gave up trying to explain. Every once in a while, with Captain Iwata's approval I would take the nuns a sack of flour, sugar, a case of canned goods, or some other scarce item of food. The good Mother would clasp her hands in delight, but I doubt the nuns got very much of the food. There were too many hungry young girls boarding at the school. Captain Iwata's wise policy of making friends with the people with whom we dealt, plus my ability to communicate with them in English, made our work very pleasant. If it weren't for the wounded who were always with us, it would have been easy to imagine that the war was far, far away.

In the evenings, after our informal English classes, Captain Iwata and I would talk about many other things. One day I told him about the way Sergeant Kido had abused me, how I had learned that he was a Nisei, and of my all-consuming desire to gain revenge. Captain Iwata listened in silence. When I finished my story, he said:

"Have you ever tried to put yourself in his shoes, Yoshida? I think it is obvious that both of you, being Nisei, were under constant surveillance. Kido, as a noncommissioned officer, had to demonstrate that he was a good soldier, and he had to make it particularly hard on you to show his superiors that he wasn't playing favorites. At the same time, he must have realized that you also had to prove you were a good Japanese soldier if you were to survive, and the most effective way to make you prove it was to keep punishing you. He must have had confidence that you could take it. And so both of you survived.

"Think, Yoshida, how often Kido must have wanted to tell you that he was a Nisei, too, but I would guess that he did not dare because he was not sure of your reaction. I think he might have felt that had you known, you would not have accepted the punishment he had to deal out. The punishment you took was physical, yes painful, but only physical. Think of the punishment Kido had to absorb within his spirit and his heart and his mind. That kind of self-punishment is much harder to absorb, believe me, than a mere physical beating."

I was far from ready to accept Captain Iwata's line of reasoning. The scars from Kido's senseless beatings were still too fresh, the bitterness born of his abuse too raw for me to buy this point of view. But the captain's words set me to thinking. Eventually I vowed to make Kido tell me first why he had treated me as he had and then pound him to a pulp.

Captain Iwata impressed me in other ways. He was a graduate of Keio University and he had the typical intellectual's disdain for military formality. He did his work diligently and efficiently because he believed he was performing a valuable service. But he resisted regulations which he regarded as silly and paid the least possible attention to official red tape. And because he was getting his job done, his superiors wisely let him have his way.

On another occasion I told Captain Iwata about Mom, and how I had failed to write her for the many months since I had entered the hospital for fear of alarming her.

"You mean you've never written her, even after you recovered?" he asked in shock.

"No, sir," I replied. "At first I couldn't get myself to tell her I had been hospitalized. I felt it was better not to let her know I was ill. Now, of course, I realize how wrong I was. It would have been very simple to send her a postcard saying I had been hospitalized due to a nutritional illness.

"But the longer I delayed, the more difficult my problem became. After I began to feel better, I kept rationalizing that soon I would have to return to combat again, and if I told her this right after breaking my long silence, I would be forcing new anxieties on her. The longer I procrastinated, the more difficult it became to write. Now I don't know what to tell her, or how I should explain my failure to write."

"I could write to her for you."

"No, sir," I said after a moment of thought. "I think I owe it to Mom to write to her myself. I appreciate your offer, but this is something I must do personally."

"Well, be sure that you do write."

"Yes, sir." In the next few weeks I started a dozen letters, but none was adequate for what I needed to say. I did not mail a single one. I kept putting off that letter home to let Mom know I was all right.

Then gradually military activity picked up in the Shanghai area. Army trucks loaded with troops careened around the streets. Antiaircraft emplacements went up in and around the French Concession where I was spending most of my time. One dark night the air raid siren began its eerie wail. This time it was no practice alert. Searchlights crisscrossed the skies. Finally they pinned a huge bomber against the black velvet of the night and the antiaircraft guns began their staccato bark. But the plane was much too high, far beyond the range of the guns. Later, someone told me it had been a B-29.

"What's a B-29?" I asked.

"Why, that's one of the B-san, the big Boeing plane that has been bombing Japan almost nightly from tremendous altitudes. Haven't you heard?"

No, I hadn't heard. But I was also thinking. Boeing. Why, Boeing was the Seattle company that had the big plant out in South Park, near the Duwamish River, not too far from Joe Nakatsu's dad's farm. I wondered whether the plane I had seen had been built in Seattle. I couldn't help but feel a swelling of pride. And yet I was worried about these planes bombing Japan. Were they dropping bombs on the cities without opposition, as the man had said? If the cities were being bombed, what was happening in the country where Mom was?

And then it happened a few days later. We heard the incredible news that a new and very terrible bomb had been dropped by the Americans on Hiroshima, and where the city had been there remained nothing but rubble. And after that, Nagasaki.

We heard Emperor Hirohito's surrender broadcast via shortwave radio. We stood at attention in the Shanghai Army Hospital grounds as the thin, reedy voice, crackling with static, was amplified over the loudspeaker system. The officers stood ramrod straight, looking directly ahead. The nurses kept their eyes on the ground. I didn't understand a word that was said, for the Emperor spoke in very formal court language, but I could guess the import of his message. The war was over and Hirohito was telling his people to put down their arms.

Suddenly I felt a vast sense of elation and fear. America had won the war! But what was going to happen to me? I had fought for the enemy. Where was I going?

I made my way back to my quarters in a daze. Captain Iwata was already there and humming a tune. He shook my hand solemnly, congratulated me, and then said: "Now we have much work to do. You will have to teach me more English, for the Americans are coming."

The tune he had been humming was "It's Been a Long, Long Time."

Ten

THE war was ended. Japan had surrendered. But for those of us at Shanghai General Hospital, very little changed immediately. It was as though our momentum sustained the routine. The wounded and the ill, en route to the hospital from inland detachments, continued to arrive daily. For those already in the wards, care went on as usual. Men died, and their bodies were taken away. Operations were performed, drugs administered, bandages changed. Hospital discipline remained as rigid as ever.

The only conspicuous change was that the officer of the day and the noncom of the day now appeared without sidearms or swords. They still wore their leather straps for their weapons, but they walked their rounds unarmed.

Overnight, however, an astonishing change took place in the International Settlement and the French Concession. Neon lights, darkened for so long, suddenly filled the night with color. Merchandise of all descriptions—watches, fountain pens, jewelry, silks and brocades, cigarettes, canned goods—reappeared like magic in store windows. Automobiles, long hidden in warehouses to avoid being requisitioned by the Japanese Army, showed up in the streets.

Nightclubs reopened their doors. Walking by a small bar in the French Concession one night, I heard someone playing "Stardust" on a piano. I made my way inside. The bar was crowded. A broad-shouldered, curly-haired White Russian was playing. He caught my eye and smiled. I nursed a beer, marveling at the pianist's skill. He had large muscular hands, but they floated over the keys, playing song after song that I remembered from my Seattle boyhood. During a break the pianist came to the bar where I was sitting and introduced himself in English as Paul, a member of a White Russian family that had fled to China after the Communist revolution. He must have stood at least six feet three inches tall. I took to him immediately, perhaps because of the kinship I felt since we were both exiles from our native land. When Paul went back to the piano he seemed lost in memory as he played a series of semi-classics. When I left late that night I put all the Chinese money in my pockets into Paul's hands and promised to return.

Captain Iwata was enthusiastic when I told him about the bar and the pianist.

"Let's go tomorrow," he said. "We will dance, you and I."

"But there are no girls there," I explained, "at least no girls that I know, no bar hostesses."

"Never mind," Iwata exclaimed. "You and I will dance together. You and I."

It took a bit of explaining to convince Iwata that in the Western world it was all right sometimes for two women to dance together, but never two men.

So we went to the bar and Iwata drank beer while I listened, misty-eyed, to all the old hits I used to know, all the songs that I had sung to myself to maintain my sanity while marching over half of China.

Meanwhile, at the hospital, Captain Iwata was quick to sense that despite the duties that kept them busy, the personnel were anxiously waiting for the other shoe to drop. The Americans had won the war; when would they arrive to take over? We had received no word. To keep everyone fully occupied, he suggested that I conduct an English conversation class. Now that was a switch. I, who had been afraid to speak English, being asked to teach English to Army personnel. A notice was put on the bulletin boards and nearly 800 signed up! Most of them were nurses.

Now it was my turn to get cold feet. I had expected some informal conversational English classes around a table. Suddenly I was faced with the prospect of lecturing to a hall full of students. The only time I'd performed in front of so many people, aside from judo tournaments, was when I had been a member of the color guard at grade school assemblies. And how do you teach a language to so many people? Finally Captain Iwata persuaded me to go ahead, and I decided to start with the alphabet first, followed by some common phrases as we progressed.

I nearly froze when I saw 800 pairs of eyes focused intently, even hopefully, on me. Then, filled with the confidence that Captain Iwata had instilled in me during coaching sessions, I began:

"The English language is based on an alphabet of twenty-six letters. I will pronounce each of the letters for you once. After that, I will pronounce them one by one, and I want you to repeat them after me."

The students responded enthusiastically and did very well until we came to the sounds that throw the Japanese every time—l, r, and v. Still, I've never seen so many people so eager to learn, and they learned very fast. I could not be aware of it at the time, of course, but this willingness of the Japanese to adapt was to stand them in very good stead as their nation struggled to reestablish itself politically and economically during the postwar years. We held a two-hour session every day, six days a week, and I was pleased to see even officers and noncoms joining us. It was impossible for me to lecture that long. I got the idea of calling for volunteers to come up on the stage and enact certain common conversational situations while I coached them. The exercises continued outside the lecture hall, too. When I met a nurse in the corridor I would say, "Good morning, nurse, how are you today?" And almost invariably the nurse, who could meet embarrassing or gruesome medical situations without flinching, would turn scarlet, lower her eyelids, and reply timidly, "Good morning, Mr. Yoshida, I am belly werr, sank you."

Each day we heard reports that American planes were flying more and more Chinese troops into Shanghai to take over its administration. Occasionally on the streets we saw some of these soldiers—lean, threadbare, sun-bronzed country boys ogling the sights of Shanghai—but there was no official change at the hospital. Then one day the Yanks arrived.

I was down on the Bund on business when I sensed a lot of excitement among the Chinese. They were pointing down the Whangpoo River and jabbering animatedly. Approaching off in the distance was a squat gray ship such as I had never seen before. It had a very blunt bow and a surprisingly broad beam. Later, I learned it was a member of the very useful family of vessels called landing ships. As she eased closer, I saw her flag—the Stars and Stripes—fluttering from the top of her mast, rippling handsomely against the blue backdrop of sky.

I gulped. I couldn't take my eyes off the flag. Such a beautiful sight it was. My skin tingled and my hands were clammy. Seeing the flag was like seeing a former girlfriend —not quite sure whether we'd broken off or whether we'd just drifted apart and lost contact, wondering whether we're still on speaking terms, marveling at the beauty I'd missed for so long, wondering how I should act: Are you still mine,

Old Glory? I've dreamed of you. Often. Oh, how I've longed for you. Do you remember how proudly I held you aloft at the school assemblies as the kids pledged their allegiance? I adored you then. I adore you now. I want to salute you—not in the Japanese military fashion, not with the three-fingered Boy Scout salute. But I don't know how the American soldier salutes. I never had a chance. Help me. I bowed to another flag. I saluted it. But it was you I wanted, Old Glory. Can you believe me? Can you forgive me?

Overcome, I bowed my head until my eyes cleared. I was afraid to wait for the ship to dock. I rationalized that I still had duties to perform. But as I hurried away from the waterfront I felt good. I was happy the Americans had come. But I had a guilty feeling, too. I had fought with the enemy although, thank God, not in direct combat against my countrymen. Not because I wanted to, but because I was unable to do otherwise.

In our English classes, I had been teaching the nurses songs I had learned in school—"Santa Lucia," "My Old Kentucky Home," "Home Sweet Home." In class that day I stood in front of everyone and sang "America the Beautiful." "Oh beautiful for spacious skies, for amber waves of grain. For purple mountain majesties above the fruited plain." The students could not understand the words, but they must have sensed my emotion. I felt very good when I finished.

Very shortly, a group of American and Chinese officers came to the hospital to meet with the Japanese brass. Through Captain Iwata I met an American major and a captain, and I served as the interpreter. The relationship was formal but not hostile. We were instructed to compile a list of all patients classified as to whether they were bedridden or ambulatory, infectious, in need of special care, and the like. The methodical Japanese, of course, had all that information and more available. Within a week, we were told, the evacuation of patients back to Japan would begin. Japanese personnel would supervise transportation of patients from hospital to dockside by truck or ambulance. There they would be loaded onto American LST's for the voyage to the homeland. Japanese nurses would accompany each contingent. I marveled at the efficiency and confidence with which the Americans moved.

A few days later Captain Iwata and I were on the dock near an American LST when I heard someone shout: "Hey Jim—Big Jim."

I whirled in astonishment. Big Jim. That's what the fellows on the Broadway High School football team called me!

Someone on the LST's deck was waving and shouting: "Big Jim, you lousy bastard, hey, Jim." He came running down the gangplank and I searched my memory for his face and his name. Then I recognized the way he ran. He was a lowly second-string lineman on the Broadway High team—big, awkward, friendly—now in the faded blue shirt and dungarees of a U.S. Navy seamen. His name was Bill, that's right, Bill, but what was his last name? I couldn't remember.

Bill came running up, right hand extended, grinning, friendly as a pup. "Jim," he exclaimed, "Christ, imagine seeing you here in Shanghai, you old sonovabitch. What the hell are you doing here?"

I grasped his hand, unable to speak for a moment. "Jeez, Bill, it's good to see you."

"Yeah, but tell me, what the hell are you doing here in China with the Japs?"

"Bill," I said, "let's go somewhere and sit down. It's a long, long story."

He wasn't interested in the details at the moment. "Here Jim, have a cigarette." He thrust a pack of Luckies toward me. "No, wait, I've got a better idea." He ran back to the ship and soon emerged with two unopened cartons—Chesterfields and Lucky Strikes.

I saw Bill many times after that while his ship was in port. Little by little I told him my story. Meanwhile I was full of questions about Seattle and the States. Was Broadway High still there? Had he heard anything about some of my friends, guys like Pete Fujino, Mud Tsuchikawa and the others who turned out for football—Shiro Tenma, Beefo Amabe, George Naito? No, he'd lost all touch with them after they had graduated from high school.

"Let me tell you something," Bill said. "Did you know that the United States Government put all you guys, all the Nisei, into concentration camps after the attack on Pearl Harbor?"

No! I couldn't believe it. "How could they?" I demanded. "We—they are Americans."

"I know it." Bill was hanging his head. "I know it, but you know how things are when people get hysterical. Well, the people with good sense were overwhelmed by the guys —the politicians and the super-patriots—who thought they saw a Jap spy or a saboteur every time they saw anybody with a Japanese face. So the Federal Government made all the Japanese Americans in Washington and Oregon and California leave their homes and go into concentration camps, even if they were United States citizens."

"But that's unconstitutional. Americans got rights."

"I know, but they did it anyway."

"Are they, the Japanese Americans, still in camps?"

"I don't think so," Bill went on. "I read something about the Supreme Court making the government turn them loose a few months ago. And a lot of the young Nisei fellows volunteered for the U.S. Army and served in Italy and France. Some of them got into intelligence service and were used against the Japs in the Pacific. Maybe some of our friends were with that Nisei regiment—I think they called it the 442nd."

It was the first I had heard of the tragic mass evacuation of Japanese Americans from the West Coast into inland relocation centers. I wanted to hear more, but Bill was very vague about the details. He just didn't know.

One drizzly day, after we had shipped out the first group of Japanese hospital patients, Bill invited me on his ship for coffee. I was never much of a coffee drinker, but the aroma was tantalizing just the same. And suddenly I thought of Mom, and how she enjoyed her hot coffee. My God, I thought, I still haven't written to her. I'll have to write tonight. Bill noticed me staring into the coffee and jolted me back to reality: "Chrissake, Big Jim, it's not poisoned. Drink the friggin' coffee."

I was astonished at the LST's mess. A big pot of coffee on a hotplate, all that anyone could drink. Big china bowls of sparkling white sugar. Bill took me back to his quarters. Some fellows had just showered. I could smell the sweet, clean scent of American soap—just like being back in the locker room with the ball players. There were big, fluffy bath towels, not like the skimpy little washrags the Japanese used. I enjoyed the scent of shaving lotion, the happy sound of American voices wisecracking, laughing, carefree. These are my people, I thought to myself, this is where I belong. Yet I knew I was an outsider, a guest, present by sufferance, a stranger temporarily in their midst. Would I ever become one of them again? I did not know. To these young Americans, I was no different from the Japanese diligently learning to speak English from me.

The presence of the Americans served to stimulate the determination of the Japanese to learn the language. Our conversation lessons brought out more than the simple differences inherent in the two languages; they pointed up a basic difference in the way of thinking. For example, with a volunteer on the stage with me, we would pretend to have a tea party. "Please," I would say, "won't you have a chair?" and invite the nurse to sit down. I would pretend to bring in a tray of tea and make-believe pastry and say: "I made these myself. Won't you try one? They're quite good." And then I would point out the difference from the proper Japanese approach, which would be: "This pastry is really quite tasteless, not very good at all, but if you will please have some . . ." The students enjoyed having these differences pointed out to them, and most of them agreed the frank and honest American approach was much better than the false modesty of the Japanese way.

About this time we were given orders that the hospital was to be turned over to the Chinese Nationalist Army's medical personnel, but not until we were sure that they were adequately trained to operate it. Surprisingly enough, although Japan and China had been at each other's throats for nearly ten years, and the troops of each side had committed unspeakable atrocities against the other, the common dedication of doctors and nurses to their profession regardless of nationality smoothed the turnover. Each day the Japanese worked with their Chinese counterparts, teaching them the numerous technical details of maintenance and operation of a vast medical complex. Captain Iwata and I ate frequently in the Chinese mess simply because their food was better.

One of my duties was to inventory medical supplies before turning them over to the Chinese. What happened after the Chinese signed for the various medicines and drugs really wasn't my concern, but we kept hearing reports that a vast percentage of the supplies was finding its way to the black market. Captain Iwata told me one day that his Chinese contacts had offered to cut us in on some of the graft.

"But that's dishonest," I protested, although frankly I wouldn't have minded a bit of cash income to supplement my military pay.

"Look, Jim," Captain Iwata said. "We are responsible only for accounting for the supplies and turning them over to the Chinese. What they do after that is their business, so I have no qualms about cooperating with them in their scheme, whatever it is. All you have to do is help them load one of the ambulances tomorrow."

"Sir," I replied, "if you don't mind, I'd rather not have anything to do with it."

"Well, suit yourself," Captain Iwata said. "I just think it's a good opportunity and wanted to share it with you."

I don't claim to be any more upright morally than the next fellow, but something about trafficking in medical supplies ran counter to my grain. Would I have agreed to a similar deal in some other commodity? I don't know. What I do know is that if I returned to Japan with a bundle of cash I couldn't enjoy it without explaining it to Mom. And I didn't relish the prospect of having to tell her I came by it dishonestly. On the other hand I didn't feel it was in my province to blow the whistle on Captain Iwata, so in that sense perhaps I would be sharing his guilt, whatever it might be.

A few days later some Chinese backed an ambulance up to one of the medical supply warehouses. When it drove away a short time later, Captain Iwata went with it. That evening when he returned to our room he said he had been given four gold bars, the only stable medium of exchange at a time when paper currency was fluctuating wildly in value.

"Two for you, and two for me," he said. When I protested he cut me off sharply with, "Oh, come off it, Yoshida. Don't think you're so pure, and besides you haven't even seen the gold. I left the bars with a friend for safekeeping."

That was a relief. At least I didn't have to cope with the problem immediately.

Captain Iwata's good humor returned quickly and he continued: "I have no idea what each bar is worth—maybe fifteen or twenty thousand dollars. If we can get them back to Japan, they ought to serve as a pretty fair nest egg. Let's say it's payment for services rendered. We aren't overpaid, you know. I'll just look after our gold bars until we can take them home."

He looked at me, shrugged and continued: "Times like these make thieves of us all. In losing a war we have also lost our sense of values. We have become greedy and self-centered. We see others amassing material riches through dishonesty, and we are envious because we are left out. We have lost the moral fiber it takes to be satisfied with our own integrity. And when an opportunity to make money presents itself, we too lose that integrity. All of us are the same—any nationality, any culture—because we share the same human weaknesses. We are honest only so long as we do not have the opportunity to become dishonest. Jim, today we found that opportunity." He laughed cynically.

The combination of a changed sense of values and opportunities affected me in another way. Suddenly I discovered that many of the shy, prim, highly disciplined, no-nonsense nurses were very much aware of men—me in particular. At first they used their English lessons as a subterfuge to approach me, but their interest in me as a healthy young male was unmistakable. Whatever appeal I may have had as an individual was not the primary issue; something biological or psychological stirred primitive desires. And because there were many more nurses than able-bodied men, things became very interesting for me. I had never experienced anything like it, and I was young enough to find the opportunities pleasant indeed. With plenty of time on my hands, I was soon seeing Sachi, one of the head nurses, regularly on the sofa of the officers' recreation room late at night when she was on duty. Fumi and I would slip into the stockroom on Wednesday nights. On Fridays it was Miyo, with others in between. If any of them became serious and even hinted about marriage when we returned to

Japan, I dropped her immediately. There were plenty of others. After so many years of a monastic existence I went overboard completely, so much so in fact that I had no interest at all when Captain Iwata suggested one night we go see some White Russian girls in the French Concession. I never told him why I was too tired to go.

Every week or two another contingent of Japanese servicemen, both healthy and ailing, would board an LST with a group of nurses for the trip back home. At first the ships were manned entirely by Americans, but as the weeks and months slipped by, I found more and more of them had Japanese seamen and American officers, a happy sign of cooperation between the Japanese and the occupation forces. Meanwhile, I found my services much in demand. There was a great deal of interpreting to be done between the Americans and the Japanese. I found I could cut a lot of red tape on both sides simply by being on the spot as the evacuation program continued. In helping to speed Japanese servicemen back to their homes, I felt for the first time that I was doing something useful. And so I volunteered to stay on with Captain Iwata until the last Japanese were evacuated.

Of course I wanted to go back and see Mom and my sisters. But I am also sure that in the back of my mind I was afraid to go back, afraid of some vague but inevitable showdown with American authorities in which I would have to explain my service with the Japanese Army, my act of involuntary disloyalty to my country. And so I was happy to have a reason for postponing that showdown as long as I could. Finally, in July of 1946, nearly ten months after the formal Japanese surrender, my Shanghai assignment neared its end.

We had already begun to pack when one day Captain Iwata received a telegram through the Red Cross. It said simply that his mother in Japan had died. I grieved for my friend. In only a few days he would have been home, able to see his mother again, but because he had volunteered to stay behind he had missed an opportunity for a last reunion. Even more I was filled with remorse that I had never once written to Mom after leaving Yoyang. What if it had been my mother who had died? I never would have been able to forgive myself for having neglected her. I pledged myself to make it up to her when I got home.

Our last two nights in Shanghai we were the guests of Chinese officials who fed us some memorable delicacies—Peking duck, black mushrooms in brown sauce, chicken broth with the head and claws floating around, sweet and sour carp, soybean cake and filets of young pork, boneless whole squab stuffed with chestnuts, and much, much more. Chinese brandy flowed liberally and many toasts were drunk to lasting friendship and peace between our two countries.

At the crack of dawn next morning the last handful of Japanese from Shanghai General Hospital—twenty-eight of us: nurses, technicians, administrators—climbed into three 2½-ton trucks with our gear and headed for the wharves. Even at that hour Chinese officers and medical staff turned out to bid us farewell.

As we bounced along Captain Iwata tapped me on the shoulder. "I don't quite know how to tell you this," he began, looking embarrassed. "The truth is, I just got cold feet. I mean, about the gold bars. So I never went back to get them from the fellow who was keeping them for us. I was afraid we would be discovered. I hope you're not too disappointed."

I covered my face to keep him from seeing my grin of relief.

At wharfside an American captain supervising our departure asked me to instruct all the Japanese to open their duffel bags for inspection. Captain Iwata nudged me. But when he and I leaned over to open our bags the American said it wasn't necessary for us to do so. This time I nudged Captain Iwata.

As the last ship with the last Japanese in Shanghai sailed down the Whangpoo River toward its meeting with the Yangtze, Captain Iwata stared out over the skyline and said softly, "Jim, I guess we were never meant to be rich." Then he threw back his head in laughter and I laughed with him.

Eleven

THE long voyage home turned out to be even longer than expected. Ordinarily the LST would have landed at Sasebo, the big Japanese naval base the Americans had taken over on Kyushu, the southern Japanese island. But while we were at sea we received a warning of a suspected outbreak of typhus in the Sasebo area and so the ship was diverted to Tokyo. That meant sailing clear around the southern tip of Kyushu and up the east coast of Japan to Tokyo Bay. We were out of sight of land most of the time and there was nothing to do but relax. I kept having the feeling that finally, so close to getting back to the family, something disastrous would happen. Like hitting a mine that would sink our ship. The crew kept a sharp lookout day and night for loose mines, but we didn't see a single one. U.S. minesweepers were doing a good job of keeping shipping lanes clear of mines sowed by the Japanese in the waning days of the war.

There was plenty of time during the voyage to sit back and think of the strange things that had happened to me —the miserable war in China, the beatings Sergeant Kido and the other noncoms had dealt me, my illness that led to the warm, satisfying friendship with Captain Iwata. And to wonder what the future held. How had Mom fared during the war? Would I ever be able to get back home to Seattle? I had long forgotten about playing college football, for the years had slipped by and I was twenty-five years old now. A football scholarship for a twenty-five-year-old freshman? That didn't seem likely. What sort of investigation would the American authorities put me through? Would I be tried as a traitor? I told myself that was unlikely; after all I was a nobody and had done nothing to hurt the United States. If they wouldn't let me return to the U.S., what would I do for a living in Japan? And what was the defeated, bombed-out Japan like under the Allied occupation? Scores of questions raced through my mind and made sleep difficult as the ship plowed on into the night through glassy seas. The others in our party were unnaturally quiet, too, and I realized they also were lost in their own thoughts and anxieties.

On the sixth morning the LST rounded the last headland and crept into Tokyo Harbor. All of us crowded the rail, anxious for a close-up look at the country we knew so well but did not know at all. Signs of devastation were everywhere. Along the waterfront, the stark framework of fire-bombed warehouses jutted into the sky. Back of them we could see neat piles of rubble, and here and there new homes and buildings rising. Despite the efforts to clean up and reconstruct, it was obvious that Tokyo had taken a devastating beating from bombs and fire. We stood in stunned silence as the ship made fast to a long wharf behind several American cruisers and destroyers.

There was no welcoming party, only a few Japanese roustabouts scampering about. A tattered sign hung from one of the broken-down warehouses: THANK YOU. WELCOME HOME. At least somebody was happy to see us return.

An American officer and a Japanese, apparently his interpreter, were waiting on the dock as we shouldered our duffel bags and straggled ashore.

"Ladies and gentlemen," the American said when we were lined up, "I must ask you to step over there to the warehouse for a medical inspection and routine dusting with DDT powder. After that we will get you on your way home as quickly as we can complete the paperwork." His tone was kind and he was trying to be helpful, but his interpreter made it sound entirely different. "All right," he snapped, "the American officer orders you to go to the warehouse for delousing. Be snappy about it."

I felt my temper rising. So this was the new Japan! Not only was the interpreter's tone insulting toward those who had served their people, but he was making the American officer look bad for those who understood no English. I was about to speak up when Captain Iwata, who was well aware of what was happening, touched me on the arm. "Don't make trouble, Jim," he cautioned. "Be quiet and let's get out of here as quickly as possible." It was good advice. I managed to keep my temper in check.

Soon we boarded trucks for the ride to Tokyo Station and the trains that would take us to our respective destinations. As the truck lurched through pock-holed streets I got a closer look at the city. Jeeps carrying unarmed Americans scooted through traffic and no one seemed to be paying them any attention. Almost all the Japanese were wearing *geta*. There were virtually no leather shoes. Many of the men, civilians now, were dressed in old Japanese military uniforms or cut-down G.I. sun-tans. Apparently there was no other clothing. Almost all the women were wearing *mompei*—baggy work pantaloons that were far from attractive. About the only girls in dresses were those walking arm in arm with American soldiers. Men were dragging carts loaded with goods, just as in China. Almost all the cabs and buses were grimy and battered and they had heavy tanks, like water heaters, mounted in the back. These were ingenious charcoal-burning gas generators which ran the engines, after a fashion, in the absence of gasoline. Small children with shoe shine kits slung over their shoulders solicited G.I. business. How young the Americans looked. I realized that the combat veterans had gone home; most of the occupation army was made up of youngsters fresh out of high school. Even though the war had ended nearly a year earlier, it was obvious that Japan was a long way from recovery. Would she ever rise from defeat? I had my answer to that question when I saw not one, but several stands selling flowers. There was hope for a people who, even in adversity, would spend money to enjoy the beauty of flowers.

The red brick Victorian-styled Tokyo Station was virtually intact, as were the blocky Marunouchi Building and the N.Y.K. Building just to the front of it. At the end of the broad avenue leading away from the station were the gray granite walls of the Imperial Palace compound with many pine trees leaning out over the moat. How peaceful, I thought. This was the home of the man in whose name a bitter war had been fought and lost. Was he aware of the savagery of war, the loss of life and dignity? Was he aware of how cruelly his people had suffered? I wondered what he would, or could, do to influence the recovery of his nation.

Captain Iwata as the senior member of our party directed all of us to face the direction of the Imperial Palace. Then he led everyone in a deep, low bow as though reporting to the Emperor that having done our duty as best we could, we had now returned home to await his bidding. I faced the Palace with the rest of them, but I could not bring myself to bow. I just didn't think it was necessary or proper. If any of the others noticed, they said nothing.

At the main entrance to the station was a weather-beaten cloth sign saying REPATRIATES, WELCOME HOME! Obviously it had been there a long time. There was a special section in the waiting room reserved for us. Passersby eyed us curiously, as curiously as we looked at them. Their eyes were unsmiling, only inquisitive. We had lost the war for them; they were wondering what sort of creatures we were. I wondered how they would have treated us had Japan won the war.

A few of our party took the first train north. I hated to see them go. A certain camaraderie had developed among us because of our mutual experience, our mutual bewilderment in a Japan that did not seem particularly anxious to accept us. We said good-bye, and then it was our turn to board a train headed down the main line south and west. A section of one car had been reserved for us, but I noticed the rest of the train was badly crowded, the coaches were grimy and many of the windows broken. The roadbed was in horrible shape from lack of maintenance during the war, and the train, hauled by a coal-burning locomotive, swayed and rattled as we made the slow run down the length of Honshu.

Little had changed in the countryside. Rice grew thick and green in tiny paddies along both sides of the tracks. On the left was the restless sea, fishing villages, sampans at anchor. On the right rocky hills, covered with pine and bamboo thickets, rose sharply. What would have happened if the Americans had actually invaded these islands? Would they have had to fight from village to village, from hill to hill, from mountain to mountain before the Japanese surrendered? Perhaps. I just didn't know. It was only when the train passed through the cities that we realized how thoroughly Japan had been bombed and burned. The smoke-blackened skeletons of factories were everywhere. Block on block of flimsy, jerry-built homes provided shelter of a sort where the houses had been razed by fire-bombs. The huge industrial city of Nagoya, Captain Iwata's home, was especially badly hit. I saw him pale as he viewed the sea of ruins. This was where we were to part, he to return to a home saddened by his mother's recent death, I to a reunion with my own family. It was hard saying good-bye to Iwata. He was the only good thing that had happened to me in the Japanese Army. He was a warm, human man, so unlike the noncoms who actually ran the Army.

As we were about to part, he asked almost as an afterthought, "Does your family know you are coming home on this train?" I admitted no one did. He insisted I send a telegram, but I had to confess I wasn't quite sure how to do it. So he took me to the combination telegraph and post office in the depot and composed a message to Uncle Saisuke Yoshida, primarily because he lived in Hirao, not far from the railroad at Yanai where I would leave the train. If Mom was not staying with him, he would know where to reach her. The message simply told Uncle Saisuke the time I would be arriving. That would be shock enough after my long silence. The details would have to wait until I reached home.

"Take care of yourself, Jim," Captain Iwata said as we shook hands for the last time. Both of us were red-eyed, and I stood dumb because I could not trust my voice. "I will write to you soon and we'll get together again." Then he was gone, and I felt as though I had lost a friend.

Now, as home and family came closer with every click of the wheels, the train seemed to crawl with exasperating slowness. Osaka and Kobe, both heavily bombed, slipped by. Then came Himeji, where the great old feudal castle on a hilltop stood unscathed, a symbol perhaps of the ancient Japanese heritage that had survived war's devastation. After that was Okayama, then the ghastly ruins of Hiroshima. I expected to see the station crowded with the crippled and disfigured from the atomic blast, but the people I saw looked like all the others. The only difference was that British forces had occupied southern Honshu island and Americans were scarce.

I grew progressively more nervous as Yanai approached, looking alternately at my wristwatch and then at the countryside basking under the hot July sun. And then I was at Yanai, the station I had departed from one wintry day three and a half years earlier. Little had changed in this quiet backwater town. Only a few passengers disembarked. I looked around for a familiar face but saw no one. I walked alone through the exit gate where the elderly ticket-taker recognized me. He snapped off a salute. "*Arigato*, thank you," he said. "It must have been very hard over there. Welcome home, I'm glad you are back."

Just then a black taxi drove up. Uncle Saisuke was in the back seat, peering out anxiously. I thought he looked very much the same as when he came to meet us at Yokohama on our arrival in Japan more than five years earlier.

Despite his age he scrambled out of the car and gripped my arm with steely fingers. "Thank God you are all right," he cried. "We were so worried, so worried. Everyone is waiting for you." I put my duffel bag in the front seat with the driver—the charcoal-burning gadget took up the entire trunk area—and climbed in the back seat with Uncle Saisuke. He seemed overcome by the occasion and had little to say, and I had no desire to talk either. The best this charcoal-burner could do was about twenty or twenty-five miles an hour. We chugged steadily along familiar country roads, barely made it up over a hill, and then down into Hirao, Dad's home town. Someone had watered the entry and the street in front of Uncle Saisuke's home, darkening the stones and gravel and giving them a cool appearance.

My sisters were the first ones I saw. Aiko, the older, embraced me fiercely, her face contorted with emotion. Then Betty was in my arms, wordless but with tears streaming down her face.

Cripes, I thought, what are they all crying about? They really must have thought I was dead.

I pried Betty's arms away as gently as I could and looked

about for Mom. Auntie Yoshida was there. So was Auntie Uyesugi, the one who had been to Hawaii. And there were several others, but no Mom.

I wondered whether she was hiding, playing tricks. But that wouldn't be like her. Maybe she was out, getting some special confection for me from the store. I wondered with a start whether she might be ill.

No one said a word. Aiko and Betty were staring at me with woebegone expressions. Uncle Saisuke kept his eyes to the ground.

Suddenly I panicked. "Mom," I shouted in English. "Where's Mom?"

Aiko and Betty burst into sobs. It was Uncle Saisuke who told me. I had seldom heard him speak English, but that was the language he used: "Mama is with Buddha."

The meaning of his words did not hit me for a moment, perhaps because I did not want to believe. The first wild, illogical thought that came to mind was that Mom wasn't playing fair; she had died without waiting for me to come home. Then my mind tried to erect a barrier against shocking fact, and I told myself that someone was playing a ghastly joke on me; Mom really was waiting for me at Uncle Denmatsu's home at Kaminoseki, that pretty little island village. I cannot remember precisely what happened after that. The others must have taken me into the house. I remember it was late evening when I found myself kneeling in front of the family altar in Uncle Saisuke's home lighting incense to console my mother's spirit, uttering what little I remembered of Buddhist prayers asking for the repose of her soul. And deep in my heart I felt a terrible guilt for having neglected to write Mom all the months I was in Shanghai. What unspeakable grief and apprehension she had felt in not hearing a word from me, not knowing whether I was dead or alive. "Forgive me, Mom," I cried in anguish. "I neglected you shamefully. I am unworthy. I am stupid. What a grievous error I made in trying to protect you from the news of my illness. I loved you so much, Mom, I broke your heart."

A few days later, still in somewhat of a daze, I took the ferry to Kaminoseki. As soon as the sampan touched the beach I ran straight for the cemetery where Mom had interred Dad's ashes. There it was, Dad's tall, gray headstone, just as Mom and I had left it. When Dad's name was chiseled on it, Mom had her name engraved at the same time. She wanted her ashes buried there together with his. Only the date had been left blank. Now I saw the freshly carved date after her name: Yoshida Suye, July 5, 1946. Mom had died only weeks before my return!

I knelt by the grave as in a trance. Now I knew for sure that Mom was gone. After a while Aunt Uyesugi walked me back to her home. The bath was ready, she told me, urging me to refresh myself and relax. I soaked in the warm water a long time, half hoping to hear Mom calling me to dinner. After a while I dressed, and as I walked by the kitchen I saw the window still with the blackout curtain Mom and I had put up together. At each turn I saw something that reminded me of her. Yet, in accepting the fact that she had passed away, I became able to ask details of her illness and talk about my own experiences. No one was quite sure how Mom had died. The doctor had not been able to pinpoint a cause; she just seemed to have weakened little by little and passed away without apparent physical suffering. I wondered if it were possible to die of heartbreak, brought about by my failure to keep in touch with her. The thought was not easy to live with. It tortured me for many years.

Meanwhile, a letter from Captain Iwata cleared up another matter. He had returned home to find his mother alive and well. The telegram about her death had been another one of those incredible foulups. Somehow Uncle Saisuke Yoshida had learned I was with a Captain Iwata in Shanghai and had sent me a message through the Red Cross in his care. Apparently garbled in transmission, the telegram came addressed to Captain Iwata, who understandably assumed without question that it was meant for him.

Kaminoseki was as lovely as ever, but the days passed slowly. I became restless and knew I had to find a job. There was no work to be had on the island. Besides, the memories there associated with Mom were depressing. I went back to Uncle Saisuke's home in Hirao where Betty was staying. Since the end of the war Betty had been working in the liaison office of the Hirao police department, meaning she was personal interpreter and translator for the chief, a Mr. Sadanobu, in his relations with the New Zealand troops who had occupied the nearby Mizuba naval base. One evening Betty came home and told me that the New Zealander in charge of local labor procurement, a Lieutenant Harry Bleasdale, had a job for someone who could speak both English and Japanese and wanted to meet me. If I was interested, she said, I was to be at Chief Sadanobu's office at 10 A.M. when Lieutenant Bleasdale would show up.

This was the best news I'd had in a long time. I had worried about what kind of work I could do, and working for the New Zealanders seemed ideal. I wondered what sort of fellow Bleasdale was, and whether I could understand his British accent. I was so preoccupied about the next day's interview that I scarcely heard the day's second piece of good news.

My sister Aiko told me about it. She said Betty had met a nice young man and they wanted to be married. Betty had put him off during Mom's illness, and now she wanted permission from me as head of the family. Betty had never had a steady boyfriend during high school days in Seattle. Now she was twenty-three years old, high time she was married.

"I want more than anything to see Betty happy," I told Aiko. "Tell her I'd like very much to meet the young man. Why don't you invite him over for dinner tomorrow?"

Only later did I realize that I hadn't even thought to ask his name. I was really thinking of the next day's job interview with Lieutenant Bleasdale.

In the morning I went to the police station and met Chief Sadanobu. He had heard of me from my sister, of course, and he remembered me as judo coach at Yanai. We were sipping green tea and making small talk when Lieutenant Bleasdale walked in. First he saluted Chief Sadanobu, then turned and shook hands with me. He was about my height but somewhat slimmer, blue-eyed, and with a sandy mustache. I guessed him to be about my age. He wore a khaki shirt open at the throat, khaki shorts, heavy black military shoes and olive stockings that stopped just below his knees. On his head was a black beret decorated with a brass crown, and the same kinds of crowns were on his shoulder boards. I also noticed he carried a leather-covered swagger stick. I took an immediate liking to him.

Lieutenant Bleasdale, speaking in very clipped English, explained he was the officer in charge of hiring all Japanese personnel for the occupation army in the Yamaguchi Prefecture area, and that he needed someone who understood both Japanese and English. He then asked if I could type. Before I could answer he said, "Never mind, if you're Betty's brother, if you want to work with me, I'd love to have you."

I accepted on the spot without even asking what my pay would be.

"Delighted, delighted," he replied. "Come to my office first thing in the morning, if that's all right. We'll put you right to work. Betty will show you where I hang out."

That evening I was seated in the garden enjoying the breeze when I heard Betty's voice outside the gate. I could hear her going into the house. There was the murmur of voices, and then Betty was asking for me.

"I'm out here in the garden," I called.

"Oh, *Niisan* [elder brother]," Betty cried happily, "I want you to meet Bert Kido."

The two were standing on the veranda in the dark shadows cast by the overhanging roof. I could not see them clearly for a moment. Then I became aware of a slim young man in light-colored trousers and a gay Hawaiian sports shirt.

My eyes focused on his face and I leaped out of my chair.

Standing there, holding hands with my sister, was Sergeant Kido.

Twelve

SERGEANT Shigemi Kido, the bastard who had made life in the Japanese Army a living hell for me. Sergeant Kido who had seized every opportunity to brutalize me. Sergeant Kido who had dredged up more hate and bitterness from the bottom of my soul than I knew existed in me. Sergeant Kido, the punk I had vowed to hunt down and beat within an inch of his life. Now he was in my home, seeking my permission to marry my sister.

I don't know how long I stood there, fists clenched, eyes staring. Yet, as I fought to control my emotions, I became aware that the Kido in front of me was not the same sneering, bullying, domineering, sly-eyed Kido I knew in a baggy Japanese Army uniform. He was different from the noncom I last saw in Yoyang. The man standing in front of me wasn't a Japanese soldier. He was a Nisei, like Pete and Mud and Joe and my other pals in Seattle. A Nisei like me. He was just a scared young guy facing up to what might be the most difficult moment in his life.

I felt the hate draining out of me and I didn't fight it. Suddenly I felt sorry for Kido. I heard myself saying, "Glad to know you, Bert. Come on out into the garden where it's cool. Sit down." I put out my hand and he took it hesitantly. We shook hands. I noticed his palm was cold and sweaty.

Kido knew me and he knew now that I knew him. He had to be aware of my bitterness. Yet he dared come to confront me, hand in hand with my sister. I had to admire his brass.

Betty was never one to procrastinate. No Japanese-style, tea-sipping, talking around and around the bush for her. She came directly to the point. She simply stated that she and Bert had known each other for nearly a year, ever since he had come home from the war, were very much in love, and wanted my permission to marry.

The thoughts raced through my head. Had Kido told Betty about knowing me in China? Apparently not, for she had never mentioned it. Did she have any idea what a mean, lowdown, no-good bastard he was? Betty was a level-headed woman, not a flighty schoolgirl who would lose her head over any man who smiled at her. She had known Kido a year, long enough to learn a great deal about anyone. Had Kido changed? I remembered Captain Iwata's wise observation that Kido might have been playing a role that saved both our skins. Which was the real Kido? Did Betty know the real Kido, the Kido I never had a chance to know? Had the war, the dirty goddam war, distorted my perspectives and destroyed my ability to think, judge, reason? Hell, the war was over. Even America, stabbed in the back at Pearl Harbor, had forgiven and was conducting an enlightened, merciful occupation. Even Japan, subjected to the ultimate cruelty at Hiroshima and Nagasaki, had forgiven and was cooperating with the conquerors to rebuild a world that would be better than the one that had been destroyed. What good would it do me now to smash my fist into Kido's face?

I heard my voice saying, "Betty, if you are sure this is the man you want for your husband, I have no objection."

Betty almost knocked my chair over as she hugged me. Then she flew into the house shouting, *"Neisan* [elder sister], *Neisan, Niisan* has given us his consent. Isn't it wonderful? I'm so happy." She hugged Aiko in ecstasy. Aiko had dinner almost ready, but Kido and Betty couldn't wait to tell his uncle and aunt, with whom he was living on the other side of Hirao. So Uncle Saisuke and Auntie and Aiko and I had dinner together. The three chattered happily about what a fine gentleman Kido-san was, what a good husband he would make for Betty, and how fortunate she was to find an eligible Nisei. Gradually they filled me in on Kido's experiences after leaving China. He had been rotated to the South Pacific. Twice the transports he was on had been torpedoed, but he managed to survive. He had been on some island for six months when the war ended. By then all their food was gone and the Japanese had been living on lizards and rats trapped in the jungle. On his repatriation to Japan, Kido had found work as an interpreter with the British Commonwealth Occupational Forces at Mizuba naval base, and there he had met Betty. After that he had visited her at home often and got to know Mom. "Kido-san really looked after your mother," Aunt Yoshida told me. "He was able to get her coffee and sugar through his connections with the British, and when she became ill he would bring her meat and vitamins and nourishing foods that weren't available on the open market. Your mother liked Kido-san very much and was hoping he and Betty would be married."

Auntie's assurances made me feel much better. No one said anything that evening about Bert and me being together in China, so I decided that for the time being I wouldn't bring it up. If Kido wanted to talk about it, that would be his business.

Before going to bed that night I knelt in front of the tiny altar in Uncle Saisuke's home, burned some incense for Mom, and reported the day's developments. Then I asked her forgiveness for having harbored so much hatred within me and promised to try to get along with Betty's new husband. I felt much better after that, but sleep came hard. I couldn't stop the memories that raced through my head. The first beating—punishment for taking the hot water for the horse—came back vividly. Then there was the time we recruits were forced to stand face to face and slug each other to help us remember to become better soldiers. And yet, I recalled, Kido had risked his life to save me when I foolishly exposed myself to enemy fire. The thoughts galloped on and on. What would I have done had I been in Kido's shoes, faced with the same pressures, and a Nisei had come into my outfit as a raw recruit? Probably the same things Kido had done, I told myself.

I remembered the long nights in the hospital bed in Shanghai when my hatred of Kido and the desire for revenge had kept me going, had given me a goal for rebuilding my emaciated body. That hatred had served its purpose, and now that I was well and home, there seemed to be no purpose in continuing to fan it. Learning what Kido had done for Mom, bringing her food and medicines, comforting her while I had all but forgotten about her, I knew that I could not continue to hate this man. And knowing what he meant to my sister, I could not hurt him. I resolved to do my best to like him, and then I fell asleep.

Betty and Bert set their wedding for October. Kido came to the house frequently, but he and I never seemed to be alone together. He never brought up the subject of China and it was just as well. If he didn't want to talk about it, neither did I.

The day after I met Kido I reported to Lieutenant Bleasdale at the labor office. Just down the hall was the Interpreter/Translator section where Kido worked. I dropped in for a moment and found Kido and four other Hawaiian-born Nisei playing poker. Their job was to translate items of interest from Japanese newspapers for the British Intelligence office. The British were on the lookout for Communist organizers or agitators and signs of local unrest. Apparently the situation was so peaceful that the translators had little to do but play cards.

Lieutenant Bleasdale had me fill out some forms, then he and I drove into town to see the Japanese labor officials. He introduced me to a Mr. Takahashi who was primarily responsible for rounding up the necessary labor. Lieutenant Bleasdale would submit a requisition for laborers, clerical help, maids, kitchen helpers—whatever kind of help was needed—and Takahashi would see that the orders were filled. There were about 250 Japanese employed full-time by the Commonwealth forces, and those hired by the day for special jobs fluctuated between fifty and a hundred. Each morning I was to accompany Lieutenant Bleasdale on his rounds of all units to determine their manpower needs, to see that the help Takahashi provided was performing adequately, to make sure that the Japanese were being treated properly and that their working conditions were acceptable.

I found the New Zealanders quite formal and reserved compared to Americans, but friendly nonetheless. Nobody seemed to have to work very hard. We had tea in the morning at nine, lunch at noon and tea again at 3 P.M. Food was still short in Japan, so Lieutenant Bleasdale arranged for me and the Nisei in Kido's office to get free lunches in the officers' mess. He was thoughtful in many small ways, and he also had a sense of humor. The housegirl assigned to clean his rooms and do his laundry was capable but homely as a mud fence. He wanted to transfer her to a major he disliked and get a prettier girl for himself, so he told me to keep my eyes open for one. One day Takahashi brought in a very pretty girl from a prominent local family. She was not accustomed to working and was taking a job only because of family need, but she was pleasant and willing to learn. Bleasdale hired her right then and there.

Next he went to the major, explained that due to his rank he was entitled to two housegirls, and told him he was assigning a second girl immediately. And having transferred the homely girl to the major, Bleasdale assigned the pretty new girl to himself. I marveled at the way the New Zealanders lived—so different from the Japanese Army. Even the noncommissioned officers had household help, one girl for every two men.

Shortly before Betty's wedding day she received the best gift anyone could give her. It came in a plain white envelope from the American consular office in Kobe. In it was a notification that her application for reinstatement as an American citizen had been approved. Her claim to United States citizenship had been verified, and an investigation had turned up no evidence that she had done anything to forfeit it. So Betty, the newly reborn American and Bert Kido, ex-sergeant in the Imperial Japanese Army, were married in a Shinto shrine in Hirao. The ceremony was brief and simple. Afterward, I shook Kido's hand and told him something I had been intending to say for a long time: "Bert, I'm happy to have you for a brother-in-law. But I want you to know that if you ever do anything to break Betty's heart, you'll have to answer to me." He looked me straight in the eye and replied: "You don't have anything to worry about." That was good enough for me.

We all drove to a big teahouse in Yanai City and I was told that Betty and Bert's reception was the biggest ever held there. Many of the New Zealand officers attended, as did the police officials, the men from the labor office, and friends of Uncle Saisuke and all of Bert's relatives. The *sake* and beer flowed liberally that night and there was a lot of gay singing and dancing. The Japanese didn't have a great deal to be happy about in those days so it was a pleasure to see them having such a good time. Betty moved into Bert's uncle's house, and suddenly Uncle Saisuke's home became a very lonely place.

Shortly afterward Lieutenant Bleasdale was transferred to Camp Ozuki, not far from Shimonoseki City, promoted to captain, and put in charge of Japanese labor matters for all New Zealand forces in Japan. He asked me to join him, and since it meant a handsome boost in pay, I was glad to go along. The New Zealanders were employing about 2,500 Japanese, so Bleasdale and I were constantly on the move. To make matters easier for me, he arranged to have me stay in the officers' billets. I was quickly accepted by the New Zealanders as one of them. What sports lovers they were. Many of them were interested in learning judo so I held classes almost every night. In turn I was invited to play rugby for the noncommissioned officers' team.

I quickly learned that American football is a sissy game compared to rugby. There are no huddles in rugby, no rest after a man is tackled. The action keeps going on and on without a stop. And the uniforms were a jersey, shorts, calf-length socks and heavy football type shoes, but no pads or helmet. I would run to tackle the ball-carrier, and just as I made contact he would lateral the ball and away they'd go. Some of the fellows could kick the ball a mile on the dead run. The amazing thing is that no one seemed to get hurt aside from skinned knees and bruised cheeks. Rugby's a great game but I found myself badly out of condition.

After a workout or a game we'd all go to the club and the fellows would drink astonishing amounts of beer. I couldn't keep up with them. In fact, I hardly drank at all but I could hold my own in arm wrestling, like I used to do with Dad on the kitchen table at home. They could teach me a lot about rugby, but not many of them were able to force my arm down, and that won me a measure of notoriety at Camp Ozuki.

Meanwhile our work load became heavier and heavier. Black market operations spread. The parents of some of the girls working for the New Zealanders complained they had been forced into prostitution. Other girls charged they had been raped. Leftists would put up posters urging the Japanese not to cooperate with the New Zealanders. Each case had to be investigated. Workers had to be discharged and replacements found for them. Many of my days were spent interpreting at military court hearings. By this time my knowledge of Japanese was adequate for this kind of work, and at the end of the day I felt I had earned my pay.

Captain Bleasdale had another Nisei in his office and about this time I got to know her pretty well. Her name was Ethel Sugako Isobe and she served as his secretary. Ethel had been born in Honolulu and she was a freshman at Farrington High School at the time the war broke out. Her father, a Shinto priest, was quickly arrested by U.S. authorities as a potentially dangerous alien. The Isobe family was evacuated to the mainland and the father chose to go back to Japan on an exchange ship. Ethel, the third youngest of six children, had no choice but to go with her parents. Ethel was a tiny girl, only about five feet two inches tall. She had Shirley Temple dimples and a personality to match. Naturally she was very popular. I saw her frequently and dated her often, but we were never more than friends. There was just too much work to be done to think about getting serious.

Frequently Captain Bleasdale and I were invited to dinner at a geisha house by the Japanese officials, and at one of them I discovered that despite his youth the captain wore dentures. It was a very gay party with an unlimited supply of *sake*, and before long Bleasdale began to feel ill.

The next morning I showed up for work as usual but the captain was late. It was obvious when he came in that he was nursing a bad hangover. But he also looked different for some reason that I couldn't quite understand. Summoning me to his desk, he said, "Jim, did I make a fool of myself last night?"

"Well, sir," I hedged, "you were a little high."

"I've got something embarrassing to tell you. At the party

I had to go to the latrine and puke. I heaved up everything—including my dentures—and they got flushed down the toilet. Jim, I need those dentures. I had one helluva time getting a pair that fit, and I don't want to go through that again. The toilets here don't hook up to a central sewage plant, do they?"

I could hardly keep a straight face.

"Jim, I would appreciate it very much if you could see about retrieving my dentures."

I took a couple of Japanese laborers with me to the geisha house and had them pump out the cesspool. We found his teeth, all right. Captain Bleasdale got some alcohol from the dispensary and soaked the dentures for a week before putting them back in his mouth.

It was a sad day when the New Zealanders got orders to go home. In the more than two years that Captain Bleasdale and I had worked together we had become as close as I had been with Captain Iwata. I rode with my friends on the military train to the port of embarkation at Kure, near Hiroshima. They were delighted to be going home. I was in the dumps because I knew I'd never see them again. When their band started to play the haunting melody of "Now Is the Hour" as the troops marched to the transport, I bawled like a baby. I think Harry Bleasdale shed a few tears, too.

With the New Zealanders gone Camp Ozuki was taken over by the company-size Reconnaissance Group of the 24th Division commanded by Captain Harold Koch. Most of the Japanese workers were released. Only a skeleton crew, including myself, was left. The Recon Company was just back from Korea, and Captain Koch was anxious to keep the fine edge his men had acquired. He would take them on maneuvers, sometimes for as long as a week, along the coast of Yamaguchi Prefecture. That didn't leave much work for the Japanese to do, and that meant business in the labor office was slack, too.

But for me, other things began to happen in a hurry. First, Betty, who had been working for the U.S. Army in Osaka, wrote to say that she had decided to go to Hawaii. She would stay with Bert's parents in Honolulu, try to get his citizenship status cleared, and send for him.

About the same time Ethel Isobe and I decided to get married. Thinking back on that decision, I can't recall anything particularly romantic. I suppose both of us had assumed that we'd be married some day, although we rarely talked about it. We were both Nisei and had a great deal in common, and since she was very attractive, it was easy to decide to take the step. We were married on Lincoln's birthday, February 12, 1949, in a Shinto shrine. A young priest conducted the ceremony, and even I could tell he was very nervous and having a bad time of it. He could hardly be blamed. Ethel's father, by then a very important senior priest, was watching his every move. Bert was my best man. When I failed to show up as the hour approached, he looked all over town for me. I was so nervous I had decided to get a last-minute haircut. Bert found me getting a shampoo.

Ethel and I moved into a large semi-Western house that had been used by a brigadier general of the New Zealand Expeditionary Force. Yamaguchi Prefecture officials practically gave me the house when they discovered I was being married, no doubt in appreciation for past services and in anticipation of future favors. It was a good thing the house was large because Bert, who was waiting to hear from Betty, and two of Ethel's brothers and a sister moved in with us. It was hardly a honeymoon cottage.

Bert and I spent many evenings talking about our chances of getting back to the States. Betty would send us encouraging notes together with newspaper clippings about other Nisei regaining their citizenship, and we'd pore over them together. We both feared that service with the Japanese Army, even though involuntary, killed our chances. I suppose it would have been simple enough to write to American embassy officials in Tokyo and inquire about my exact status, but the fear of being turned down prevented me from doing it. If the officials said no, that would be the end of it. But as long as they didn't know about me, as long as my status did not become an issue, I felt there was hope. Still, I was intensely curious. I composed a letter of inquiry many times in my head but never had the courage to write it. One day I heard that a Seattle girl, Rose Hamada, was working for the U.S. diplomatic mission in Tokyo. I wrote her a personal letter asking what I should do to determine my citizenship status.

Rose wrote back quickly assuring me that many Nisei who had been caught in Japan by the war were being cleared to go home. What was most important, she said, was that the Nisei have a record of not having done anything to hurt the United States, that he must not have voted in a Japanese election, and that he must be in good health. Bert and I were both healthy and we had never voted. But what about that bit about a clean record? We were just as confused as ever.

Bert's problem was cleared up a short while later. Betty wrote saying the authorities had ruled he could enter Hawaii as "the spouse of an American citizen." We laughed about that as we read the documents. It didn't matter who Bert was or what he had done; he was being permitted to go home because he was a male war bride! The news cheered me immensely. If Bert could go, perhaps there was hope for me. As he left to catch the boat in Yokohama, Bert pledged to do everything he could to get me to Hawaii.

Ethel gave birth to our first child, a son, on January 19, 1950. It started out as a dark, cold day, and suddenly the weather didn't matter any more. I had been hoping for a boy and even had his name picked out—Kenneth, after Kenny Kuniyuki, my first judo teacher. Little Kenny was such a tiny, red-faced, squalling handful that it seemed to me he'd never grow up to play football or throw an opponent in judo. Ethel's parents were as delighted as Ethel and I. Kenneth was their first grandson. Ethel's father gave him a Japanese name, Kenichi. So I had a new responsibility, a helpless little bundle with the impressive name of Kenneth Kenichi Yoshida. Would he grow up to be a Japanese or an American? I didn't know. He was all the more reason I had to try to get home to the States.

Thirteen

By June of 1950 I was working in the labor office of the U.S. 24th Division at Kokura, on the southern island of Kyushu, about an hour's train ride from home. The division employed some 4,000 Japanese on the regular payroll with about another 1,000 working from time to time. Without the Japanese the division as it was then set up could not operate. Most of the traditional K.P. duties were handled by the Japanese. They provided labor for the work details that dug ditches, laid pipes, repaired barracks, distributed supplies, patched the roads, hauled the trash. The pay these Japanese drew kept the local economy afloat, so in my supervisory capacity I felt I was helping both sides. Our office took care of personnel records and payrolls. Vouchers were submitted to division headquarters which in turn passed them on to the Japanese government, which made the actual payments. These disbursements were charged off to war reparations. Often when we were busy, which was much of the time, I stayed at Kokura, going home only on weekends to see Ethel and the baby. Ethel's parents had moved in with us, so I knew she wasn't too lonesome.

I was drawing a fairly comfortable salary by Japanese standards, my work was challenging, I had plenty of responsibility, and I should have been happy. Yet there was that nagging urge to get my citizenship status cleared up and go back to Seattle. Occasional letters from Betty and Bert in Honolulu stirred my hopes, but there didn't seem to be much I could do about the matter at the moment.

Then one day a telephone call changed a great many things. Over the crackling of the interference I finally recognized the voice out of the past. It was Junks Kurose, friend of my boyhood and football teammate at Broadway High. Junks was with the U.S. Army on occupation duty. Somewhere he had heard of my whereabouts and finally had been able to reach me.

Junks brought me the first direct word about some of my friends. All the Japanese in Seattle, in fact all of them on the West Coast, had been shoved into concentration camps by the Army after the attack on Pearl Harbor, Junks said. Succumbing to the fear and hysteria that followed the outbreak of war, the United States Government had put men, women and children of Japanese extraction behind barbed wire. The only crime they were accused of was that of being of the same race as the Japanese enemy. And finally, when the Government realized its error and asked the Nisei to fight for their country, hundreds stepped forth from the camps to put on a uniform and demonstrate their loyalty. Dozens of them were my friends.

"What happened to my friend Pete Fujino?" I asked, hardly able to contain my excitement.

"Pete was killed in action in Italy."

Lanky, fun-loving Pete. Dead. A hard, cold knot grew in the pit of my stomach. I hardly had the courage to ask the next question.

"What about Joe, Joe Nakatsu?"

"Joe volunteered the day after Pearl Harbor. He went to Europe with the other Nisei guys in the 442nd Regimental Combat Team and made it okay. I think he was a sergeant in a rifle company."

Junks called off the names as he remembered them. George Tatsumi, killed. Beefo Amabe, killed. Tak Shibuya, okay. Bill Nakamura, killed. Bill Yanagimachi, okay. Skid Arita, okay. Ken Omura, died while serving with U.S. military intelligence in the Southwest Pacific. Tak Okawa, okay. The list went on and on, and when Junks could recall no more, I counted fourteen Seattle friends and acquaintances among the dead. What a price they had paid to prove the loyalty of Nisei to the United States!

We talked a long time and finally Junks asked the question I'd been dreading: "What about you?"

I told him of my service with the Japanese Army in China.

"Yah, yah, I heard all about that, but that's not what I mean. Don't you want to go back to Seattle?"

"Jesus, Junks, I'd give anything to get back there, but they tell me I can't. I lost my citizenship."

"Well, don't give up," Junks urged. "I heard some other guys like you got their citizenship back. The war's over, you know. Things might change."

"Do you think so, Junks? Do you really think so?"

"Sure. Keep trying, boy. Keep giving it the old college try."

That very afternoon I telephoned the United States consular office in Fukuoka, the one nearest Kokura. The officials were somewhat less encouraging than Junks had been, but they promised to send me some forms to be filled out. I struggled over them for several nights and then returned them in due time.

In the days following, my thoughts returned often to Pete, Beefo, Bill Nakamura and the others who had died in defense of their country . . . my country. Had I been on the other side of the Pacific, I would have been proud to serve alongside them, to have died with them if necessary. I mourned their loss. Such blithe spirits, so full of the happy juices of life, gone. Who was to be blamed? I cursed the madness that causes war. There is no glory in it. Pete and the others had volunteered to fight for a cause they believed in. They had died for their country. But so had the Chinese I had bayoneted, and the Japanese youths who had been carried in and out of my hospital room while I, too, lay near death. And to what avail? I could make no sense of it all.

Late in June the division provost marshal, Captain Kenneth J. Peterson, asked my boss if I could be detached for some temporary interrogation work on Japanese trains. I didn't know what was up, but the newspapers were reporting an unusually heavy movement of Korean nationals from Japan back to their country. Captain Peterson told me I was to be attached as an interpreter to military police teams boarding trains headed for Shimonoseki, the closest port to the Asian mainland, to question all Korean travelers. Since few Americans understood Korean, and virtually all Koreans spoke Japanese fluently, English-speaking Japanese interpreters were the pivot men in a three-way conversation. The captain also warned me this was hush-hush duty since the Army wanted to avoid alarming the Japanese. The only thing I could tell my wife was that I was busy on a special job and might not be home for many days.

The assignment kept us constantly on the move and was grueling but interesting. What I enjoyed most was working together with Americans—not for them, but with them, because they depended heavily on my interpreting and quickly accepted me as one of the team. I would ask the Koreans where they were from, where they were going, the last time they had been in Korea and why they were going home at this time. Almost all had the same answer—they had been brought to Japan to work in factories during the war years and were en route to see their families. Most said their homes were in North Korea, but this too was understandable as the north is the industrialized half of the country and the most likely source of trained manpower. We had no reason to detain any of them, but their uneasiness under interrogation aroused the suspicion that something was up. We found out soon enough.

At dawn on June 25 (June 24, American time), two Communist North Korean columns led by Russian-built tanks struck across the 38th Parallel and raced down the Imjin River plain toward Seoul, the South Korean capital. Out-gunned South Korean defense forces crumpled and soon were in flight. All American forces in Japan were placed on alert. Three days after the attack began President Truman ordered General Douglas MacArthur, Supreme Commander of Allied occupation forces in Tokyo, to go to South Korea's aid. On June 29 Communist forces captured Seoul and the next day the first contingent of American infantry landed in Korea.

My M.P. team had been ordered back to Kokura as soon as fighting broke out. The entire 24th Division was rushing to get ready for the move to Korea. I don't know who was busier—the troops preparing weapons, ammunition and supplies, or the G.I.'s making last-minute arrangements to see that their Japanese girlfriends were amply supplied with groceries and cigarettes while they were gone.

The bustle of activity reminded me of nothing more than a football team preparing for an out-of-town trip. And suddenly I was filled with a wild idea; I should be going along with the M.P.'s! I belonged with them! I had proved I was a member of their team, hadn't I? They needed me!

I suppose that somewhere in my consciousness I still had a deep-seated guilt feeling about having served in the Japanese Army while my boyhood buddies were fighting and dying for the United States. Perhaps I felt that going along with the G.I.'s would be a way of vindicating myself. But no such deep thoughts were in my mind when the idea of volunteering struck. I just wanted to go. Impulsively I went to the leader of my interrogation team, Sergeant John F. West, and told him what I wanted to do.

Sergeant West was a career soldier, perhaps in his middle forties. He was somewhat shorter than I, but he weighed about 200 pounds, had a ruddy complexion and looked a little like Phil Harris, the comedian. He was in charge of the Investigation Section, and I don't think he ever was surprised by very much, but my request stopped him. He put down the snub-nosed .45 automatic he was cleaning and scratched his head before replying, "Jeez, Jim, I don't know. You'd be a helluva good man to have with us, but there are regulations, you know." He was one to go through channels. "Why don't you ask Captain Peterson?" Having thus divested himself of the responsibility, he returned to his chores.

I hurried to see Captain Peterson before my nerve ran out.

"You crazy, Jim?" he exploded. "We're not going on a picnic. For all I know, none of us may come back, the way the gooks are going."

"Sir," I pleaded, "I think that you know I'm a Nisei. I think I'm just as American as you and the boys—"

"God damn it, Jim," he broke in, "I know all about you and you don't have to remind me. I'd be proud to have you in my outfit. But I'm not running the show. We have rules and regulations in the friggin' Army and I'm not about to break them." Seeing my woebegone expression, he put his arm around my shoulder. "Besides, if you got into this man's Army, you'd have to cut off that long, black hair of yours."

"Well, thank you, sir, for giving me your time," I managed to say. "I'd sure like to go along, though."

I spent most of the afternoon walking aimlessly about the camp, feeling like an outcast, an unwanted outsider, a rejected foreigner. Late in the day I made my way to the camp barbershop staffed by some Japanese women and took an unoccupied chair.

"*Obasan* [Auntie]," I said, "please shave all my hair off."

"*Doshite* [Why]?" she asked, astonished. "Do you have lice?"

"No, no, never mind why. Just shave my head, please."

I looked in the mirror when she was finished. It was a sickening sight, the hair showing blue-black through the pale skin of the bare scalp, every ridge and bump of my skull visible. After I had my head shaved in the Japanese Army I had vowed never to have my hair cut short again, but this was for a very special cause.

That evening I knocked on Captain Peterson's door.

"Yes? Who's there?" The voice reflected irritation.

"Sir, this is Jim. Jim Yoshida, sir."

"God damn it, Jim, what the hell do you want now?"

This was it. Make my point now or back down forever.

"Sir, may I see you for a few minutes, sir? It's very important."

As I entered the captain flicked on the overhead light. He had been reading on his bed. He stared in astonishment at my head gleaming under the light.

"What the goddam hell happened to you? You some kind of a nut?"

"No, sir. But I guess you will have to take me now."

Captain Peterson's face turned purple. I could see the pressure building up. He sat up and I expected him to explode momentarily. Suddenly he covered his face with his hands. I stood ramrod-straight, more frightened than I had ever been waiting for Sergeant Nakamura to dress me down. Why didn't Captain Peterson jump up and shout at me? Then I noticed his shoulders were shaking—as though he was trying to suppress laughter.

He rose from the bed, unfolding his big, powerful frame until his cold blue eyes looked straight into mine.

"Jim," he said, "I'm sticking my neck out. Don't do anything to foul me up, because it's going to be my ass."

"Yes, sir. I mean, no, sir."

"We'll have to have something in writing, just in case." I reached for a piece of paper in my hip pocket. "Will this do, sir?" I had typed:

To Whom It May Concern: I, Jim Katsumi Yoshida, hereby volunteer my services in Korea with the 24th Division Military Police of my own free will. In the event of sustaining any injuries, or getting disabled or killed in any action, my family consisting of my wife and son will not ask for any compensation from the United States Government. I further agree that I will not be paid and that I am serving strictly on a volunteer basis.

I had signed the statement and had it witnessed by Sergeant John F. West, Sergeant Joe Metzger and Corporal Victor Castro.

"You sonovabitch, you really want to go with us, don't you?" Captain Peterson said with admiration in his voice.

"Yes, SIR."

He picked up the telephone and called the post supply sergeant: "Sergeant, I'm sending Jim Yoshida over. Equip him with whatever he wants. Yes, firearms, too. Thank you."

I vaguely remember thanking the captain and running out before he changed his mind.

I burst into the supply warehouse. "Hey, Sarge, the provost marshal sent me."

"Yes, I know."

I wanted to be sure I got the important items first.

"Give me a .45. It doesn't have to be new."

"Okay. How many clips do you want?"

I was in! He was going to issue me a pistol! The rest would be easy! "Couple's enough. I'll need a carbine, too, and some extra clips, and a dog tag—"

"What the hell you talking about? You lose your tags?"

I didn't want to get into a long-winded explanation. "No, Sarge. The provost marshal asked me to get one without a serial number. Some special deal, I guess. Just my name and blood type. Jim K. Yoshida, type B. And don't forget the black rubber guard that goes around the tag."

"Yeh, yeh, I'll fix it for you."

As the sergeant searched for a set of fatigues, I snapped the canvas ammunition belt around my waist, hooked the holster to it and snapped the cover over the .45. Its weight was reassuring. The sergeant gave me everything I needed —underwear, socks, messkit, canteen, steel helmet, plastic helmet liner, M.P. armband, a brand new duffel bag and shoes that fit. Boy, what a difference between this and the Japanese Army. This outfit has shoes that fit!

Loaded with all my gear, I hurried off to the recreation room where some of the fellows were playing cards. The game came to an abrupt stop when I burst into the room. "I made it," I shouted. "I'm in. I'm a G.I. now!" They shook my hand and pounded me on the back. Several of them helped me put my gear together. Sergeant West gave me a quick course in the operation of the .45 and carbine. When I discovered I had forgotten to pick up a pair of brass "U.S." collar insignia Corporal Castro gave me some spares he had.

I bunked with Castro that night, but I lay awake long after he was snoring. Now that the excitement had died down, my stomach was filled with butterflies. I knew I had done the right thing, even if it seemed foolish. There was no backing down now, no turning back. But how would I explain all this to Ethel? I hoped she would understand.

All the next day motorized equipment shuttled between the camp and the piers at Moji, just across the channel from the port of Shimonoseki. The bulk of the 24th Division in southern Japan—34th Infantry Battalion, 19th Infantry,

24th Recon, the 21st Gimlets—were already in Korea. The military police had supervised the movement and our outfit, the Military Police Interrogation Section and the provost marshal's office, was to be the last to leave Kokura, with only a skeleton force staying behind at the camp. We were to sail out of Moji after dark, and our outfit was restricted to the pier compound or headquarters. There was not even time to hurry home to see Ethel and little Kenny. The telephone was such a cold, inadequate instrument for telling her what needed to be said that I kept putting off calling my wife. Over and over in my mind I rehearsed the way I would break the news to Ethel. But when I finally reached her I forgot my prepared speech. I told her only that I would be very busy on a hush-hush mission and would not be home for a while. If she needed anything, I told her, the acting provost marshal at Kokura would take care of it.

"I'll get in touch with you as soon as I can. Try not to worry about me. I love you very much."

"I love you, too. Take good care of yourself."

As I hung up the telephone I had a feeling that Ethel knew exactly what I was doing, and more than that, she understood why. I felt like a heel.

Captain Peterson revived my spirits when he summoned me to outline my duties. I was to be his clerk, interpreter, bodyguard, driver, messenger, and liaison man with the Korean military police who no doubt would be attached to us. As the captain's personal driver, I was put in charge of a jeep with big white letters reading PROVOST MARSHAL under the windshield. Sergeants West and Metzger would also ride in the jeep. Obviously I wasn't going to Korea as just a hanger-on, an errand boy; the captain was giving me responsibilities; I was an important member of his team. And I knew I looked the part with my green fatigues, M.P. band, steel helmet, carbine and .45.

Sergeant West gave me further advice and reassurance:

"You've got a lot to learn, but don't worry about it. Stick close to me and I'll teach you the ropes. One more thing, don't tell strangers who you are or what you are—it's none of their damned business. So far as we're concerned, you're just one of us. Okay?"

Okay. You're damned right, it's okay.

That evening my jeep led a column of vehicles out of the camp, through Kokura, over the narrow black-topped road to Moji twenty miles away. We parked on the wharf alongside an American military transport, boarded the ship and leaned over the rail as we watched the vehicles being lifted into the hold. The crew worked swiftly and purposefully. We were permitted to stay on deck, and there was plenty of coffee and sandwiches for all hands. I marveled at the freedom of the American Army. We were treated as human beings. In the Japanese Army we had been herded below decks like animals. Here I was going off to another war, but this time in dignity and voluntarily. And gladly, too. I fingered the dog tag around my neck and knew I was an American again. Maybe not quite, but almost.

Presently the hawsers were cast off, the freighter backed out of its slip and made a wide arc as it headed westward in the channel. Across the waters on the far shore I could see the lights of Shimonoseki. Seven years earlier I had been on another ship, sailing from that port for the same destination, Pusan. But how totally different things were this time.

A Japanese ferry, its lights ablaze, cut across our bow. None of the passengers seemed to be paying any attention to us. Presently our engines settled down to a steady throb. The night breeze was cool. One by one the G.I.'s moved away from the rail. Some lay down on the hatch covers to nap. Cigarettes glowed in the dark. Under a hooded light on the after deck a crap game got started. I wondered how many of these fellows would make it back to Japan. They were so young, so inexperienced in combat. I wondered whether I would be among the fortunate, but the thought didn't stay with me for long. It was enough to be with a Yank outfit. By dawn of the morrow, July 3, 1950, I would be in Korea, the war-torn Land of the Morning Calm.

Fourteen

No sooner was the ship made fast to the wharf than the unloading began. There was not a moment wasted. Captain Peterson instructed Sergeant West to look after our vehicles and personal gear while he and I went to the harbor master's office. There intelligence officers gave us a quick briefing. South Korean troops had pulled out of Seoul and were trying to set up a new defense line in the city of Osan south of Seoul. The first American troops, Task Force Smith —an understrength infantry battalion from the 24th Division plus an artillery battery—had joined the South Korean Army at Osan and was about to be committed to battle. Their mission was to hold off the Communists until reinforcements could be rushed north. The South Korean government had moved its capital to Taejon, sixty miles southeast of Osan. An intelligence officer pointed out the towns on a wall-size map of the Korean peninsula. Taejon was roughly halfway between Pusan and Seoul, and apparently a major stand would be made there if Osan were lost. Captain Peterson was ordered to move his M.P.'s up to Taejon as quickly as possible. A small detachment of

Republic of Korea (ROK) military police would show us the way.

When the briefing was over Captain Peterson took me aside and said: "Yoshida, it looks awfully rough up there. You don't have to go, you know. You can still hop on the ship and go back to Japan if you wish."

"No, thank you, sir. I volunteered and I guess you're stuck with me."

"Good boy. We've got a lot to do and you can be a big help. Let's go meet the ROK's."

Our man was Lieutenant Kim. Kim is Korea's most common name. There must be millions of Kims. Our Kim was a wiry young fellow, no more than five feet three inches tall, with the typical high cheekbones of the Korean people. He saluted Captain Peterson, flashed a big grin, and began to introduce himself in English. His accent was so scrambled I could hardly make out what he was saying, and it was obvious Captain Peterson wasn't catching a word.

"Just a minute," Captain Peterson broke in. "This is Jim Yoshida. He speaks Japanese. You speak to him in Japanese."

Lieutenant Kim grinned even more broadly and fired away in Japanese which I translated into English; then I translated the captain's reply into Japanese. Lieutenant Kim had about twenty men with him and he marched them down to the wharf. Already there was more darned mechanized equipment there—jeeps, deuce and a half trucks, tanks, self-propelled artillery—than I had seen in all of China. Our company, which had been the last to board the ship, was the first offloaded and was ready to move. Sergeant West was waiting with my jeep with all our gear under a tarpaulin in the trailer it was hauling.

I was to drive the lead jeep with Captain Peterson beside me and Sergeants West and Metzger in the rear seat.

Lieutenant Kim was in the second jeep. The other Koreans boarded a truck, and our column headed northwestward out of Pusan toward the front. Our first destination was the city of Taegu, seventy-five or eighty miles by road. The road led through narrow valleys between ripening rice fields, patches of taro and soybeans. Rugged, sparsely forested mountains rose sharply from the valleys. Brief stretches of the road were black-topped, but mostly it was gravel. The jeeps kicked up clouds of fine gray dust that billowed behind the column. The longer stretches of road were lined with poplar trees. Pedestrians who saw us coming would duck behind the trees, partly to escape the dust, partly to enjoy their shade while waiting for us to go by. We passed dozens of tiny villages tucked into finger valleys leading off from the main ones. Hardly larger than a garage, the farmhouses had dirt-colored walls and heavy thatched roofs. This rugged, chopped-up countryside was totally unlike the broad plains of China. Even I could tell that if we had to fight over terrain like this we'd be in for a very difficult time. But south of Taegu the land was so peaceful it was hard to imagine that only a hundred miles or so up ahead towns were burning and men were killing and being killed.

Taegu turned out to be a nondescript city on the broad plain of the slow-flowing Naktong River. We drove right into town and parked the jeeps on the playground of a middle school. While Captain Peterson went to confer with officers of the U.S. Military Advisory Group attached to the Korean Army, the rest of us took a lunch break. It was my first experience with K-rations—cold, greasy meatballs eaten from an olive-colored can with a little plastic fork, stale crackers, and a packet of cigarettes. It was my first G.I. field meal and I can't say I enjoyed it. The Koreans also were issued the same K-rations and they didn't think much of them either. Lieutenant Kim promised me we would have rice as soon as we were settled. The G.I.'s astonished me by flipping off their steel helmets and sitting on them in the shade while they ate. In the Japanese Army sitting on one's helmet was absolutely taboo; a helmet protected one's head, was worn on the head, and therefore was to be used with care. Well, I was a G.I. now, so I too sat on my helmet.

After chow I had time to stretch out in the shade and think about my first half-day in Korea. If we were the Japanese Army, we would have force-marched up to Taegu instead of riding in jeeps. And right after the lunch break we would have been marching again. Instead, some of the fellows spread a blanket over the hood of one of the jeeps and got a crap game going.

Captain Peterson returned and told us we were moving on another eighty miles to Taejon, warning us that anywhere north of Taegu could be considered enemy country. A "point" jeep was sent off ahead of the column. We were now fourth in line and the vehicles were spaced out so that there would be less chance of many of us being hit if we should run into hostile artillery. Every man carried a bullet in the chamber of his weapon, and where the valley choked down to a narrow passage, we eyed the hills anxiously. Every mile or so we encountered bands of refugees headed south, trudging in long columns on the side of the road, men and women with bundles on their backs or balanced on their heads. There would be as few as fifty men, women and children in a band, or as many as several hundred. I assumed that whole villages were moving south as a group ahead of the advancing Communists. Dusty, weary, sunburned, they presented a pitiful sight. They must have known we were Americans rushing to the front in defense of their country, yet not one stopped to wave or smile at us. I could hardly blame them. They had nothing to be happy about, fleeing for their lives with only as much of their meager possessions as they could carry with them. Invariably the women wore long white national costumes, and I wondered how they kept them clean.

Occasionally we saw soldiers walking with the refugees and we stopped several for questioning. They must have had the right answers, for Lieutenant Kim let them go. He said they were on the way to join their outfits in Taegu. As we neared Taejon we drove by the bodies of several South Korean soldiers sprawled by the side of the road. No one had gotten around to burying them. Close by, four or five American jeeps and trucks were piled into roadside ditches. Several had bullet-shattered windshields. One truck was burned out, apparently caught in a guerrilla ambush. The reality of war was closing in now.

Captain Peterson turned to me and asked: "Hey, Jim, are you scared?"

"Hell yes, sir," I replied, and we all laughed and kept moving.

A steady stream of civilians was leaving Taejon, but we could see G.I.'s everywhere, building roadblocks, stringing barbed wire, patrolling streets.

"Hey, you mop-pushers," some of them shouted when they saw the M.P. armbands, "what are you doing up here with us Doggies?" But it was easy to see they were happy to have us. The time might come when every man would count.

We drove into another school compound. The 24th's medics had opened a field hospital there in anticipation of casualties from Osan. Some of the 24th Engineers had set up shop, too. The school was a two-story frame building, just like the kind one sees in all parts of Japan. The floors had been polished by the feet of a generation of school children, but G.I. boots were rapidly scarring them. Upstairs classrooms were being used for offices and sleeping rooms. The school lunchroom had been converted into a mess. Outside the lunchroom was a low concrete trough with a half dozen faucets above it. The trough had been built for grade school children and we had to double over to let the water sluice over our faces. The latrine was out in back—a long galvanized tin urinal and toilet receptacles set flush with the floor. They drained into a horribly unfragrant cesspool. We washed up, spread our bedrolls in one of the classrooms, then went down to the messhall for our first hot meal in Korea.

Facilities for washing our messkits hadn't been set up in the kitchen yet, so Sergeant West and I walked down a slope on one side of the schoolhouse to a stream, planning to rub away the greasy remains with wet sand. A series of bridges guarded by our troops spanned the channel. As we watched, two 2½-ton trucks approached the bridge several hundred yards downstream. Before Sergeant West and I knew what was happening, a G.I. guard not far from where we were standing opened fire on the trucks. Some men in ROK uniforms jumped out and fired back. Then the men in the school compound up above us opened fire. Pistols in hand, Sergeant West and I worked our way up the slope and took cover along a wooden fence. I could hear bullets whining all around us. Sergeant West fired several times. I tried to fire, too, but the trigger wouldn't budge. By the time I realized the safety catch was on, Sergeant West had vaulted the fence and crawled back into the school grounds. My first impulse was to jump the fence after him, but suddenly I realized that with my Oriental face I was taking a chance of getting shot at by my own buddies. I unfastened my M.P. armband, held it up high, found a hole in the fence and crawled to safety. Only then did I realize that when I pulled the trigger of my .45 I had no idea who or what I was shooting at.

By this time Captain Peterson came charging out into the compound roaring at everyone to stop shooting, demanding to know who was firing at whom. The gunfire ended as abruptly as it had broken out. None of our men was injured, but the ROK's had one man killed and four wounded. The G.I. who started it all was a young private from the 24th Engineers guarding a footbridge across the stream. I had no idea why he had fired on the trucks. Perhaps he had heard too many stories about North Korean infiltrators and forgotten that we had Koreans on our side, too. The incident underscored Sergeant West's warning: Almost all our troops, including many of the noncoms and junior officers, had never been in combat. They were young and inadequately trained. They were soft from garrison duty. We would absorb some bloody lessons before the G.I.'s became an effective fighting force.

Later that night I learned once more how totally unprepared even our outfit was psychologically for combat. Each of the M.P.'s was scheduled for an hour of guard duty. A pretty fair poker game was under way when it came time for one of the corporals to go on duty. "Jim," he said to me, "I'll give you twenty bucks if you'll take my turn on guard, just for an hour. These cards are too hot to leave." I took the offer. Since I wasn't being paid, I figured I could use the money.

Next morning Lieutenant Kim took me to call on the local chief of police who turned out to be a graduate of Keio University in Japan. Naturally he spoke Japanese fluently, much better than I did. The chief assigned two boys scarcely in their teens to do Captain Peterson's laundry and keep his room clean. They had been orphaned in the fighting up north, the chief explained, and would be happy to go wherever we went just for food and shelter. I was glad to have them because they would simplify my relations with the captain. I was happy to be his driver and interpreter, but I didn't relish the idea of being his houseboy. The chief also gave me three live chickens for Captain Peterson.

Thinking to give the captain a surprise, I butchered the chickens, boned them, cut the meat into bite-size pieces, rubbed them with salt and pepper, added a dash of soy sauce and a bit of garlic, and deep-fried them in the company kitchen. I had learned the dish from my aunts in Japan and occasionally, just for fun, I'd cook chicken this way for my friends. Captain Peterson was delighted. He gave me a standing order to prepare the dish for him any time chicken was available. I took that to mean he wanted me to make chicken available, so I kept a sharp lookout for stray fowl.

Meanwhile, the M.P.'s were kept busy all day long processing the refugees passing through Taejon on their way south. Word from the north was that elements of the 24th Division were locked in a bitter battle against vastly superior North Korean forces. Task Force Smith was reported to have taken such heavy losses that it was no longer an effective fighting force. The 21st Gimlets had been badly mauled. Still they hung on, fighting for time, grudgingly yielding only yard by yard. The fighting was beyond earshot; we knew only what we heard from couriers and the wounded making their way back. Our contribution to the effort was to secure the rear, and that meant keeping the refugees moving and checking them for infiltrators.

At first we were very lenient with the refugees. The examination at our checkpoint was superficial. "Okay, Mamasan," the M.P.'s would say, waving a woman on, "hubba-hubba (hurry, hurry) and don't try to come back for a while." This kind of examination outraged Lieutenant Kim and his men. Soon they set up their own checkpoint several hundred yards down the road from us for a more thorough inspection. One morning, shortly after we had let a woman with two young children through our gate, we heard gunfire at the ROK checkpoint. Sergeant West and I ran there as fast as we could. A large group of Korean refugees was shouting and milling around. A woman was writhing in the dirt while blood pooled darkly in the dust. I recognized her as the one with the babies. Another woman was carrying one of the children, but the second child was still strapped to the mother's back by a wide sash. Sergeant West lunged at the Korean sergeant in charge, demanding to know what had happened. I relayed the question in Japanese. The ROK sergeant simply pulled back the woman's blouse. Tied around her waist were three Russian-type grenades. I looked about for a medic but it was too late. The woman was dead. When we turned her body over we found another grenade clutched in her hand. The baby on her back apparently was killed by the same bullet that killed the woman. Some of the refugees spat at the woman's body. I never did learn what happened to her other child. We took the ROK sergeant in for interrogation but he was soon released. What he really deserved was a commendation for his alertness. Chances are he saved some American lives by uncovering an infiltrator.

After that the ROK M.P.'s built a wooden "gate" shaped like a low sawhorse. They required all refugee women to straddle the device and walk past while the ROK's examined them for concealed weapons strapped to their thighs. Lieutenant Kim said up north it was the women who were carrying grenades and cartridges for the infiltrators. Of course it was totally impossible to distinguish a North Korean from a southerner. We simply had to be alert for anyone who seemed different or especially nervous. But after examining hundreds of refugees, they all looked alike and equally nervous. The government had ordered all refugees to stick to the roads, warning that anyone trying to move south through the mountains would be shot, so the stream of refugees through the checkpoints was almost endless.

Regardless of our efforts there were many instances of grenades being thrown at G.I.'s and ROK troops after dark on the streets of Taejon. Within a few days our military police at the checkpoints were as rough and ruthless as the ROK's. The checkpoints were closed at dark and anyone moved at his own risk. Except for men on guard duty, we kept pretty much to the compound at night, and there were plenty of the usual crap games, card games and bull sessions.

One night I had been telling Corporal Castro about judo when he suggested that Sergeant Metzger and I engage in an arm wrestling contest. Metzger was of Polish or German extraction. He was a powerfully built brute, about six feet three inches tall, and he had the reputation of being able to lift one end of a jeep by himself. He said very little, and even though he had signed the paper in which I waived all claims against the government, I had never been able to get through to him. I had no wish to get into any kind of a wrestling match with him, but before I knew what was happening everyone in the room was demanding that we tangle. The crap game stopped. The dealer put down his cards.

"You willing, Metzger?" Sergeant West asked. Metzger grunted approval.

I couldn't back down; I had no choice but to take him on.

We sat down face to face across a table. Sergeant West explained the rules; it would be a two out of three match. The fellows crowded around, and some pretty hefty bets were being laid. Metzger was the favorite since he was a much bigger man and his physical strength was well known in the company.

When Metzger gripped my right hand in his, I knew I was in for a real battle. *Wham!* Down went my arm. I had lost the first match almost without resistance. Cries of dismay and encouragement rose from the crowd.

As Metzger and I gripped hands again I noticed his arm was several inches longer than mine. That forced me to hold my arm at an awkward angle, so I asked Metzger if he would mind lowering his arm a bit. When he did this his wrist was farther from his shoulder and his leverage was lessened. This gave me the advantage I wanted. We seesawed back and forth, neither enjoying any advantage.

Just when it seemed my strength would give out I felt
Metzger weaken, and with a yell I forced his wrist down to
the table.

We were both dripping with sweat now as we prepared
for the deciding match. This time I wedged one of my
knees against a crossbar under the table to give me additional support. On Sergeant West's signal I managed to turn
my wrist toward me. It was all the leverage I needed. I
locked my shoulder muscles and put the full weight of my
body behind my effort. Slowly I forced Metzger's arm down.
My arm was dead from fatigue, but I had won. The fellows
cheered and pounded me on the back.

Metzger was a good sport about his defeat. He shook my
hand, nearly smashing my fingers in his enthusiasm. We
became good friends after that. The incident reminded me
of the time Pete Fujino and some of the other fellows and
I tangled with the college kids at a parking lot back in
Seattle. They were belligerent until we demonstrated that
we were better fighters than they, and immediately afterward they wanted to be friends. Never underestimate the
value of power under any circumstances.

Sergeant West and Corporal Castro later gave me sixty
dollars. "We put some money on you," West said. "This is
your share of the winnings." I protested, but they insisted
I keep the money.

"What if I had lost?" I asked.

"You didn't," West replied with a grin.

Neither the money nor the fact that I had defeated Metzger were the important things to me. What really counted
was that I was now one of the gang. I felt wanted. I was
no longer merely an outsider who had been permitted to
tag along on the whim of the commanding officer.

But there would be precious little time to enjoy my new
status. Combat units of the 24th Division under Major
General William F. Dean south of Osan were being forced
closer and closer to Taejon. As North Korean columns

lapped around his overextended flanks, increasing numbers of infiltrators disguised as refugees penetrated our lines. Soon there would be pitched battle in the streets. We knew the 24th was buying time to enable the 25th Division to land at Pusan, and the 1st Cavalry also was reported on the way. But there was no assurance that Taejon could be held.

Fifteen

SEVERAL mornings later at breakfast we got the word we had been expecting. Bug out. Pack up real quick and take off as quickly as possible. For some unexplained reason the gooks had crossed the Kum River and there was nothing to stop them. While we hurriedly loaded the trailers we could hear the nearby rattle of machine gun fire and the whomp of out-going mortar shells. Then we learned Russian-built T-34 tanks were already in Taejon. The engineers were supposed to have blown up the bridges over the Kum. How had the tanks made the crossing? That didn't matter now. The important thing was to get out of Taejon with our skins intact. Our M.P. company didn't have a thing to be used against tanks. Even the infantry had only a few bazookas, effective only at close range.

Captain Peterson shouted at us to hurry, but he could have saved his breath. I clambered in behind the wheel and Captain Peterson scrambled in from the other side. Sergeants West and Metzger jumped into the rear and I spun the wheels taking off. I don't know how many jeeps were in the column behind us but that wasn't my concern. My orders were to head south out of town as fast as possible.

Near the southern outskirts of Taejon we came on four jeeps overturned by the side of the road. Several were burning and all were riddled with shrapnel. Scattered about on the ground were about a dozen G.I.'s. The grotesque posture of some of the bodies told me they were dead. But others were wounded and crying for help. I slammed on the brakes.

"No, no, keep going," Captain Peterson bellowed. I glanced at him in disbelief.

"Keep going," Captain Peterson shouted again. "The medics are right behind us and they'll take care of the casualties! Our job is to get down the road and set up some kind of a defense line!"

I punched down hard on the throttle again. In back of me I could hear West and Metzger firing their carbines. At what I didn't know. I was too busy watching the road ahead.

About five miles down the dusty highway toward Taegu we came on a makeshift roadblock manned by infantry and some of our M.P.'s. Captain Peterson ordered a halt and conferred with the major who seemed to be in charge. Shortly he returned and told us the major had received word the Communist tanks were still in Taejon and for the moment they didn't seem to be planning to head down the road. The captain's orders were to take the M.P.'s on down to Taegu and set up a base there. It wasn't until a long time afterward that we heard what had stopped the tanks. General Dean at the head of a handful of infantrymen armed with bazookas had stalked them in the rubble-strewn streets of Taejon. He and his men had knocked out a half dozen or so of the tanks, blunting the North Korean spearhead, before the Americans were surrounded and captured. General Dean spent the rest of the war in a Communist prisoner of war camp, but his courageous stand had given the survivors of his 24th Division enough time to get out of Taejon and set up a new defense line. No American was more deserving of the Medal of Honor.

Meanwhile we continued our retreat toward Taegu in

silence, sullen, angry. It bothered me that we were running away. Americans weren't supposed to retreat. Captain Peterson seemed to sense what I was thinking. "Jim," he said, "this isn't a retreat. It's a scientific, pre-planned withdrawal to trap the enemy." For a moment I missed the irony in his voice. I thought he was being serious and I almost voiced what was on the tip of my tongue: "Don't give me that crap, sir." Then I realized that he was as unhappy about being driven out of Taejon as I was, and I clamped my mouth shut.

The jeep rattled and bounced back down the rocky road over which we had advanced only a few days earlier, and I began to wonder what madness had moved me to volunteer to serve with the Americans. The Military Police were supposed to direct traffic, guard prisoners, conduct investigations, yet we were plunged into battle just like the infantry, but without the necessary arms and equipment. I began to feel sorry for myself until I realized that all my buddies in the company were in the same boat. In football, the worst thing that can happen to a team is for everyone to become discouraged at the same time. What the hell, we weren't licked yet! I had asked for an opportunity to fight; I would give it everything I had.

The 24th Division had held Taejon just long enough to let the 25th Division and the 1st Cavalry get into position for the defense of sun-baked, flea-bitten Taegu along the broad Naktong River. Our company moved directly into Taegu and set up headquarters in a school building. At night we could hear the cannon thunder, and flashes lit the sky, but except for the endless refugee and military traffic in the streets the war seemed to be far away. Long processions of refugees straggled slowly down the dusty roads, the men bowed under the weight of the possessions piled on A-frame pack boards, the women with cloth-wrapped loads balanced on their heads. In the evening when they camped in pine groves back of the roads, the women made their way down to the streams to wash their flowing white robes. They had nothing as sophisticated as soap. They pounded the clothing on a flat rock, rinsing and pounding, rinsing and pounding until miraculously the cloth turned out snow white.

A day or so after we reached Taegu, the city chief of police invited Captain Peterson to dinner. Captain Peterson took a rather dim view of Korean delicacies, and besides he was very busy so he asked me to go in his place. I drove the captain's jeep and parked it in front of the chief's home. What a meal the chief's wife dished up! Shredded chicken fried in oil and topped with sesame seeds, thin-sliced beef barbecued with hot Korean sauce, soybean cake flavored with soy sauce, garlic and sesame seeds. Hot white rice—the first I'd had since leaving Japan—was served together with *kim chee,* which is Chinese cabbage pickled in red pepper juice together with chestnuts, apples and great quantities of pungent garlic. I made a pig of myself while the chief and his wife beamed. When it was time to leave the chief's wife brought out five long, slim bundles of rice straw. There were ten eggs in each bundle, each egg wrapped separately and placed in the bundle so that they were like beads in a necklace except that they didn't touch each other and were completely protected by the straw. Fifty fresh eggs! A treasure! They were a gift for the captain.

I thanked my hosts profusely, opened the door, stepped out and found my jeep on four blocks. The tires were gone.

The chief was mortified. Bowing again and again, he apologized and swore he would punish the thieves to the limit of the law. I flagged down an M.P. jeep that happened to be going by, and pretty soon a truck from the motor pool came by with replacement tires. Captain Peterson was so delighted to get the eggs that he didn't raise much of a fuss about the tires. I prepared a Japanese-style omelet for him, flavoring the eggs with salt, sugar and soy sauce. He finished it off appreciatively, then remarked: "Eggs are great, but how's about getting the mama of the eggs? I sure enjoyed the way you fixed chicken for me up in Taejon."

A few days later when Sergeant West and I went on an inspection tour I found an opportunity to satisfy the captain's appetite. We drove into a tiny abandoned village. There were no living things except forty or fifty chickens clucking and scratching in the dust. The two of us tried to round them up, but they were far too agile for us.

"How are we going to catch them?" Sergeant West asked. "Shoot 'em?"

"Let's cut some bamboo poles over in the thicket there," I suggested. We each cut a pole and Sergeant West ran after the chickens, swatting at them futilely as though he were chopping wood.

"No, no, watch me," I said. I knelt and held my pole at one end so that it stretched out in front of me a few inches off the ground. Creeping up on the chickens, I swept the pole in a wide arc parallel to the ground, left to right and back again. The pole would whack the chickens' legs and snap the bone, crippling them so they couldn't run away. We picked up forty of them in no time.

"Hey, that's a damned good trick," Sergeant West exclaimed. "Where did you learn to do that?"

"I just know," I replied. I wasn't going to explain that I learned the trick on a foraging raid with the Japanese Army in China. The captain and the noncoms had plenty of chicken that night. Shortly afterward Captain Peterson received word he had been promoted to major. That was reason enough for Sergeant West and me to go out once more on a chicken-hunt, and we celebrated with another deep-fried chicken feast.

These days in Taegu gave me an opportunity to compare the differences between the Japanese and American Armies. After battles in China, we would return to our barracks in Yoyang and face the almost sadistic hazing of the noncoms. If their purpose was to make barracks life so miserable that we preferred combat, they succeeded. In the U.S. Army time away from line duty was a time for rest and relaxation. The G.I.'s would sit around shooting the breeze, write home, read comics, pitch horseshoes, play cards, shoot craps, wash and clean up, oil weapons, or sleep. The American system appeared undisciplined, and yet I knew that at a moment's notice they could swing into action. It might be said that American industrial power won World War II, but that war also proved that no nation has better infantry soldiers than the United States. The easy-going American system had overwhelmed the harsh discipline of the Japanese system. It was, to my way of thinking, a triumph of the human spirit even in the inhumanity of war.

One very hot day, while driving back toward the compound, I overtook a young Korean woman walking along the side of the road. I stopped and offered her a ride. When she looked up at me I saw a face of delicate, classical beauty. The features were unusually fine, the eyes large and luminous. She was exceptionally tall for a Korean. She was, in fact, one of the most beautiful women I'd ever seen. Tiny beads of perspiration stood out on her forehead. She hesitated for a moment, then stepped into the jeep with a word of thanks.

"Why do you speak Japanese?" she asked. "Why don't you speak Korean?"

"Because I am Japanese," I said.

She pulled back with a start, her eyes alarmed. "I thought you were a Korean in American uniform. If you are Japanese, why are you dressed like an American soldier?"

"I'm a Japanese American. My parents were Japanese. But I was born in the United States, so I am an American."

"I don't believe you," she retorted, anger rising in her voice. "Americans have white skins and blue eyes and red hair. You are an Oriental. You are Japanese. I hate the

Japanese for what they did to my father and to my country. Stop the jeep and let me out."

"Look, young lady," I said as gently as I could in my best Japanese, "it's a very hot day and it doesn't make any sense to walk when you can ride. I'm not going to hurt you, even if my ancestors were Japanese. Tell me where you want to go and I will take you there and then I will go about my business."

I dropped her off at a tiny house not far from the Military Police compound. After supper that evening I lay down on my cot and thought about the Korean girl's reactions. My American uniform was what first caught her eye. She knew Americans were friendly. Then she saw my face, assumed I was a Korean, and accepted my offer of a ride. But when she discovered I was Japanese rather than Korean, she became hostile. Suddenly it didn't matter any more to her that I was wearing the uniform of a friendly nation.

I couldn't blame her at all for the way she acted. After all, her country had been invaded and brutalized by the Japanese occupation, and I was a stranger who had thrust himself on her, no matter how innocently. Still, her reaction, the finality with which she rejected all "Japanese" as bad without looking beyond surface impressions, offered a challenge to change her mind. I decided I wanted to get better acquainted with her.

The next time I had a few free hours I picked up a thirty-pound bag of rice from the South Korean Military Police through Lieutenant Kim and went looking for the Korean girl. I found her home easily enough, and much to my surprise she invited me in.

"I must apologize for having been so rude," she said in flawless Japanese. "I'm afraid I was upset, with the heat and the war and all. I failed even to thank you for the ride."

She told me her name was Duk-Chu. She was a schoolteacher living with her mother and a younger brother. Her father had been killed by a Japanese soldier. She was somewhat vague about the details and I didn't feel I should press her for them. She went on to say she had family friends in Pusan where they might seek refuge if Taegu were threatened, but so far had remained in their home because the long trip would be so hard on her mother. For ordinary civilians there were no trains, no buses, and of course no private cars. The only way to get from one place to another was by foot. I could hear the older woman puttering around in the back room but she didn't come out to meet me and Duk-Chu did not offer to introduce her. After a very pleasant evening I left the rice as a gift and returned to the compound. It would be presumptuous to think I had made more than a casual impression on Duk-Chu. Yet she had invited me, a "Japanese" in her view, into her home and we had passed a very pleasant evening. I chalked up one imaginary mark for understanding.

The encounter also had another and unlooked for result. Until then the plight of the South Korean refugees fleeing southward from the Communists had been largely an impersonal matter. Of course I felt sorry for them. But they were merely an endless sea of faces, sometimes concealing the enemy, and there had been no reason to identify myself with them. Now, however, after meeting Duk-Chu, the situation changed. I realized Duk-Chu could well be my sister Betty. Duk-Chu's mother could well be my mother. What would Mom and Betty have done if the Americans had invaded southern Japan? Would they have dared hide out from the pre-invasion bombardment and waited for the Yanks to land? More likely they would have fled inland in fear and terror, just as the South Koreans were fleeing, just as Duk-Chu and her mother and brother would have to flee if Taegu were threatened. I knew I had to help Duk-Chu and her family if the opportunity ever arose.

That opportunity came much sooner than expected. Major

Peterson sent me on an assignment to Pusan. It was just an errand boy's mission, but it was a chance to get Duk-Chu down to her friends. When I explained the problem to Major Peterson he gave me permission to take the Korean family along. Lieutenant Kim managed to find several hundred pounds of rice that his outfit didn't need, and he gave it to Duk-Chu to help tide her over. I loaded the rice and some of the family's belongings into the trailer. Duk-Chu sat up beside me in the jeep. Her mother, a wrinkled prematurely old woman who bore no resemblance whatever to the beautiful Duk-Chu, sat in back along with the boy. It was the first time I had seen the mother. She said not one word during the entire drive. But when I finally delivered them to their friends' home in Pusan, the old woman's face broke into a big grin and she embraced me in gratitude. Duk-Chu held both my hands in hers and gazed at me with misty eyes. I wanted very much to kiss her. In fact, if I weren't married, I would have liked to come back and get better acquainted and perhaps ask Duk-Chu to become my wife. She invited me to drop by and see her the next time I was in Pusan. I promised I would, but I never saw her again.

Duk-Chu and her family had gotten out of Taegu none too soon. Day after day the North Koreans hammered at the Naktong River perimeter, probing sharply at night in search of weak points. Even though the 2nd (Indian Head) Division and the First Marines, plus a couple of regimental combat teams, had arrived in mid-August to reinforce our defenses, there were many lightly held sectors, and it was likely that Taegu would have to be given up shortly. Communist artillery shells landed frequently in the suburbs. The civilians who were still left were warned to get out as soon as possible, and soon the streets were all but deserted.

One day Sergeant West and I were patrolling the abandoned streets when we came across a large gray building. It was obviously a warehouse of some kind. The steel door was padlocked. We tried to break the lock with a tire iron but it refused to give. Apparently something important was in the warehouse and we resolved to find out. We hurried to the 24th Engineers and Sergeant West borrowed a welding torch. In no time at all he had cut through the lock and we opened the door.

A stale smell met us. As our eyes adjusted to the darkness I saw huge piles of what looked like half-dried carrots, all of them forked. I quickly realized they were ginseng roots—a government warehouse full of ginseng.

"Sarge, there's a fortune here," I exclaimed. Then I explained to Sergeant West that the root of the ginseng plant is highly regarded throughout the Far East for medicinal purposes. Somewhere I had read that ginseng is considered so valuable that its cultivation is a Korean government monopoly. The plants are carefully tended for six years before the roots are dug up and dried. A tea is brewed from the roots, and tiny bits of it are slowly chewed and swallowed. It's alleged to prevent or cure colds, overcome anemia, restore vigor after fatigue. Many swear by ginseng as a highly effective aphrodisiac, although I suppose the secret is that if you're feeling well, your sex drive increases.

"What do you think this pile of roots is worth?" Sergeant West asked.

"Oodles of yen, Sarge. Millions and millions of yen. Millions of dollars, maybe."

"Will this stuff go in Japan?"

"Faster than hotcakes."

We held a quick council of war. It didn't take long to rationalize that since Taegu was likely to be in Communist hands very shortly, it was fair to consider that the South Korean government had abandoned this warehouse of ginseng. And, if we were to help ourselves to a supply, we would be denying that much to the enemy while incidentally laying open the possibility of making a few bucks for ourselves. Some burlap sacks were stacked in a corner. We grabbed them and began to stuff them with ginseng. The roots in some piles were white. Other piles were reddish. I didn't know which was more valuable. To play safe, I told the sergeant to fill his sacks with white ones while I filled mine with red roots. Soon we had eight sacks, each bulging with ginseng root, but what would we do with them? Sergeant West had the answer. He sent me to borrow the M.P. company's paddywagon.

Corporal Castro was the noncom in charge of the paddywagon. He was instantly suspicious. "What do you want the wagon for?" he asked. "You got something going?"

I had no choice but to tell him. "We'll cut you in," I assured him. "A three-way split, maybe four if Major Peterson finds out." Corporal Castro knew about ginseng. His Japanese girlfriend's mother in Japan used to buy it, and since he had to come up with the money, he was aware of its value. He needed no further encouragement. The three of us loaded the sacks into the paddywagon and pledged to tell no one.

After chow we three met at the paddywagon to make our plans. Castro said he had connections in Japan where he could unload the roots. Sergeant West said he knew how he could exchange big amounts of Japanese yen into U.S. military script. All we had to do was find a way to get the ginseng back to Japan—and stay alive long enough to enjoy the profits. Our imaginations soared. We calculated that we had about one million dollars' worth of ginseng at the going retail price, and maybe half that much if we had to dump it all on a wholesaler. Corporal Castro said he would marry his girlfriend and buy her a cocktail bar. Sergeant West just wanted to feel the cash in his hands; he'd worry about investing it later. I had the odd sensation that I was part of an old James Cagney gangster movie. I was afraid Major Peterson would find out and punish us, and I kept feeling like a thief.

"For Chrissake, Jim," Sergeant West admonished me.

"You know the South Koreans abandoned them roots. The goddam North Korean gooks are going to get it anyway. We should have taken everything in the warehouse instead of just eight piddlin' sacks."

We agreed that one of us would sleep under the truck each night to make sure nothing happened to it, and I drew the first watch. As I stretched out on my bedroll under the truck, I kept worrying about the South Korean government investigating us. And what if we didn't have to evacuate Taegu?

I needn't have worried. The North Koreans chased us out the next afternoon. They lobbed mortar shells into town and followed up the barrage with heavy machine gun fire. We took off for Masan, a pretty little city on the ocean on the west coast of the Korean peninsula. I hated to be retreating again, but having been driven out of Taegu my conscience was clearer. Now the question was not whether we'd be caught, but whether we would survive the war to enjoy our prize.

There seemed to be no way of stopping the North Koreans. The best-trained, best-equipped U.S. divisions couldn't hold the line against the enemy's determined onslaughts. Our foothold in Korea was pinched down to little more than a beachhead on the southern tip of the peninsula and our backs were almost to the sea. One more powerful Red offensive and we'd be faced with another Dunkirk. Perhaps the only factor that kept the Reds from slashing us up at will was that we had almost complete air superiority.

But air superiority didn't mean a thing when Bedcheck Charlie came calling.

He came one night in a tiny, single-engined propeller-driven aircraft. At first we thought it was one of our artillery spotter planes but when we found it wasn't, we panicked like schoolgirls. "Air attack—douse the damn lights," someone cried, and we all ducked for cover. The pilot dropped two mortar shells. He probably just tossed them over the side, then took off into the night. The shells didn't land close enough to do any damage, but they shook up our nerves plenty. The same plane came over every night after dark. He'd cut off his engine somewhere in the distance and glide quietly over our camp, drop his shells, restart his motor and take off again, probably threading his way through the peaks around Masan to get back to his base. Naturally he was named Bedcheck Charlie, just like the Japanese light plane pilots who harassed Yank troops the same way in World War II. It was inevitable that someone should suggest that the pilot was a Japanese flying for the North Koreans, but I didn't think so. At least I didn't want to think he was Japanese.

Sixteen

THE Allies' Pusan Perimeter defense line was anchored on the east coast of the Korean peninsula at the town of Pohang. It extended westward in a broad half-moon to just south of Taegu, which we had recently evacuated, then straight across to the southwest coast at Masan, where we now were. One more big push and the North Koreans could run us completely out of Korea. If the Allies were to keep from being driven into the sea, the port of Pusan had to be held. Every ton of supplies for the Army was brought ashore at Pusan. Without its docking facilities we were finished. Thus every possible man was thrown into the lines to keep the North Koreans at bay. That meant even the military police were sent into outlying areas to help man the outposts.

The 24th Division M.P. headquarters were moved up to Miryang, about thirty-five miles northeast of Masan. Small groups of our men were detached temporarily to join infantry battalions in forward areas. I remained with Major Peterson, but from time to time we toured our lines to see how our men were getting along. Shortly after my twenty-ninth birthday Sergeant West, Sergeant Metzger and I drove to Chirwon to check on the military police there. Chirwon lay at the confluence of two major rivers, and there we found the M.P.'s engaged in a gruesome game—fishing the corpses of North Korean soldiers out of the water and recovering American wristwatches. Apparently the North Koreans were stripping watches and other valuables from the bodies of American dead. Later, when some of these North Koreans were killed in battle their bodies would come floating down the river. We were told that one gook had twelve watches on his wrists when his body was pulled ashore. The M.P.'s complained that only a few of the watches were waterproof and most of them were ruined by the time they were recovered.

Sergeant West didn't like what the fellows were doing, but he had no authority to stop them. All he could do was warn them to be careful. It was a timely warning. Shortly afterward we learned that the North Koreans had discovered what the G.I.'s were doing and booby-trapped some bodies before throwing them in the river. That soon stopped the fishing expeditions.

As we were leaving Chirwon we came on a 24th Division Signal Corps van parked in a dry river bed. Suddenly, *kerwham,* an artillery shell exploded not far away. Even before Sergeant West shouted at us to take cover we had grabbed our carbines and bailed out. Cowering together in the meager shelter of a small depression close to the stream bank, we watched in fascination as the enemy gunner expertly "walked" his shells in fifty-yard strides closer and closer to the van. Then, right before our eyes, the van disappeared in a great puff of smoke and dust. The Red gunner had scored a direct hit! There was nothing left of the van or of the men who had been in it. I jumped up to get a better view of this amazing sight. Sergeant West grabbed me by my belt and jerked me down savagely. Almost immediately the ground shook with a tremendous explosion.

Earth and rocks rose in a dirty brown geyser and showered down on us.

It seemed as though we lay flat on the ground for an hour waiting for the next shell to land right in our midst, but it never came. Presently we rose. Just behind the spot where I had been standing was a tree. Sergeant West beckoned to me. Imbedded in the trunk, at about the height of my head, was a jagged piece of shrapnel. Sergeant West dug it out with his knife and tossed it to me. The bit of steel, about three and a half inches long, an inch or so wide and a half inch at its thickest, was still warm. As the realization of what that chunk of metal could have done to me sank in, I began to tremble. Sergeant West must have noticed how pale I had become. "Let me take the jeep for a while," he said casually, and I gratefully turned the driving over to him.

The broad backs of West and Metzger, looming over me as I sprawled out in the back of the jeep, were warmly reassuring as we drove back to headquarters. I remembered how another sergeant, Kido, had saved my life under somewhat similar circumstances, tackling me as I foolishly exposed myself to Chinese gunfire. I remembered also the punishment that followed, when we men were forced to line up face to face and punch each other. Even if the U.S. Army had sanctioned such disciplinary measures, Sergeant West would not have resorted to physical punishment. He was wise enough to know that he had made his point with me. Nor did he think it was any of his business to tell Major Peterson what had happened, so I did. The major simply reminded me of his responsibility for my welfare and told me to be careful.

A few days later I had an opportunity to repay my friends in a small way. The major sent me to the divisional medics for a supply of codeine pills for his recurring migraine headaches. I found that some of the medics were fellows I had done favors for back at Kokura in Japan. One of them slipped a case of grain alcohol into the jeep. "Take it back to the boys," he said. "Typical snafu here. We've got more than we can use in ten years." On the way back I detoured by way of a quartermaster's depot and exchanged several bottles of alcohol for a case of canned orange juice and a case of canned pineapple juice. For a while we must have been the only outfit in Korea that enjoyed a cocktail hour before evening chow. Japanese troops were inclined to get mean when they drank, but not the M.P.'s. They were simply great.

And thus did the torrid, humid Korean August give way to early September. The days were sunny and dry, but after sundown the crispness in the wind hinted of the fearsome cold that soon would sweep down from the Siberian steppes. Along the perimeter, our troops continued to fight desperately to maintain the line. Our South Korean allies, given a chance to regroup and reorganize, were able to carry some of the burden. No longer were they frightened, disorganized rabble fleeing for their lives. Some of them even launched a counterattack and retook Taegu. Up front, death was a daily visitor. Back where we were, duty was less hazardous but not always pleasant. There was the day, for instance, when Sergeant West, a South Korean sergeant named Soon and I were dispatched to investigate a rape.

The G.I. suspect was reported to be holed up in a Korean farmhouse. We drove into the village and one of the elders pointed out the house. We had to duck to get through the doorway, and there was the G.I. with his rifle pointed at us. Sergeant West ordered him to put down his gun. There was a silent confrontation for a long moment and I thought I detected the glint of madness—or fear—in the G.I.'s eyes. Then slowly he lowered his rifle. Sergeant West walked up to him, grabbed the gun and delivered a solid punch to the gut. As the soldier doubled over I sprang in and put an armlock on him. We led him out of the house screaming protests that we were trying to help the "gooks." Meanwhile Sergeant Soon was questioning the villagers and was told that the suspect had raped a thirteen-year-old child and her grandmother. We found the grandmother and she told Sergeant Soon of the attack. Soon became more and more agitated. Suddenly he jumped up and ran at our prisoner, screaming in anger. Sergeant West stepped in and held off the Korean sergeant until he cooled off. We took the prisoner to the stockade. Sergeant West kicked him, hard, in the seat of the pants as the other military police led him away. I had no idea what Sergeant West wrote in his report but I wondered whether some of our troops knew why we were in Korea, whether they understood that the South Koreans were our allies, and that not all people with Oriental faces were to be dismissed simply as gooks. I sympathized with Sergeant Soon who was so deeply moved by the grandmother's account that he might have slain the suspect. Yet, I realized that most of the Americans were good men, and hundreds of them were giving their lives for a country and a people they hardly knew. The next time I saw Sergeant Soon I would try to explain all this to him without making it sound too corny.

Meanwhile, unknown to us, a bold and imaginative military maneuver was under way. A huge Allied amphibious force was sailing up the west coast of Korea. On September 15, Marines stormed ashore at Inchon, the port of Seoul. Opposition was light. The Marines quickly established a beachhead and drove inland toward the capital twenty miles away. General MacArthur, unable to make yardage through the middle of the enemy line, had executed a neat end run. The Communist forces in the south were now in imminent danger of being cut off from their bases in North Korea. Abruptly they broke off the engagement and hurried back up the peninsula in an effort to escape before the trap could be closed.

Now the 8th Army under General Walton H. Walker,

which had been hanging on for dear life, set off in pursuit. Mechanized columns raced northward to link up with the Marines outside Seoul, bypassing major pockets of Communists in the mountainous spine of the country. They would have to be mopped up later. Once more our outfit rolled up the now familiar highway, through Taegu, on into Kumchon and back into Taejon. And everywhere we went, so did Corporal Castro's paddywagon loaded with our fortune in ginseng roots.

Taejon was in ruins. Few buildings were intact and soot-blackened bricks and tiles and charred timbers were everywhere. Only the foundations remained of the school where the military police had maintained their headquarters. Only half the Korean police headquarters building remained standing. Almost before Taejon was secured, the former residents began to trickle back. Some, apparently, had been hiding in the hills during the Communist occupation and others had found shelter with relatives in remote villages. Still others, no doubt, had hurried back from Pusan on the heels of the 8th Army, displaying the remarkable resilience of the Korean people.

Probing through the wreckage of the police building we discovered what appeared to be a shallow grave. A little digging unearthed a corpse, the partly decomposed body of an American soldier. His hands were still tied behind his back. Part of his face had vanished, apparently blown off by a bullet that had been fired into the back of his head at close range. The man, whoever he was, had been executed, no doubt in cold blood. We dug elsewhere in the police compound and uncovered more bodies, almost all of them with their hands bound, most of them executed in the same manner. So this was what had happened to some of our comrades who had stayed behind in Taejon to cover our withdrawal! If there had been any doubt about the savagery of the Communist enemy, there was none now. In all we exhumed the bodies of twenty-six G.I.'s in that one area. There was no way to tell how many other Americans lay buried under the wreckage and rubble of what had been Taejon. Our discovery caused an abrupt change in our plans. Major Peterson's unit was ordered to remain in Taejon to make a full investigation as well as to process prisoners.

What we had seen made us much more tolerant of the way the South Korean M.P.'s handled captured Communists who now were surrendering in droves. Thousands of prisoners passed through Taejon and each man had to be registered and interrogated. Most of them were simple farm boys who were only too glad to be out of the fighting, but occasionally there would be hard-core Communists who refused to say anything. The South Koreans knew how to make them talk. They would get a pole about four inches in diameter, three or four feet long, and place it lengthwise behind the prisoner's knees and then force him to squat on it. The man's weight bore down on the pole, exerting pressure on the leg muscles that produced excruciating pain. Sometimes the South Koreans would persuade a prisoner to become even more cooperative by beating him over the head, or standing on the ends of the pole to add their weight to the pressure. The prisoners would scream in agony. We Americans would turn away but we never interfered. The South Koreans knew that they could expect the same kind of torture, if not worse, if they were captured by their cousins from the north, and we reasoned that after all it was their war.

Any bit of mercy we might have held for the prisoners vanished the day some of the refugees led us to a wooded hill back of Taejon where an estimated 2,400 South Korean civilians had been massacred by the enemy. According to witnesses, the civilians had been forced to dig their own graves, then were mowed down by their executioners so they toppled into the holes. Afterward the bodies were lightly covered with earth. Perhaps it was the shade from the trees that prevented complete putrefaction of the bodies. Fighting nausea, we watched in awe and astonishment as an endless number of Korean men and women trudged up the hill to dig up bodies in search of friends and relatives. Weeping, they would try to clean the dirt and mud off decomposing faces in an effort to make positive identification. When a loved one was found, the corpse was wrapped in white cloth and carried off for decent burial. As the sun's heat hit some of the corpses the bellies became horribly bloated until the gas escaped. Witnessing this sort of activity was almost more than we could take. I wondered at the stoicism of the Korean people and of the love that bound them to their kin. But I wondered, too, at the fetish we make of the mortal remains of the dead. How much less gruesome it would have been if the dead had been permitted to remain where they lay and a memorial service conducted over them. Yet I suppose that would not have satisfied these people's sense of obligation to each other.

When civilian government of sorts was restored in Taejon and most of the Communist stragglers cleared out of the countryside, our outfit was ordered north. By this time Seoul had been recaptured, and troops driving up from the south had linked with the Marine landing force. On October 1 Republic of Korea troops drove across the 38th Parallel, the demarcation line between North and South Korea, and pushed on toward Pyongyang, the Communist capital. A week later U.S. troops also invaded the north. No announcement was made as to our ultimate objective but for those of us in the field it appeared the intention was to drive up into the heart of North Korea and smash the Communist armies in one final battle. Despite our rapid advance, the Reds were still a force to contend with. Thousands of Communist troops had been captured, but other thousands had escaped. In fact the main body of the North Korean invasion force had fled to the east side of the peninsula before the Allied trap could be closed and had run away to fight another day.

Pyongyang was captured on October 20. By the time our outfit set up camp on Pyongyang's outskirts the city was firmly in Allied hands, and combat spearheads were pushing up the narrow valleys of North Korea toward the Yalu River. On the other side of the Yalu was Manchuria, home ground of some of Red China's best troops. High level strategists weighed intelligence reports to determine whether the Chinese would come to the aid of their North Korean comrades. If they did the "Korean Incident" would be a brand new war, perhaps the kickoff of World War III.

But for our shivering company of military police on the windswept plain outside Pyongyang, there were more immediate matters to worry about. Winter had set in. Icy blasts raced down from the north and each night the frost settled a little deeper in the ground. Fortunately the quartermasters were well-prepared, and before long we were issued warm winter clothing and down-filled sleeping bags. With them, sleeping under the paddywagon was no problem. A potbellied stove appeared from somewhere to keep the squad tent comfortable, and we even found a mobile generator to provide us with electric lights. Surely the United States does more to look after the creature comforts of its servicemen than any other country.

It was outside of Pyongyang that a number of promotions caught up with us. Major Peterson made lieutenant colonel. He had been only a captain when we came to Korea five months earlier. Now he was entitled to wear silver oak leaves, and I think I was as proud as he was. I located some silver paint and one of the Korean M.P.'s fixed up the insignia on the colonel's helmet. Lieutenant Kim, who had accompanied us in all our travels, was promoted to captain at the same time. This was reason enough to celebrate. I went foraging for some chickens, finally located a supply, and we had another one of the fried chicken feasts Peterson liked so well.

By mid-November it was time to move north again. ROK patrols were reported to have pushed all the way to the Yalu. On November 21 we heard that elements of the U.S. 7th Division also had reached the Yalu and the entire 8th Army was advancing toward the border all along the front. The boys in camp were chattering happily about chasing the gooks clear into China and of getting back to Japan in time for Christmas. But the closer we pushed to the frontier, the fiercer the fighting became. Each night before we settled down we were under orders to dig foxholes. I had the job of digging one for Colonel Peterson as well as for myself. The colonel insisted that his foxhole be at least four feet deep, two feet wide and six feet long. With the ground frozen to a depth of a foot or more, this was almost an impossible task.

I was grumbling about it one day when one of the Korean kitchen helpers let me in on a secret. He took me to the ruins of what had been a house or a building and scraped away the broken tiles, ashes and other rubble that covered the ground. He showed me that the soil underneath was not frozen. Elsewhere it might be as hard as concrete, but the litter served as insulation and the dirt under it was easy to dig. After that digging the colonel's foxhole was a cinch. All I had to do was make sure his tent was pitched near a ruined building. My own foxhole didn't have to be anywhere as large as the colonel's. I could be satisfied with a very small shelter when I had to dig two of them.

One day Sergeants West and Metzger, Captain Kim, Sergeant Soon and I went to check out a tiny village which had been by-passed by the infantry. The village seemed to be deserted, but suddenly I heard a slight noise. With .45 in hand, I peered around a farmhouse—and came face to face with a youth in North Korean uniform. I don't know who was more startled, he or I. I saw him draw back and reach into his quilted jacket. Instinctively I squeezed the trigger. The roar of the shot deafened my ears and jolted my arm. I saw the North Korean spin away, as though kicked by a horse, and twist and fall. He tumbled into a heap and lay still. The others came running, pistols drawn. We straightened the man out, but he was already dead, a bloody hole in his chest. His right hand was still inside the jacket. When we pulled the hand out it was clutching a little white safe conduct pass which our planes had been dropping by the tens of thousands in an effort to get enemy troops to defect. This guy was ready to surrender—he was trying to surrender—and I had killed him!

I sat down, stunned and confused. I wondered if I'd be sick, but nothing happened. I felt nothing. Under the so-called rules of war, I knew that my action was fully justified. It just happened that he was reaching for a safe conduct pass; he could just as well have been reaching for a grenade with which to kill me, and I had only done what was necessary.

Our two ROK's were burdened with no doubts about the death. They quickly frisked the dead enemy for documents —orders, letters, a diary—that would interest the boys in intelligence. Then they kicked the corpse into a roadside ditch, and we continued the patrol. That evening when I told Colonel Peterson what had happened he commended me. "You did absolutely right," he said, looking very serious. "If in doubt, shoot first and ask questions later. There is no place in war for gentlemen, nor can we afford to feel sorry for the enemy. I'm sure he doesn't waste his time feeling sorry for us."

On patrol again the very next day we came across a most un-warlike—and un-Korean—cache. It was a big supply of cheese and smoked ham. There were no labels on the packages so their origin was unknown, but there was no doubt in our minds that they were Russian. The cheese was quite moldy, but it was excellent after the mold was scraped off. Colonel Peterson sent a generous supply to the officers in the Interrogation section and to other senior officers in the area with his compliments. I was sure in my mind that a high-ranking Russian military adviser had brought the delicacies in for his personal use, but who knows? It might have been a senior North Korean officer who acquired a taste for cheese and· smoked ham on a visit to Moscow.

As Thanksgiving approached, the weather grew even colder. In the morning I could feel the ice forming in my nostrils if I breathed deeply. By agreement Sergeant Metzger, Corporal Castro and I quit sleeping with the paddywagon. It was just too uncomfortable. The only thing that kept us cheerful was the promise of a hot turkey dinner, with all the trimmings, on Thanksgiving Day. We swapped stories of other Thanksgivings we had known, and I remembered the traditional football games and the wonderful clam chowder that Dad used to make for our turkey dinners. We tortured ourselves by talking about being back in Japan in time for Christmas and entertained each other with tall tales about what we intended to do.

That's when it happened. The Chinese got into the war.

We were camped twenty miles south of the Yalu River when we got the news. On the night of November 25 a large, well-armed force of Chinese struck viciously at Allied units on the western side of the front, sending our troops reeling. Intelligence reports were alarming. Tens of thousands of Chinese were reported pouring across the Yalu into North Korea. Other tens of thousands seemed to materialize out of nothing in the bleak Korean mountains where, apparently, they had been massing for days if not weeks. Our lines were overextended. We had to pull back and regroup if we were to stop them. We got the word: Bug out. Fast.

The numbing cold had been playing havoc on our vehicles. Sometimes, after a night in the open, they became quite temperamental. Now that we needed them, several refused to start. Among them was the paddywagon. Corporal Castro fiddled desperately with the carburetor, but it was no use.

"We've got to get going," Colonel Peterson shouted. "There are a lot of men up the road headed back in this direction. We can't afford to stay here and block their way. If a vehicle won't start, we'll just have to abandon it and double up."

Corporal Castro looked at Sergeant West and me with an utterly miserable, forlorn expression. Then he slammed the hood shut and jumped into another jeep in the column. Sergeant West stood up in the back of my jeep, raised his carbine and fired a clip into the paddywagon. Time and again in the movies I had seen cars burst into flame when someone fired even a single bullet into them. But the paddywagon sat there, cold and inert, unchanged except for a row of bullet holes through the hood and body.

"What the hell was that for?" Colonel Peterson demanded.

"I just wanted to make sure those damned Chinamen wouldn't get our paddywagon, sir," Sergeant West said. The column started out and I didn't look back. It hurt too much to think we were abandoning a fortune in ginseng, a fortune we had watched over so carefully in our travels virtually the entire length of the Korean peninsula.

The retreat southward in the miserable cold was slow and bitterly fought. The 24th Division and the British 27th Brigade alternated as the rear guard. While the British held off the Communists, we would hurry down the road about ten miles and dig in. Then the British would pull back, leapfrog past us, and set up new defenses while we protected them. We engineered the retreat in well-disciplined ten-mile leaps, slowing the Chinese advance and giving other units of the 8th Army an opportunity to reorganize. By December 15 General Walker had established a strong defense line north of Seoul, generally along the

38th Parallel. We were right back where we had started from, and still without assurance that a new invasion of South Korea could be stopped.

If General Walker had plans for turning the tide, he never got the opportunity of executing them. Two days before Christmas our headquarters received word of a serious collision somewhere up toward the front in our sector. Sergeant West, Corporal Castro and I were ordered to investigate. A light snow was falling as we set out. We found a jeep had collided with a weapons carrier driven by a South Korean soldier. The jeep was General Walker's. Apparently his driver had been traveling on the wrong side of the road. When the weapons carrier loomed out of the snow the driver had skidded the jeep broadside into the heavier vehicle. The jeep flipped over on top of the general, killing him instantly. His driver was injured but conscious. We covered the general's body with a blanket, roped off the area for investigators, and radioed for the medics. When they arrived to treat the injured G.I. and take custody of the general's body, we took the ROK driver back to headquarters with us. Sergeant West had warned everyone on the scene that General Walker's death was to be classified information until 8th Army made the official announcement, but within an hour someone's radio was blasting out the news for all the world to hear. Three days later I heard South Korea's President Syngman Rhee apologize for the death of General Walker due to the carelessness of the driver of the weapons carrier. I hoped nothing happened to him. From what we had ascertained, it wasn't his fault at all.

General Walker's death spread a pall over Christmas, which was miserable anyway because we were hanging on desperately again whereas we had hoped to have the war won and be home for the holidays. None of us knew the general, of course. But we had fought with him, we had listened to his exhortations to stand firm or die on the

Pusan Perimeter, and we had driven almost to the Yalu with him. We felt an affection for this stocky bulldog of a man, and each of us took his loss personally.

But the worst was yet to come. On New Year's Eve the Chinese began the second Communist invasion of South Korea. Seoul was evacuated for the second time less than a week later. Civilian refugees fled for their lives once more, this time down frozen, snow-swept roads. Their courage, their determination to stay free, was deeply moving. I was proud to be fighting on their behalf and heartsick that our efforts were not more effective.

Somewhere south of Seoul a few weeks later, I received an unexpected letter at mail call. It bore the return address of the United States Consulate at Fukuoka, not far from my home in Japan. Something told me the letter was very important. Trembling with excitement I tore the envelope open. It was a formal letter from the American consul in typically stilted language and I had to read it twice to make sure it meant what I thought it said. Stripped of its verbiage, the letter simply said my application for clarification of my citizenship status was in the works, and I'd better get back to Japan and round up the documents I'd need to make my case.

Seventeen

EVER since we had come ashore in Pusan that hot day in July I had driven Colonel Peterson wherever he wanted to go. Now, on the bone-chilling morning of January 17, 1951, he insisted on chauffeuring me to the little dirt airstrip where I could hitch a ride back to Japan on a Military Air Transport Service C-47. I had spent 198 days in the Korean combat zone in United States Army uniform but the fact would never appear in the records. In fact, because my very presence was illegal, there would be no record that I had ever gone to Korea with the 24th Division Military Police contingent. My name had never appeared on the unit roster; if I had been killed, chances are I never would have made the casualty list. I had been happy to serve in the U.S. Army even as a non-person. Now I was happy to be going home.

Sergeant West had nearly crushed my fingers when we shook hands in farewell. I turned over my .45, carbine and helmet to him, trying to be casual by saying: "Where I'm going, Sarge, I won't be needing these." That didn't sound quite the way I wanted it to, but we laughed and he slapped me across the back.

Now it was time to crawl into the C-47 and I turned and saluted Colonel Peterson. He returned my salute gravely, shook my hand and said: "Good luck, Jim, and thank you for everything. If there is anything I can ever do for you, just let me know."

"Thank you, sir," I replied and I didn't trust my voice to say more. I turned and entered the plane without looking back. I never saw Colonel Peterson again.

It is only a short hop across the Korea Strait from Korea to Japan, but there was plenty of time to study the passengers who, like me, were strapped into the uncomfortable bucket seats with our backs to the plane's wall. Some were the walking wounded, going back to Japan for specialized treatment. Others were on rest and recreation leave, which meant booze and girls and darned little rest. A few must have been on official missions of some kind. Most of them sat impassively, staring into space, and soon I, too, was lost in my thoughts.

I had to admit to myself that I was relieved that the letter from the U.S. Consulate freed me from the self-imposed obligation of remaining in Korea with the military police. I had volunteered on an impulse. I had enjoyed a priceless comradeship with my buddies, an experience that I wouldn't have missed for anything. And I had served my country. But when the glamour and excitement of playing soldier wore thin, I was too proud to ask for permission to quit. In good conscience, I couldn't. I don't think I ever would have told Colonel Peterson I wanted to go home. Chances are I would have remained in Korea until I was killed or wounded, or until the outfit was rotated back to Japan. So I was delighted to have a good reason for returning to civilian life, delighted to be going home to Ethel and the baby, delighted that at last the wheels had begun to turn on my appeal for reinstatement as an American citizen. But tempering that happiness was a deep-down sense of guilt that I was abandoning my buddies, that I really belonged in the cold and mud of Korea with my outfit rather than in a plane flying to the peace and quiet and comfort of Japan.

Not even in my wildest daydreams had I seen myself performing some great feat of valor that would win me recognition, a medal and perhaps instant restoration of my citizenship. My experience in the Japanese Army had taught me that for the most part military life is dull and dirty and mean, that glory is for the storybooks and that opportunity —which must appear before any man can demonstrate either courage or cowardice—is denied in war to all but a few. Still, I felt that what little I had been able to do in the service of my native country helped in some small way to make amends for what I had been forced to do in another war.

My thoughts were disrupted by the imminence of landing. We circled the vast concrete expanse of Ashiya Air Base, and I was struck by its contrast with the facilities in Korea. Except for Kimpo Airfield outside Seoul, the planes in Korea landed and took off from dirt strips which, more often than not, adjoined burned-out villages. At Ashiya huge hangars were available for maintenance crews, and other buildings were drawn up around the field in straight, neat rows. Nearby villages basked peacefully in the pale winter sun. Little children played in courtyards. Outside a junior high school young girls in middies romped and ran. These children were far too young to remember World War II; hopefully, if the war in Korea could be contained, they would never see World War III.

Ashiya was a major staging base for combat and cargo flights to Korea. There was plenty of vehicular traffic moving in and out of the base and I had no trouble catching a ride to Camp Kokura. There, I found that aside from the fact that only a skeleton force of G.I.'s remained, almost nothing had changed. I hurried to my old office in the labor administrator's department. My desk, neatly dusted, was still there. Some of the Japanese clerks looked up in surprise. "Welcome back, we haven't seen you for a long time," one of them said.

"I've been on a long, long assignment," I replied with a grin. If they knew I had been in Korea, and they probably did, they certainly were aware that I had been there without authority. But they obligingly continued to play the know-nothing game, and I was grateful that they accepted my long absence without questions. One of the office girls hurried off to get me a cup of tea while I picked up the telephone and put through a call.

Presently I heard Ethel's familiar voice saying, *"Moshimoshi,"* which is the way the Japanese say hello.

"Ethel," I shouted in English. "This is me, Jim." I heard her gasp, as though she had heard a voice from the dead. "I'm back. Are you all right? How is little Kenny?" I was so excited I didn't give her a chance to talk. "I'm at Camp Kokura now. I'm taking the next train and I'll be home in just a little while."

Ethel, looking her prettiest, had a hot bath waiting when I arrived home and took her in my arms. Nothing would do but that I enjoy the luxury of a Japanese style bath before anything else. Immersed up to my neck, I let the hot water soak out the aches and loosen the grime accumulated by life in the field. I emerged feeling like a new man. Ethel and I had so much to talk about, so much time to make up for, so much playing with Kenny to catch up on. My son had been but an infant when I left in July. I returned home just two days before his first birthday and found him a sturdy youngster able to stand erect and pull himself around by holding on to the furniture. Soon he would be walking by himself. That night, as Ethel and I lay close to each other in bed, I asked her forgiveness for having run off without even consulting her.

"That day you called," she said tenderly, "I knew what you were about to do. I knew it was something you just had to do. It would have been wrong to try and stop you. I knew I had to get along alone until you were ready to come home." She kissed me, and I was finally sure I had done the right thing.

Several days later I took the train to Fukuoka to visit the U.S. Consulate and inquire about the papers that would be needed. The amount of red tape that would have to be cut was staggering. I needed documents that showed where I was born, where I went to school, where I worked; documents to certify that I had never been in trouble with the police, another document to prove I had never voted in a Japanese election, etc., etc., etc. How could the U.S. Army be so casual about things and the Department of State so fussy? I also learned at the consulate that Betty and Bert had been in touch with that office on my behalf, asking the officials to expedite my application and asking what could be done from Hawaii to help. It was reassuring to know they were pulling for me.

From Fukuoka I went to Hirao and then to Kaminoseki, mainly to gather documents from the local officials, but also to drop in on my uncles and to visit my parents' graves. Neither of my uncles seemed to know that I had been in Korea, so to avoid a lot of explanation I made no mention of my experience. While at Hirao I picked up papers attesting to my employment at Yanai Commercial School where I had taught judo before being conscripted, a certificate from the police department attesting to my good character, and a document from the Japanese labor office regarding my employment with the British Commonwealth forces. I also picked up a copy of the Yoshida family register at the village government office showing that my name had been entered on the record in infancy, thus making me a Japanese citizen under Japanese law.

I spent a quiet hour at the cemetery in Kaminoseki, lighting incense to the spirits of my parents in the traditional manner. I grieved that both my father and mother had died so young, and yet I was grateful that they, unlike so many unfortunate civilian victims of war in China and Korea who had been buried hastily in unmarked graves, rested together on this beautiful island. Finally I prayed to Dad and Mom. I thanked them for looking after my family while I was in Korea and for guiding me safely back home. Did I really believe that their spirits had an influence over what happened to me? That is a difficult question to answer. I think it is sufficient to say that nothing untoward happened to my family while I was gone and I had come home unscathed; someone was looking after me and certainly it wasn't improper to thank the spirits of my parents. Finally, I told my parents of my growing hopes for returning home to America and asked their understanding, and then I turned away, not knowing when I would be able to visit their graves again.

One by one I assembled the necessary documents. A certificate from the Kodokwan Judo School. An affidavit stating I had been drafted into the Japanese Army. My birth certificate and high school graduation diploma from Seattle which Betty had obtained and forwarded to me. All of these many, many documents were duly filed with American officials in Tokyo to support my application for clarification of my status as an American citizen. After that there was nothing to do but wait while my plea proceeded with glacial speed through the tortuous official channels.

Meanwhile, I kept busy at my job in the labor office. The biggest demand now was for carpenters and cabinetmakers. The American Graves Registration Service needed a saddening number of coffins for the bodies of American dead from Korea, and for the wounded who died in American military hospitals in Japan despite everything that could be done for them. Day after day the carpenters hammered out coffins, and each of them was shipped back to the States with the body of an American. What a price the United States paid to insure the freedom of Korea!

Spring of 1951 slipped into summer. The hot, humid days returned. The first anniversary of the outbreak of the Korean War came and went and the fighting continued to rage. On July 10, 1951, United Nations and North Korean representatives sat down for the first time to talk about a truce, but there was no letup in the fighting. And still I heard nothing from U.S. officials. I began to wonder if they had forgotten about my petition, or whether the papers had been lost in some bureaucratic pigeonhole.

A new element entered the picture in November. Congress passed what was known as the McCarran Immigration and Naturalization Act, sponsored by Senator Pat McCarran of Nevada. Principally, the Act removed race as a qualification for naturalization. Japan-born residents of the United States—like my parents if they had been living—were now eligible to apply for American citizenship. Other Asians who had been in the same boat—ineligible for naturalization because of race—could now become citizens. An insulting slight based on race had been corrected. A second provision of the Act established an immigration quota for Asian nations, so that now a few hundred Japanese could enter the United States each year as immigrants. None of this affected me directly for I was contending that I was an American by birth and that citizenship could not be taken away from me. But an obscure section of the McCarran Act affected my job. The way 8th Army Headquarters in Tokyo interpreted the legislation, I would have to cease working for the Occupation Forces. What was involved was that although I was employed by the U.S. Army, I was being paid in Japanese currency by the Japanese government from reparations funds, and now this was no longer possible. I didn't try to find out what the problem was all about. All I knew was that I was out of a job.

Fortunately my friendship with many Americans who knew of my service in Korea paid off in the offer of other employment. The Troop Information and Education Center (TI&E), which had quarters close to the labor office, was looking for someone to supervise distribution of *Pacific Stars and Stripes,* the daily newspaper published for servicemen, in all of southern Japan, and I was offered the position. My pay was to be the same as I had been drawing— 136,800 yen a month, or the equivalent of $380, which was a very handsome salary in Japan in those days. The difference was that I would be paid from non-appropriated TI&E funds and not through the Japanese government.

I had never worked on a newspaper but lost no time in taking the job. *Pacific Stars and Stripes* was edited and printed in Tokyo. Each day the papers were flown from Tachikawa Air Base near Tokyo to Ashiya. I hired a crew of some thirty district managers. Some of them picked up the papers at Ashiya and dropped them off at the railroad station for outlying areas. Others supervised delivery of papers to messhalls, post exchanges, and dependents' housing areas. I was responsible for gathering up all the money collected from the sale of the papers, depositing the cash in the Bank of America branch at Camp Kokura, and sending daily reports to the newspaper's business manager in Tokyo.

More months sped by, and still I heard nothing from U.S. officials about my citizenship application. Little Kenny was now a mischievous toddler and soon he would be old enough to start school. One day Ethel's father and mother left for Hawaii. The Shinto congregation he had served there invited him to come back, and American immigration officials saw fit to give him an entry visa even though he had been arrested immediately after the outbreak of war as a potentially dangerous alien. Of course this had been a precautionary move and he was no more subversive than any of the other men of influence who had been seized in the federal dragnet. I was pleased that he could return to Hawaii even though he was an alien, but I could not help but resent the irony of the United States Government's failure to act on my application.

Then, early in December, 1952, I received a telegram from Tokyo. It was from Katsuro Miho, a prominent Nisei attorney in Honolulu. He asked me to meet him at the Imperial Hotel in Tokyo to discuss my citizenship appeal. I took the train the next day.

It was a dark, overcast, typical winter day in Tokyo when I entered the carpeted lobby of the Imperial, at that time Japan's leading hotel. Miho greeted me warmly. He was a short, chunky individual, brisk-mannered, in early middle age. He told me he had been retained by Harry Isobe, Ethel's brother in Honolulu, and her parents, to do what he could to expedite my case. Over many cups of tea at the Imperial I told him the full story of my experiences. He interrupted me many times with questions about details and his manner bolstered my growing confidence in him. Finally he said, "There is one way to break up the bureaucratic logjam which is delaying action on your case and that is to file suit in federal court against the United States."

I was astonished. I couldn't imagine me, Jim Yoshida, a nobody seeking a favor from the United States, going to court to try to force the government to take action in my favor.

"What you must understand," Miho explained, "is that the government in all its majesty often is wrong, or it is reluctant to take a necessary action, and in such cases the courts are available to every citizen in his search for justice. You have a right to have your case heard in a court of law. That is one of the beauties of the American system." He told me he thought my chances of regaining my citizenship seemed good and he would file suit on my behalf if I approved.

"Mr. Miho," I said, "I don't know how much it's going to cost and I don't know how I'm going to pay you, but I want my citizenship more than anything else in the world."

"Good," he replied enthusiastically. "Don't worry about paying me. The Isobe family has guaranteed my fee so you can make your arrangements with them. I'll get the paperwork started as soon as I go back to Hawaii. Just keep your nose clean and don't lose fight."

Lose fight? I assumed he meant that I shouldn't lose courage. Much later I learned "never lose fight" is a common Hawaiian pidgin expression meaning never lose your fighting spirit. I thought about that a lot during the long train ride back home.

Christmas soon arrived, then New Year's Day. Even in postwar Japan New Year's is the big holiday. It is a time of celebration and feasting on exotic dishes, of joy that another year has come, of anticipation of better things in the twelvemonth ahead. Japan's economy had improved so much that the New Year season of 1953 was an especially gala one. There was abundant food on the festive tables— broiled fish, herring roe, rice cakes, seaweed, sweetened black beans, burdock root, shrimp, taro, bamboo shoots, chicken: On New Year's Eve we visited the temples while the great bronze bells tolled away the old year. On New Year's Day we paid duty calls to friends, neighbors, employers and employees, just as Dad had done in Seattle. And we gorged ourselves. In the excitement of the holiday season I almost forgot the visit with Katsuro Miho, but obviously he hadn't. Early in January, less than a month after my trip to Tokyo, the United States Government issued me a Certificate of Identity. It amounted to a special visa which would permit me to go to Honolulu to take part in the suit to regain my citizenship. I was as excited as a child. I wanted to take the certificate to bed with me for safekeeping but Ethel persuaded me to put it away with my important papers. A few days later I received a money order from Bert and Betty to cover my boat fare. I promptly booked passage on the next available ship, the S.S. *President Cleveland* sailing from Yokohama on March 2. After so many years of frustrated waiting, all the details were falling into place with miraculous precision. Ethel was just as excited as I, even though she would have to stay behind until the suit was settled. She packed and unpacked my suitcases. She fretted about gifts to be taken to her parents and to Betty and Bert. I telephoned Aiko, my older sister, who by then was living in Wakamatsu City and told her the news. She insisted that I spend a week with her but I begged off. Aiko would cry when I left and that would make me cry, and I wanted none of that. But a few days before I was to leave for Yokohama I visited Kaminoseki one last time. Uncle Denmatsu and Auntie and I talked late into the night. They recalled their days in Hawaii and told me about local customs, the balmy climate, the wonderful fruits to be had. "Hawaii is just like Japan," Auntie assured me. "Almost every other person is Japanese and it isn't even necessary to know English." I smiled wryly. She just couldn't understand that I was trying to get away from Japan.

Next day, alone, I went to the cemetery for the final farewell. I was still there when the ferry chugged into the harbor, and I barely made it aboard. Somehow the word must have gotten out that I was on my way to America, for almost everyone in the village lined the shore to see me off. Despite all that I could do the tears came to my eyes. Some of my most pleasant—as well as most trying—moments in Japan had been spent here.

I would have preferred to drop in on Uncle Saisuke Yoshida at Hirao for a quick and simple good-bye, but he would have none of it. My stay lasted two days. Friends and relatives came to call each day. Both nights we partied. I finally broke away on the plea that I had to go home to see Ethel and pack.

Uncle Denmatsu and Uncle Saisuke both insisted they were going to escort me as far as Yokohama. It would be a long, weary train ride for them, and I would have preferred to go on alone, but I argued in vain. Nothing would do but that they accompany me on the first leg of the trip to America, just as they had escorted Mom and my sisters and me on the last leg of the trip to Japan a dozen years earlier. Knowing the confusion that would ensue at the railroad station, I persuaded Ethel to remain at home. I kissed her tenderly and assured her once more that I would certainly win in court and when that happened I would send for her and Kenny immediately.

The familiar Japanese landscape flitted past the train windows but I saw nothing, for I was locked deep in thought. My uncles seemed to understand for they did not try to engage me in conversation. I remembered when Mom and I took this same train to Tokyo when she enrolled me in judo school. What would have happened to us if we had made it on the last ship to the States in 1941? Would Mom still be living? Would I have gone into the U.S. Army with my pals? Would I have married someone other than Ethel? Where would I be and what would I be doing to make a living?

My uncles took very seriously their self-appointed responsibility as escorts. They accompanied me right to the gangplank, and they remained on the wharf waving, waving, waving, long after everyone else was gone. I was caught in a most uncomfortable dilemma. I needed desperately to go to the bathroom. Yet I couldn't very well duck away while my uncles were on the wharf. Finally, when the other passengers began to drift away from the rail, I ran in search of relief. What a way to leave Japan, I thought as the pressure eased, and yet it seemed somewhat appropriate.

My cabin mate was a young Hawaiian Nisei named George Nakamura. He was on his way home after a brief visit in Japan. He talked about Hawaii as though he were an employee of the chamber of commerce. At the same time he said he liked Japan even better than Hawaii, and I found him hard to figure. Even so he was friendly and companionable, and after dinner we'd stroll around the decks together for exercise.

The days were sunny and comfortable but I dreaded the nights. While others slept, I wrestled far into the small hours with the doubts raised by hundreds of questions: Did I have a chance of winning my case? How would I conduct myself in court? Would the U.S. attorney bully me, confuse me, put words in my mouth so that I would convict myself? Would I be branded legally in court as a traitor? What would I do if the court ruled that I had indeed lost my citizenship? What would I do for a living in America if I regained my citizenship? Seattle certainly must have changed in twelve years; did I really want to go back there? Betty and Bert were in Honolulu; Ethel had grown up in Hawaii; would Hawaii be a better place to settle down? The United States Government was opposing my efforts to go home to America—would the officials hold a grudge against me if I won my case and try to deport me on some pretext or make it tough for me to get a job? Hawaii was only a territory and not a state; would winning the right to remain in Hawaii be only half a victory? Why didn't I demand a trial in Seattle, my home, instead of Honolulu where I'd never been? Was Katsuro Miho as good a lawyer as he had appeared to be when I met him? The questions raced on and on. I tossed and turned, resenting the sound of George Nakamura's deep breathing, hating the monotonous throb of the engines that took me steadily closer to the federal courtroom in Honolulu. Some nights the sky was turning light before I finally fell asleep.

I had just dozed off on the morning of March 10 when George shook me awake. It wasn't quite daybreak yet, but far in the misty distance I could see the dark outline of a mountain range against the lighter sky behind it. This was Oahu, beautiful island, thrust violently up from the mid-ocean floor in some mysterious, distant age. I washed and dressed and hurried out on deck. It was more light now. White foam flecked the tops of blue waves. White puffs of clouds hung close to the highest peaks, but beyond the sky was clear and blue. I remembered Bing Crosby in another time singing the praises of "Blue Hawaii."

The rhythm of the engines slowed and the *Cleveland* turned toward land. George was pulling at my sleeve. "Over there," he said, pointing, "that's the entrance to Pearl Harbor." How peaceful it seemed. This is just the way it must have appeared on that Sunday morning in December when it all started. I stared in silence.

The ship glided slowly into the narrow confines of Honolulu Harbor, and two busy little tugs bustled up to nudge her gently toward her slip. George pointed out the Aloha Tower greeting all newcomers. It looked startlingly like the tower of the King Street Railroad Station in Seattle. Down on the wharf Betty and Bert were waving wildly to attract my attention. I put two fingers in my mouth and whistled a shrill greeting.

The formalities of health inspection, immigration and customs examination passed in a blur. Somewhere along the way my friend George disappeared and I never did get a chance to say good-bye to him properly. Then abruptly I was outside the bureaucratic barriers and in the happy hubbub of the waiting room. Betty was the first to come to me, with Bert a half step behind. She gazed at me a long moment. Then she draped a fragrant flower lei over my head and threw her arms around me. I hugged her tight, and suddenly I remembered when she charmed the sentry and came to visit me with food soon after I had been drafted into the Japanese Army. What a debt of gratitude I owed my little sister!

Bert dropped another lei over my head and shook my hand. He introduced me to his two brothers, and each of them presented me with a lei. He introduced me to his sister. She placed still another lei around my neck and when I bent down she kissed me. The leis were up as high as my nose. I felt like a fag behind all the flowers, but I knew I would like Hawaii.

Bert whisked me in his car to his parents' home where he and Betty were staying. I was astonished at how clean and fresh Honolulu appeared compared to drab, wintery Japan. Everywhere I looked there were Orientals. Even the police officer directing traffic was an Oriental; there had been nothing like that in Seattle.

"First thing we have to do," Betty said when we reached home, "is to get you dressed like a Hawaiian." She led me to the room I was to use and there on the bed were several short-sleeved, open-neck Aloha shirts in vivid floral prints and a pair of neatly tailored slacks. "You look like an old man in that white Japanese shirt and those dark trousers. When in Hawaii you have to dress like Hawaiians."

I put on the most conservative shirt but even then I felt the colors were screaming. That evening Bert had some of his friends over to meet me. Bert's mother had prepared some Japanese goodies. The charcoal was good and hot in the hibachi, and soon the steaks were sizzling. I thought I was getting away from Japan, but here I was in the midst of friendly Orientals eating Japanese food and cooking over a charcoal brazier.

The conversation was lively and happy—and different. Everyone spoke English as well as I did, but when they got together for an informal party they reverted to the pidgin they knew in childhood, with scant regard for tenses or syntax. "Hey, no do that," I heard someone shout, "you going broke it!"

By this time I was positive I would like Hawaii.

Eighteen

KATSURO MIHO had bad news for me. The Smith Act trial
of the so-called Hawaii Big 7 labor leaders, accused of Communist links, had dragged on endlessly. Other action in the
federal courts had come to a virtual standstill. The calendar
was so badly jammed that no one could tell when my case
would be heard. The one glimmer of good news was that
the time available to us would be utilized to sharpen up
my case.

I had been under the impression I would be the defendant since I was trying to defend my rights as an American citizen. But Miho explained that I was the plaintiff.
I was challenging the United States Government's contention that I had lost my citizenship. The defendant, in name
only, was John Foster Dulles as Secretary of State. The suit
had been filed in the U.S. District Court for the district
of Hawaii and it was designated as Civil Suit No. 1257.
My attorneys were the firm of Fong, Miho, Choy and Chuck.
That doesn't sound like an American law firm but it was
one of Hawaii's most distinguished. Hiram Fong, of Chinese
descent, went on to become United States Senator from

Hawaii. Choy and Chuck were brilliant young men of Korean and Chinese descent respectively, while Miho, of course, was of Japanese stock.

The government, in a document called a Certificate of Loss of Nationality, charged that I had expatriated myself "by serving in the Japanese armed forces as a Japanese national." Section 401 of the Nationality Act of 1940 specifies that an American citizen "shall lose his nationality by entering or serving in the armed forces of a foreign state" unless expressly authorized by the laws of the United States.

There was no denying that I had served in the Japanese Army. Miho explained that my case would be based on the contention that service was compulsory and involuntary, that protests would have been to no avail, and that I had no choice but to serve when ordered. There were to be no witnesses other than myself.

One day several weeks after reaching Honolulu, Miho introduced me to Abraham Lincoln (Al) Wirin, a well-known civil rights attorney who practiced together with Fred Okrand in Los Angeles. Wirin was in Hawaii in connection with the defense of the Big 7 and Miho said he had become greatly interested in my case and wanted to talk to me. I judged Wirin to be in his middle fifties. He was nearly six feet tall and he had the wind-blown, rumpled look of a professor. His most distinguishing feature on first sight was the hair that protruded from the nostrils of his rather prominent nose. Wirin had a way of looking directly at whoever he was talking to and his speech was deliberate. I liked him instantly. He invited me to the modest apartment he had taken near the Waikiki Theatre, and there I told him my life story just as I had related it to Miho in Tokyo. Wirin took copious notes on a pad of yellow legal paper. Finally, when we were through, he said he would like to join Miho in presenting my case because of the important principles involved.

"I'd be proud to have you represent me if Mr. Miho approves," I began hesitantly, "but the cost—"

He waved me off. "No need to worry about that. I think you have a very good chance of winning and I want to do what I can to help improve those chances. If you do win, it may help a lot of other Nisei boys who were caught in the same kind of fix. Some rather significant precedents will be set by the court's decision."

He must have noticed the worried look on my face for he went on: "This would seem to put a heavy responsibility on you, but there's nothing to be afraid of. The main thing is to remain calm. The government attorney may try to work you over, asking the same questions many times in different ways in an effort to confuse you. Stick to your story just the way you've told it to me. Keep your temper. Try not to lose your patience."

The interview with Wirin filled me with new confidence, but the delay led to another problem. My Certificate of Identity enabling me to enter Hawaii was not valid indefinitely. Since I was engaged in a lawsuit against one branch of the government, it seemed somewhat improbable that another branch would look favorably on an extension. There seemed to be a very good chance that I would be forced to return to Japan before my case ever came to trial.

"Jim," Miho said one morning, "we'll have to take a drastic measure to head off any attempt to deport you. I want you to sign a petition for naturalization."

My jaw dropped. "Why?" I demanded. "I don't want to be naturalized. Aren't we arguing that I never lost my citizenship? If I apply for naturalization, doesn't it mean that I'm admitting that I'm an alien?"

Miho patiently explained that the petition for naturalization was simply a device to block possible deportation, that the court would recognize it as such, that the Immigration and Naturalization Service was sure to deny the petition, and the petition would have no effect on the outcome of my suit. He also explained that under prodding from the Japanese American Citizens League, Congress had revised U.S. naturalization laws so that race was no longer a consideration. In other words, Japanese and other Asian aliens could seek American citizenship on the same basis as Europeans.

I wasn't convinced that Miho's strategy was a good one, but after all, he was my attorney. Reluctantly I signed the "petition," No. 13063, dated April 7, 1953, respectfully requesting the privilege of becoming a naturalized American citizen. It was a ridiculous document. It stated that I had been physically in the United States "for at least 23 days" and that I had resided in Honolulu "continuously since at least March 13, 1953." Bert Kido and a YWCA social worker named Mildred Towle witnessed the affidavit.

The days dragged on without a hint as to when the court would hear my case. Due to my uncertain status I wasn't allowed to take a job. I had nothing to do all day long but fret and worry. Bert and Betty tried to be kind but they had their lives to lead and work to take care of—Bert as a salesclerk in a fish market, Betty as a seamstress. Left to my devices day after day, I killed time by wandering over the beaches, sitting in the parks, walking the downtown streets, looking at people, thinking about myself. I never tired of Hawaii's lush tropical beauty, the blue ocean and white beaches. I was fascinated by the cosmopolitan atmosphere—the best foods and nicest customs of many ethnic groups had been blended into the delightful Hawaiian way of life, and Japanese and Chinese and Koreans and Hawaiians and Caucasians of various origins all intermarried, worked together, played together, lived together in happy harmony. I wanted to become part of this life, but I knew that until I could appear before a federal judge and convince him of my right to my American heritage, I didn't belong in it. Until that time I wasn't a citizen of anywhere. What I was in my heart didn't necessarily make me an American, for there were laws that had to be satisfied.

In my darker moods I asked myself what I would do if the court ruled against me. Could I stand to be deported to Japan after this taste of America? I wanted to belong to America so badly that the knowledge that a judge could exile me with a simple stroke of the pen was excruciating. I almost wept one day at Ala Moana Beach Park when I came across a neatly painted sign that said THIS IS A PUBLIC PARK—HAVE FUN. Where but in America would there be such concern for the common people?

Three months dragged by. One day in July Miho telephoned to say that, as expected, my petition for naturalization had been denied. The reasons were that I had entered Hawaii under irregular circumstances and that a ruling on my citizenship status was pending. But the petition had the desired effect, Miho assured me. The Immigration and Naturalization Service had officially recognized my suit and therefore I would not be deported prior to the trial. The news lifted a big load off my back—but Miho was about to make me shoulder another. He asked me to meet some other Nisei who also were seeking to establish their American citizenship.

That afternoon there were nearly a dozen men crowded into Miho's office. All had spent the war years in Japan. Some had gone to Japan in early childhood, had been educated in Japanese schools, understood little English and were Americans only in a technical sense. Still, if they had been born in the United States, they were entitled to the rights and privileges of citizenship. Others of the group had completed their schooling in the United States before visiting Japan. All, like me, had served in the Japanese armed forces and now were seeking to reestablish their American citizenship.

Miho explained that he and Wirin were agreed that my case, for a number of reasons, was the strongest. Therefore, they would use my suit as a test case. If my challenge were successful it would be cited as a precedent affecting all the others and further trials would be unnecessary. The responsibility staggered me; the futures of all these guys would hinge on me.

After a long moment of thought I said: "All right, Mr. Miho. If we lose my case, it's their funeral as well as mine. As for me, I don't care who hangs on to my coattails. I just want to get the trial over with. The waiting is what's killing me, one day at a time."

The deliberate pace of the courts was infuriating. There was scant consolation in the thought that justice must not be hurried. Twice my hearing was scheduled, then postponed both times. Each time I built up to a high state of expectation, then had to cope with a painful emotional letdown.

Finally the hearing was scheduled a third time—for 10 A.M., October 12, 1953, just one day short of seven months after my arrival in Honolulu. I steeled myself for another postponement, but this time the date was firm. Bert took a day off to accompany me, and we met Miho at his office. Chatting affably, Miho led us through the morning cool to the three-story, cream-colored stucco Federal Building that also housed the postal and customs offices. Miho's calmness was maddening. I was wound up like a spring; he acted as though he appeared in court every day. Then it occurred to me that he probably did, and I should quit worrying because I was in good hands. But it was impossible to turn off the adrenalin, just like that. Near the entrance my eye caught sight of a grim reminder of the times we live in, a fading sign with an arrow pointing to a stairway and the words, FALLOUT SHELTER—CAPACITY 670 PERSONS. Miho led the way to the elevator. Federal buildings seem to have the world's slowest elevators and this was no exception. It crawled up to the third floor. On the highly polished marble wall was a directory. I found what I was looking for: UNITED STATES DISTRICT COURT. JUDGE JOHN WIIG. COURTROOM 1.

Courtroom 1 was to the right. My hands were cold and clammy as we turned toward it. I could feel the perspiration soaking into my shirt. The tall, paneled double doors of Courtroom 1 were standing open and I could see into the high-ceilinged interior. Miho asked me and Bert to wait while he went inside. In a moment he reappeared and signaled us to join him. The room was perhaps forty by sixty feet. At one end, on a slight elevation, was the judge's bench. To the left of the bench was a silk-textured American flag on a gold-colored staff topped by an eagle with wings outstretched.

The jury box was on the left. It would not be occupied for my hearing; Judge Wiig would preside without a jury. The government attorney's table, with three chairs around it, was to the left. Our table was to the right. This was the first courtroom I had ever been in.

Bert gripped my arm in a good-luck gesture and took a seat in the section reserved for the public. I sat up front with Miho. A tall, lean man was standing at the other table talking to someone in low tones. Miho leaned over and whispered: "That's Louis Blissard, assistant United States attorney. He'll conduct the government's defense. He's the one who will be questioning you." I knew I would not like this man. At that moment Wirin hurried into the courtroom, breathing heavily as though he had run up the stairs. He apologized to Miho for being late and patted me on the back.

A bailiff suddenly said in a loud voice: "His Honor, United States District Judge John Wiig. Everyone please rise." The door to the judge's chambers opened and a lean, slightly built man in long black robes swept into the room. I estimated him to be in his forties. His straight brownish hair was combed back and he had a small black mustache. Smiling faintly, the judge took his chair and everyone in the room also sat down. "Here we go, Jim," I muttered to myself. "This is what you've been waiting for."

Judge Wiig examined some papers, noted that this was Civil Suit No. 1257, Katsumi Yoshida, plaintiff v. John Foster Dulles, and then nodded to Mr. Miho who stood up to make a few introductory remarks. Then it was Mr. Wirin's turn. Speaking in a low, deliberate voice, glancing occasionally at the legal notepad in his left hand, he cited some cases in California in which Nisei strandees had regained their citizenship. The tension that had gripped me slowly began to ease. This hearing, it seemed, wasn't going to be too bad after all. Wirin reviewed my statement which had been submitted to the court. Then it was Blissard's turn to speak. He ignored me, addressing himself completely to the bench.

Then all too suddenly I heard my name being called. I was told to rise and enter the witness box. A clerk swore me in with a Bible. It didn't occur to me at the time to tell anyone I was a Buddhist.

Blissard started gently enough, as though trying to establish in my mind that he was a nice fellow. He asked my name, which of course he knew. He asked my age when I left Seattle. I was nineteen. Walking away from me, he observed to the judge that a person nineteen years old was of military age. Abruptly he whirled, fixed me with his greenish eyes and demanded to know whether I had gone to Japan to avoid being drafted into the United States Army.

I thought: *He's being nasty. That's a dirty question. He's trying to make me look bad. He knows that's not true.*

I replied: "No, sir. I accompanied my mother to take my

247

father's ashes back to Japan, and to take a training course to further my judo skills."

He asked: "The relations between the United States and Japan were very shaky at that time, and knowing this you went to Japan?"

I was nineteen years old, interested in football and girls. I wasn't paying any attention to international affairs.

I replied: "I did not know anything about relationships between the two countries."

He asked: "You knew you were leaving the United States for good, didn't you?"

You didn't even read my statement. I had a football scholarship. I had every intention of coming home and going to college and playing football.

"When my mother and sisters and I left Seattle, we expected to return to our home in a few months."

He asked: "When did you realize the two countries had cut ties?"

Is he going to try to prove that we knew Japan was going to attack the United States? He should be smarter than that.

"The first time was in July of 1941, when we were informed that shipping across the Pacific had been suspended and we were stranded in Japan. The second was December 8, 1941, Japan time. I heard on the radio that Japan had attacked Pearl Harbor."

"Were you surprised?"

What a silly question. Of course I was surprised.

"Yes, sir. Very surprised."

"Did you try to enlist?"

"No, sir."

I shot a glance at Judge Wiig. He was looking on very calmly. His eyes were kind, compassionate. Somehow I felt that he could understand my fear and loneliness, my yearning, my resentment at the line of questioning. Somehow I knew that I would find justice in his court.

"Did you go to the American embassy?"

"No, sir. We just didn't know what to do or where to go to make inquiries. Besides, we were living in a little country town a long way from Tokyo."

"When did you realize you were a dual citizen, that you had Japanese citizenship and were subject to Japanese laws?"

"After the war started. My mother told me."

"At the time of enlistment, did you try to refuse?"

That's another dirty, insinuating question. He knows what the answer is. He read it in my statement. He's trying to make me look bad.

"I did not enlist. I was conscripted. I had no choice."

"Why? You knew you were an American—why didn't you refuse to go into the Japanese Army?"

"I couldn't. I had no choice."

Al Wirin, I need you. Why don't you come to my rescue? Explain it for me, please, please.

Almost as though he heard my silent plea, Wirin rose. "If it please the court," he broke in, "I beg to interrupt to establish a point of fact."

"Proceed," Judge Wiig answered.

Wirin reached into his briefcase and pulled out a sheaf of papers. Referring to them, he told the court: "Article 6 of the Constitution of Japan reads: 'A subject of Japan will obey the laws and have obligations of military service.' Articles 74 and 75 of the Japanese Military Service Law are as follows: 'Article 74: Any person who evades military service by deserting or hiding, injuring wilfully one's body, or acquiring disease and by other acts of fraud will be punished to penal servitude of three years or less.' 'Article 75: Persons called for military service who delay entering the barracks for more than ten days, without any legitimate reasons, shall be punished by imprisonment of six months or less; during wartime, when five days have elapsed, shall be punished by imprisonment of one year or less.'

"I submit, Your Honor, that this was the Japanese law

in effect at the time, and which the plaintiff was obliged to obey as a dual citizen." Wirin sat down.

Thanks, Mr. Wirin, thanks for helping me out. No one refused the Japanese Army in those days.

Blissard resumed the questioning: "Mr. Yoshida, wasn't penal servitude better than fighting against the United States?"

"I wanted to refuse service, very much. I didn't because I didn't know where or how to refuse. I also had to think of my family. I feared if I caused trouble, my mother and sisters would have been deprived of their food rations. I had to think of my relatives who might have suffered from my actions. I would like to get the record straight on one point. I fought in China. I did not fight the United States."

"Did you know of anyone refusing to serve? Did they kill anyone for refusing?"

"No, sir. I don't think anyone refused. No one dared refuse."

"It is my understanding that you were athletically inclined. Did you do your best to keep up with the rest? You did get promoted rapidly."

"No, sir, I didn't do anything outstanding. I just followed the others. My first promotion was automatic. After basic training everybody gets promoted."

"Why did you work for the Occupation Forces in Japan? Why didn't you go to the American embassy to ask about your American citizenship status?"

He's insinuating that I didn't want to come home. How can I make him understand how it felt to be cut off from home, from one's native country? How can I explain the tears and heartache of involuntary exile?

"My Nisei friends in Japan, who had made inquiry, told me that any American who served in the Japanese military automatically lost his citizenship. I made my own inquiries and failed to get a clear-cut answer. I went to the Occupation Forces because I had to make a living. My knowledge of the English language was an asset, and I also felt I was helping the Occupation Forces."

Blissard changed his line of questioning: "On April 7, 1953, you submitted a Petition for Naturalization."

God, he's got me in a corner now. I knew I shouldn't have let Miho talk me into that.

Blissard went on: "The records show that you were denied the petition. Is that why, now, you are here attempting to regain your citizenship?"

Why don't Miho or Wirin jump up and object, like they do in the movies? My citizenship suit was in the works a long time before that naturalization petition and Blissard knows it. He's just trying to make me look bad. How should I answer him?

"Because of the lengthy Smith Act trials, the hearing on my case was delayed for so long that I was afraid I would be deported before any action could be taken. I was looking desperately for any means that would have allowed me to stay here. The denial of the petition has nothing to do with my suit."

Blissard changed course again: "It's stated here that you went to Korea with the U.S. 24th Division. Did you go thinking that this would help regain your citizenship?"

What's wrong with that? Is there a more convincing way to demonstrate loyalty?

"I volunteered for service in Korea. I wanted to prove to myself that I was an American."

"Maybe, by volunteering, you thought you could get three square meals a day?"

That was dirty and uncalled for. I've got to hold my temper. He doesn't want me to be an American again, and I've got to show him I'm a better man than he is.

"Hunger had nothing to do with my volunteering. I was very well set. I had the highest paying civilian job at Camp

Kokura. In addition, I had dining privileges at the officers' mess."

"Did you get paid for going to Korea? How much?"

"Not one cent. I went strictly on a voluntary—"

"That's enough," he broke in. "No more questions." He hadn't even let me finish my sentence.

My lawyers didn't even bother to question me. There was a bit of legal pulling and hauling, and then Judge Wiig announced he would take the case under advisement and court was adjourned. Only then did I realize how exhausted I was. Both Miho and Wirin were cheerful. "You made a good witness," Miho told me. "I think we have a good chance, but we'll just have to wait and see how the judge rules."

Judge Wiig rendered his "decision" nearly two months later, on December 4, 1953. He reviewed the case in a five-page document which was delivered, most undramatically, through the mail. Miho summoned me to his office and we went through the decision together. The news I had been waiting for was contained in two totally unemotional sentences:

"The defendant offered no evidence proving expatriation, and has failed to rebut the presumption that plaintiff's service in the Japanese Army was involuntary . . . It is the opinion of the Court that plaintiff's conscription into the Japanese Army under the circumstances of this case was not his free and voluntary act within the meaning of Section 401 (c) of the Nationality Act of 1940 and that his service in the Japanese Army did not cause him to lose his status as a national of the United States."

I was speechless with gratitude, and not even Miho's stern warning that the government still had the right to appeal could stem the warm feeling that started in my toes and swept all the way through my body. For the first time since arriving in Hawaii ten months earlier I felt free.

The final step, the action that would establish my citizenship unequivocally, was yet to come. That would be a "judgment" signed by Judge Wiig, but he would not issue it until he was sure the decision would not be reviewed by a higher court. Miho, however, was so confident of the outcome that he persuaded the Immigration people to let me get a job.

I found work as a carpenter's helper with a contractor named Ben Hayashi. Building concrete forms was rough, hard work but I enjoyed the physical exertion. To save money I moved in with Ethel's parents. There were debts to pay off—for my boat fare, the attorney's fees, the money Ethel and Kenny had been living on while I was in Honolulu. And on that happy day when I legally became an American again, there was passage to buy to reunite my family under the Stars and Stripes.

On April 16, 1954, Judge Wiig took the most unusual step of assembling all parties to Civil Suit No. 1257 in his courtroom to hear his "judgment." With Mr. Miho at my side, I stood to hear Judge Wiig intone the unforgettable words:

"Now, therefore, it is ordered, adjudged and decreed as follows: That the plaintiff Katsumi Yoshida was born at Seattle, Washington, on July 28, 1921, of parents born in Japan. At all times since his birth, plaintiff has been and he now is a national and a citizen of the United States of America with all the rights, privileges and immunities of such a citizen. The plaintiff, Katsumi Yoshida, did not lose his United States citizenship by virtue of or because of his service in the Japanese Army from February, 1943, to July, 1946."

Judge Wiig gravely put down the document, turned to me and broke into a wide smile. It was as though the sun had broken through a heavy overcast and I basked in its warmth.

"Congratulations, Mr. Yoshida," he said. There were a

few more remarks, and then he said a most gratifying thing: "The fact of your service with the armed forces in Korea played no part in my decision. But I want you to know your country is grateful, and so am I."

Blissard strode over to shake my hand but I hardly noticed him. I was looking for the flag, and the tears streaming down my cheeks made it very hard to see.

Since 1954...

ETHEL and Kenny joined me in Honolulu soon after Judge Wiig returned his "judgment." My first job was selling Venetian blinds. Subdivisions were springing up all around Honolulu and the new homes needed blinds. I was able to pay off my debts in about two years. Several years later Ethel and I were divorced. It was an amicable parting, both of us agreeing that we had married under less than ideal circumstances and really weren't suited for each other. A couple of years after that I met and married Helen Vincent, a native of Hawaii of Korean descent. We have one daughter, Aileen.

As this is written, my son Kenneth is a noncommissioned officer in the United States Army, stationed in Vietnam. My brother-in-law, Bert Kido—the Sergeant Kido who gave me such a bad time in China and who was so helpful in my fight to win back my citizenship—is dead, victim of a heart attack. His widow, my sister Betty, works in a Honolulu bank. I am a property developer and importer now. I import ginseng products from Korea and jade from Hong Kong. My wife Helen is prominent in her own right in the Hawaii beauty industry.

Hawaii has been good to me. No one was happier than I when the Territory of Hawaii became the fiftieth State in 1959. As my small contribution to the working of democracy I take part in politics on the grass roots, door-knocking level. Not many Americans, I would say, have more reason to love the United States, or a greater desire to keep its principles strong.